"As the war on terrorism continues, Klein's book provides chilling insight into the thoughts and beliefs of the leading fanatics who could very well have a role in shaping both our future and the next presidency."

—Denise Wheeler, *Huffington Post*

"Our sworn enemies tell Mideast-based, twenty-something U.S. journalist Aaron Klein whom they'd like in the White House, *kvetch* over showbiz types like Madonna, Britney, Spielberg, Mel Gibson, bigmouths Jane Fonda and Sean Penn and conservative talkers Limbaugh and Hannity, plus Richard Gere, who did a commercial urging Palestinians to vote. Well, they did. And elected Hamas."

—Cindy Adams, *New York Post*

"How refreshing to hear a member of the Fourth Estate telling it like it is. How refreshing to hear terrorists debunking with their own words such mealy-mouthed Western canards as 'ignorance and poverty make them do it,' 'they act only out of desperation,' or 'they are merely defending themselves against occupation.' For those under the sway of the Western media, many of the frank (proud, even) revelations, motivations, and goals offered by Klein's subjects will come as a very rude awakening."

—*Jerusalem Post* Book Review

"A hawkish young man in his mid-twenties, Klein uses his book as a rocket launcher aimed at terrorists, 'cowardly' Israeli politicians, Jews who knuckle under to Palestinians, and Americans who can't grasp the stake they have in the rat's nest of Mideast politics."

—*Philadelphia Daily News*

"Klein's book...provides the necessary proof that willful ignorance and cowardice play a strong role in the current widespread distribution of sympathy for the Arab Palestinian narrative."

—*American Thinker*

"Klein is the most accurate, talented reporter in the Middle East. He has better access to the terrorist bad guys than Muhammad would if he came back from the dead."

—Radio host G. Gordon Liddy

"Klein is the Middle East insider you need to know. Most network, cable, and print correspondents talk about the Middle East. Aaron Klein lives it."

—U.S. radio host Michael Reagan

"Klein's style is conversational and personal: he never hides his own perspective…. And yet those whom he interviews, although occasionally bridling at some of Klein's questions, are perfectly comfortable meeting with him and articulating their views and goals."

—*Aish HaTorah* Review

"Klein's interviews show that Palestinian leaders have repeatedly perpetrated a vile hoax on their acolytes."

—*Philadelphia Jewish Voice*

THE LATE GREAT STATE OF ISRAEL

THE LATE GREAT STATE OF ISRAEL

HOW ENEMIES WITHIN AND WITHOUT THREATEN THE JEWISH NATION'S SURVIVAL

By Aaron Klein

Edited by Benyamin Korn

WND Books

THE LATE GREAT STATE OF ISRAEL
A WND Books book
Published by WorldNetDaily
Los Angeles, CA
Copyright © 2009 by Aaron Klein

Jacket design by Linda Daly

WND Books are distributed to the trade by:
Midpoint Trade Books
27 West 20th Street, Suite 1102
New York, NY 10011

WND Books are available at special discounts for bulk purchases. WND Books, Inc. also publishes books in electronic formats. For more information call (310) 961-4170 or visit www.wndbooks.com.

First Edition

ISBN 13-Digit: 9781935071082
ISBN 10-Digit: 1935071084
E-Book ISBN 13-Digit: 9781935071624
E-Book ISBN 10-Digit: 1935071629
Library of Congress Control Number: 2008944358

Printed in the United States of America

10 9 8 7 6 5 4 3 2 1

TABLE OF CONTENTS

It has been four long, thrilling years since I first arrived as a journalist in the Middle East. I've reported for months on end from the rocket-battered Jewish communities of the Gaza Strip and the war-torn Israeli-Lebanese-Syrian borders. I've stood in the trenches during massive nationalist protests and Israeli evacuations of Jewish homes. I've observed from the *plenum* intense Knesset sessions and have entered the viper's den of Palestinian terrorism, conducting extensive in-person interviews with some of the world's most dangerous jihadists. I've traveled throughout the Middle East and have had the privilege of interviewing some of the region's leaders and newsmakers as well as its ordinary citizens. I've conducted extensive investigations and have forged trusted sources across the political and defense spectrums. I've dodged rockets and mortars and have broadcast from some far-off, remote locations.

Four years of this work have led me to a frightening conclusion: Israel is teetering on the brink of destruction, and hardly anyone has noticed.

After following Middle East events as closely as I could from the sidelines in America, I found that the decision to become a journalist focusing on Israeli-Palestinian affairs more or less forced itself upon me in the spring of 2004. That was when the Israeli government, led by aging warrior Ariel Sharon, decided upon a total retreat from the Gaza Strip and began uprooting the territory's Jewish communities, treating its long-sacrificing Jewish residents as outcasts, and evacuating all Israeli military personnel stationed there.

Like so many others concerned about Israel's security, I had for years watched as the Jewish state embarked on its so-called land-for-peace policy of handing over strategic cantons of territory to the Palestinians, only for much of that land to be converted into staging bases for attacks against Jews. Once it became clear that Israel would attempt an historic and complete withdrawal from Gaza, fraught with the likelihood of disastrous consequences, I felt compelled to do my part to report the possible ramifications of an Israeli retreat.

The warped picture coming from the news media about Gaza overwhelmingly painted Israel's Jewish communities there as fundamentalist settlements built upon stolen Arab land, while welcoming an Israeli withdrawal as a major step toward regional peace. Actually, as I was soon to witness firsthand, the true story was far different.

My interest in Middle East news goes back to a few years earlier, when Osama bin Laden's global jihad network—still unknown to most people in those pre-9/11 days—carried out a series of terrorist attacks against Western targets overseas. I was frustrated with the way the news media covered the issue of terrorism at the time, often describing it as regionalized conflict, as a tool used by "militants" to gain specific political or ideological ends. I knew there was more. Something told me Islamic terrorism wasn't just about remote pieces of territory or getting U.S. troops out of the Middle East.

So I decided to investigate things for myself. In 1999, as a student at Yeshiva University in New York, where I headed the undergraduate newspaper, I arranged to spend a weekend in London with the leadership of an Islamic extremist organization called al-Muhajiroun. My hosts supported the goals of al-Qaida and staged rallies in Britain calling for the downfall of America, Israel, and the U.K. and for the establishment in these countries of Islamic regimes. The top members of al-Muhajiroun patiently explained to me that the international news media were wrongly portraying jihadist attacks against the West as being about local politics. Indeed, the leaders exclaimed, Islam was on the rise and seeking to spread its belief system around the world. Knowing that I was a Jew with particular interest in Israel, the group members also told me they viewed the "Zionist entity" as an outpost of the West that must be removed to achieve regional Islamic hegemony.

I penned a piece called "My Weekend with the Enemy," which was published in a few major newspapers, including the *Boston Globe* and the *Jerusalem Post*. It forewarned of the growing threat of Islamic terrorism and highlighted the simplistic Islam-versus-the-West lens through which al-Muhajiroun viewed the Israeli-Palestinian conflict and the world.

And then terrorism hit at full force. In the summer of 2000, after walking away from U.S.-brokered negotiations and an Israeli offer of a Palestinian state, Yasser Arafat returned to his perch in the West Bank to launch his *intifada*, or terrorist war against Israelis, utilizing extreme violence targeting civilians to "liberate Palestine." Suicide bombers detonated themselves in Israeli buses, cafés, hotels, and nightclubs. Their fellow jihadists shot Jews on the highways. Just months later, the 9/11 attacks rocked the U.S. and changed everything we thought we knew about terrorism. Or at least they should have.

The news media continued to insist that terrorism was just a local, regional issue. In Israel, Palestinian violence was still portrayed as a response to "Israeli occupation," instead of as the front line in the global jihad targeting Israelis, Americans, and the West in general. The U.S. government continued to push for agreements between Israel and the Palestinians, creating a separation between terrorism against Jews and terrorism targeting everyone else. The Israeli government persisted in its drive to give away territory, this time in hopes of separating itself from the Palestinians by retreating from the Gaza Strip.

To my eyes, the chasm grew between the reality on the ground and the news media's portrayal of events. It became clearer to me that this was true not only of Israel's retreat from Gaza, but of a host of other key issues in the Israeli-Palestinian conflict. I again decided to investigate things for myself, this time on a full-time basis. I relocated from the U.S. to open a news bureau in Jerusalem, initially traveling frequently to Gaza's Jewish communities, where, in a tree-lined neighborhood under constant rocket attack, I lived until Gaza was ethnically cleansed of Jews—by a Jewish government.

And now, following a slew of willful retreats and military losses, Israel faces disaster. Enemies surround her who grow more emboldened than ever, while a maniacal Iranian regime, on the brink of going nuclear, rants about Jerusalem's annihilation. Israel remains committed to negotiating a Palestinian state—in talks strongly urged on by the Obama administration—with a "peace partner" whose official institutions indoctrinate its citizens with intense anti-Jewish hatred and violence; whose gunmen make up one of the deadliest anti-Israel terrorist groups; and whose leadership is weak, corrupt, and at serious risk of being overthrown by radical Islamists.

Israel is also under relentless pressure from an international community that favors terrorist gangs over a forward-looking Westernized democracy; that balks at any assertion of Israeli self-defense; that pressures the tiny Jewish country to evacuate vital territory; that perpetuates the Israeli-Palestinian conflict by artificially maintaining a festering "refugee" crisis; and that provides legitimacy, and at times money, weapons, and advanced training, to Israel's terrorist foes.

And a gang of internationalist politicians rules the Jewish state itself—some of whom seem more interested in making a quick buck than saving the country they are supposed to lead. Most of them are hell-bent on pursuing the same failed policies that have resulted time and again in large numbers of Jewish deaths and the handover of strategic land to terrorists, fueling a worldwide perception of Jewish weakness.

But the greatest threat, the one that magnifies all others exponentially, is that only a few in Israel or abroad are aware of the real extent of the dangers facing the Jewish country—both from within and without. This is due in part to an international and Israeli news media so entrenched in their accepted narratives that they will completely invert the truth or blindly repeat proven falsehoods, even when this requires covering for the terrorists. At times, as I will show, the Israeli and U.S. governments are just as guilty of distorting the truth, suppressing the disastrous results of their failed policies and actions, and masking the murderous ways of their Palestinian or Arab state "partners."

Few have any idea how the country is being torn apart by an Israeli war against the "national religious"—a battle of Jew versus Jew in which those in power who want the country to resemble a secular, Europeanized state suppress a significant segment of the population that wants to keep Israel a Jewish country defined by its profoundly Jewish history, traditions, and character.

Most don't know how the Hamas terrorist organization actually blasted its way to control over the Gaza Strip and how the pre-takeover stage of that same process is being played out now in the West Bank—territory slated for evacuation despite its proximity to Israel's population centers and the country's international airport. Most don't grasp the true ramifications of Israel's 2005 retreat from the Gaza Strip, of its mismanaged war in Lebanon two years later, of its failure to achieve its goals during the twenty-two-day confrontation against Hamas in Gaza that ended in January 2009, or of its longstanding negotiations to hand over more land to a weak and corrupt Palestinian regime.

There are other crucial stories that have yet to see the light of day: how the U.S. knowingly funds Palestinian terrorism; how Israel and the international community legitimize the jihadist Hamas movement; how the Jewish state has already essentially forfeited the holy Temple Mount—Judaism's most venerated site; and how, scandalously, the Israeli government has allowed hundreds of thousands of Arabs to live illegally on Jewish-owned land in Jerusalem that may, as a result, shift parts of Israel's capital to future Palestinian control.

Also minimized and little understood is the misplayed fiasco of Israeli diplomacy: how Israel legitimized the tyranny in Syria, ending its isolation even while Damascus plays host to terrorist leaders and furiously acquires thousands of advanced missiles; and how Israel has emboldened Iran to surround the Jewish state, to position its proxies on the regional chessboard such that Tehran now possesses the capability to wreak havoc on Israel.

This book is the culmination of four years of in-the-field reporting and research that has brought me to the front lines of the Middle East news cycle. While each chapter is thoroughly footnoted, the vast majority of the manuscript consists of original reporting, with many issues presented here for the first time. The book contains nearly one hundred original interviews not only with Israeli and U.S. officials, but also with leaders in Lebanon, Syria, the Palestinian Authority, and even Hamas, including the top chiefs of that group. I believe readers from all sides of the political spectrum—from those with little knowledge of regional affairs to news connoisseurs who consider themselves in command of the facts—will learn anew about a conflict at the center of the world's attention.

I intend these words as a wakeup call, written in the hope of stimulating debate on and change to the failed policies that have now led Israel to an existential crisis. As I write, both America and Israel have ushered in leaders who promise change. Meanwhile, Israel's "peace partner," the Palestinian Authority leadership, is shaky and could soon be overthrown. The policies of these new administrations remain to be seen (although, as I will document, we can expect the same failed policies to be repeated), but the region's calamitous downward spiral will be difficult to reverse. While the Psalms reassure us that "the Guardian of Israel neither slumbers nor sleeps," the current leaders of Israel are fast giving away the land and strength with which the Jews have been blessed. It is not yet too late for Israel, but if these perils are not taken to heart—and if the Israeli leadership, along with the rest of the world, continues to sail the present course—the only remnant of the Jewish country may be an epitaph: "The Late Great State of Israel."

CHAPTER ONE

MEET ISRAEL'S "PEACE PARTNER"

inutes before midnight, a terrorist cell hid quietly in a
darkened vehicle under cover of a shrubby hill. Above a
road on the West Bank frequented by Israeli motorists, the well-
armed jihadists waited in ambush for a Jew to drive by. A car
bearing easily visible yellow Israeli license plates (as opposed to
the green plates issued to Palestinian drivers) drove up the road.
At the wheel was unsuspecting Ido Zoldan, a twenty-nine-year-old
father of two and a decorated officer in Israel's prestigious Golani
Brigade. Upon seeing the Israeli plates, the terrorists sprayed
Zoldan's vehicle with a hailstorm of automatic gunfire. Ido was
mortally wounded in the attack. Though paramedics soon arrived
at the scene, they couldn't revive him.

In typical fashion, the next day, a Palestinian group publicly
took "credit" for the terrorist shooting. The al-Aqsa Martyrs
Brigades is the self-declared military wing of Israel's partner in the
"peace process," the U.S.-backed Fatah organization founded by
Yasser Arafat. The statement the Brigades released to the media
announced they would continue "resistance" operations—meaning
terrorist attacks aimed mainly at civilians—until "the liberation of all
our lands," a euphemism for the entire state of Israel.[1]

Dates are important here. Zoldan's murder took place on
November 19, 2007, only eight days before the opening of a U.S.-
sponsored peace conference in Annapolis, Maryland. The Annapolis
conference was a major Mideast summit at which Israeli Prime
Minister Ehud Olmert and Palestinian Authority President Mahmoud
Abbas, the chief of Fatah, were to commit to negotiations aimed at

creating a Fatah-led Palestinian state in the coming year. The Annapolis process was widely expected to lead to Israel's surrender of most of the West Bank and eastern sections of Jerusalem.

Fast forward two weeks to December 2, 2007. The Annapolis conference was deemed a great success. Olmert and Abbas pledged immediately to launch direct talks. Then the Israel Defense Forces dropped a bombshell—that Israeli security forces had caught the Fatah perpetrators of Zoldan's murder on the very night of the deadly shooting, meaning that the Fatah operatives had already been in Israeli custody just days before the Annapolis summit.[2] Astonishingly, the arrested culprits constituted a cell of Fatah's al-Aqsa Martyrs Brigades composed of gunmen serving simultaneously as paid police officers in a major U.S.-funded and trained Fatah security organization, the Preventative Security Services. The PSS had received a shipment of U.S. assault rifles only one month earlier, so the news that PSS members may have used U.S.-supplied weapons to murder Israeli civilians just days before a U.S.-sponsored "peace conference" was shocking indeed.

The IDF revealed that two of the Fatah suspects, Abdullah Braham and Jafar Braham, were arrested on the night of the murder. A third terrorist, Fadi Jamaa, was apprehended days later by Palestinian security forces.[3] With the Annapolis conference safely concluded, however, the news that forces of Fatah—Israel's "peace partner"—had committed Zoldan's murder did not receive much media play in Israel, or anywhere else, for that matter. The three major Israeli newspapers, all of which supported the Annapolis process, merely published back page articles reporting the arrests, but two of the three reports failed to mention that Fatah operatives had been responsible.

This incident is troubling on many levels. Fatah security officers in the West Bank carry out a terrorist attack days before a major peace summit. At this summit Israel's leaders pledge to hold intense negotiations with Fatah's chief, leading to an agreement to cede parts of the West Bank essentially to the control of Fatah security officers. When Israel arrests the Fatah operatives days before Annapolis, it knows its "peace partner" is responsible for

Zoldan's murder, but waits to announce Fatah's culpability until after the conference is over. *And no one considers this a big story.*

Asked why the IDF would withhold publication of the arrests until after Annapolis, a spokeswoman for the army referred me to a superior, who declined to comment. According to one informal explanation, the IDF waited because they were acting on intelligence from the arrested Fatah members. Possibly. But more likely is that the Israeli government did not want to expose Fatah's involvement in terrorism so close to the summit. Nationalist Knesset (parliament) member Nissan Slomiansky speculated, "If the reason why they did not publicize was in order to ease the Annapolis summit, this is a scandal of unprecedented proportions—and it must be stopped by simply refusing to hold the next round of talks with Abbas."[4]

Unfortunately, Slomiansky overstates it when he characterizes the situation as unprecedented. Rather, it is the norm. Fatah gunmen regularly carry out terrorist anti-Jewish attacks, including just before negotiations with Israel, and sometimes even while actual negotiations are going on. Israel routinely arrests Fatah terrorists, often at a rate of several arrests per week. Israeli news media regularly downplay these arrests, usually misidentifying the Fatah gunmen as belonging to another group or minimizing Fatah's involvement. Meanwhile, Fatah itself brags about its involvement, or at least takes no great pains to hide it. Evidently they are confident that their Israeli "peace partners" will cover things up for them.

DECEPTIVE SINCE ITS INCEPTION

Fatah is a reverse acronym from the Arabic name *Harakat al-Tahrir al-Watani al-Filastini*, which means "Palestinian National Liberation Movement." *Liberation* is a key word in Palestinian discourse, almost always referring to the "total liberation of Palestine," meaning all of Israel. The group was founded in 1954 by several principal Palestinian leaders, including Yasser Arafat, who, over the next fifty years, pioneered many tactics used by terrorist groups worldwide. Upon its founding, Fatah's main method of garnering international attention to its cause was carrying out attacks, including bombings, airline hijackings, and guerilla-style raids. The targets were not only Israeli, but at times also European and American. Often, Arafat maintained a degree of separation from these assaults by using "affiliate" groups, such as Black September, to carry out attacks at a deniable distance from Fatah. However, these groups unquestionably were controlled and directed by Arafat and other Fatah officials.

In one particularly notorious Black September attack, on March 1, 1973, eight operatives of Arafat's Fatah faction stormed the Saudi Arabian embassy in Khartoum, Sudan, taking as hostages U.S. ambassador Cleo Noel and the U.S. embassy's *chargé d'affaires*, George Curtis Moore, along with several others. The siege occurred during a publicly announced diplomatic reception honoring a local U.S. diplomat, leading many to suppose that the Americans were the main targets. The next day, Arafat's men machine gunned the two U.S. diplomats, Noel and Moore, to death. We know now that Arafat directly ordered these murders. Yet twenty-five years would pass before this crucial information would be revealed.

James J. Welsh was the U.S. National Security Agency's Palestinian analyst at the time of the murders. In 2001, Welsh began telling anyone who would listen that the NSA had tapes of Arafat ordering the executions of the American diplomats.[5] As a one-time primary analyst and interpreter of Arafat's communications for the NSA, Welsh revealed that in 1973, just before Black September took over the embassy, he had intercepted a transmission directly from Arafat involving an imminent operation in Khartoum. Welsh's NSA superiors were alerted. The next day, the Black September operation took place. There was immediate information that Arafat had personally given the order for the execution of the American diplomats to the terrorists via a radio broadcast in which he uttered: "Why are you waiting? The people's blood in the Cold River cries for vengeance." "Cold River" was reportedly known to American intelligence as the code phrase for executing the captives. The reported NSA recordings of that call have since disappeared.

In 1985 and 1986, Congress requested Attorney General Edwin Meese to investigate Arafat's complicity in the murders of the diplomats. Meese didn't come up with much. On February 12, 1986, some forty-seven U.S. senators, including Al Gore, petitioned Meese "to assign the highest priority to completing this review, and to issue an indictment of Yasser Arafat if the evidence so warrants."

No evidence was produced by the NSA, the Central Intelligence Agency, or the State Department; had there been any, it obviously would have undermined Arafat's image as a statesman who wanted peace with Israel and the West.

Then, in 2006, two years after Arafat's death, the U.S. government admitted that for thirty-three years it had possessed evidence that Arafat had ordered the killings of Noel and Moore. A declassified State Department document from 1973 outlining U.S. findings into the Khartoum operation states:

> The Khartoum operation was planned and carried out with the full knowledge and personal approval of Yasser Arafat, chairman of the Palestine Liberation Organization and the head of Fatah. Fatah representatives based in Khartoum participated in the attack, using a Fatah vehicle to transport the terrorists to the Saudi Arabian Embassy.[6]

This was a monumental admission. The U.S. knew Arafat had arranged the killing of its diplomats but went to great lengths to hide that information, instead building up Arafat as a legitimate statesman and showering him with money and weapons. Israel ceded key territory to Arafat, who received a Nobel Peace Prize and became one of the foreign dignitaries to visit the Clinton White House most frequently. Later, after Arafat turned down an Israeli offer of a Palestinian state in 2000 and instead launched an *intifada*, or Palestinian war of terror aimed at "liberating" Israel, the U.S. and the Jewish state worked to isolate Arafat until his death in 2004.

After Arafat's death, when his deputy, Mahmoud Abbas, became Fatah's leader and the president of the Palestinian Authority, the duplicity began anew and has now reached a fever pitch.

Fatah has not changed much ideologically from the days of Arafat. It continues to indoctrinate generations of Palestinian children to hate Israel. Official Fatah textbooks label Israel as "occupied Palestine," teaching extreme anti-Jewish propaganda similar to rhetoric from Nazi Germany. Fatah imams and clerics routinely incite violence against Jews in their sermons, broadcasts, and publications. Fatah's official media outlets incessantly celebrate terrorism and suicide bombings, as has been thoroughly documented in other books and by organizations such as Palestinian Media Watch and the Middle East Media Research Institute. A brief browsing of official Fatah media on any given day yields glaring examples of intense anti-Semitic and anti-Israel propaganda.

FROM INCITEMENT TO MURDER

Less understood and almost entirely unreported is Fatah's primary role in the Palestinian terror apparatus. Absolutely central to Fatah is its declared military wing, the al-Aqsa Martyrs Brigades, which statistically is responsible for more terrorism than the leading fundamentalist Islamic group Hamas or any other Palestinian terrorist group. Israeli and American policy considers Fatah to be moderate even while the State Department labels its subsidiary, the Brigades, as a terrorist organization.

Together with the Islamic Jihad Movement in Palestine, a Syrian-backed group, Fatah's Brigades took responsibility for every suicide bombing inside Israel in 2005, 2006, and 2007. The Brigades is responsible for thousands of shootings and rocket launchings from the Gaza Strip aimed at nearby civilian Jewish centers. After several recent suicide bombings, knifings, and shootings, the al-Aqsa Martyrs Brigades publicly boasted that it was the dominant force behind each attack. Israeli news media largely downplayed or else entirely ignored Fatah's involvement.

In a suicide bombing in Tel Aviv during Passover 2006, an American teenager and ten other civilians were murdered. Both Islamic Jihad and the Brigades took "credit" for the attack. The Brigades announced it had recruited the bomber from the northern West Bank city of Nablus (biblical Schechem), planned the attack, and infiltrated the bomber into Israel. It said Islamic Jihad merely provided the suicide belt as a symbolic act of participation in the "holy martyrdom operation." Driving home Fatah's culpability for the attack, Nasser Abu Aziz, deputy commander of the al-Aqsa Martyrs Brigades in Nablus, gave me an on-the-record interview in which he boasted of planning the attack. Still, most Israeli media reported the bombing as an Islamic Jihad operation.

The al-Aqsa Martyrs Brigades can fax reporters their statement of responsibility for a terrorist attack and the Israeli media will still ignore Fatah's direct culpability. I remember a particularly farcical situation when on September 15, 2008, the al-Aqsa Martyrs Brigades claimed responsibility along with Islamic Jihad for firing a Qassam rocket from Gaza aimed at the nearby Israeli town of Sderot. An official al-Aqsa pamphlet faxed to news agencies, including mine, stated, "We will not respect the cease fire and will continue to launch attacks against the Zionist enemy." I confirmed with the Brigades that they faxed the same statement to Israel's major newspapers.

In a deed worthy of news stories about themselves, Israeli newspapers and television networks reported only that Islamic Jihad had fired the rocket. Israel's *Ha'aretz* newspaper, for instance, featured an article headlined: "Islamic Jihad claims responsibility for Qassam attack on Sderot."[7] Similar reports appeared on the Web site of *Yediot Aharonot*, Israel's most widely circulated newspaper, and on the popular Army Radio.

When the Israeli and international news media do report on al-Aqsa Martyrs Brigades attacks, the reports many times characterize the Brigades as a "violent offshoot" of Fatah, as if Fatah no longer bears any responsibility for the Brigades's attacks on Jewish civilians. Israeli and U.S. policymaking circles have likewise created some sort of mythical separation between Fatah and its al-Aqsa Martyrs Brigades, as if the Brigades acts independently of Fatah leadership, when, in fact, the Brigades is part of Fatah's leadership.

Any real separation between Fatah and its terrorist branch exists largely in the minds of those who wish to ignore reality. On the ground, Fatah openly and fully integrates the al-Aqsa Martyrs Brigades into its ranks.

Some Fatah parliament leaders are also well-known Brigades members. Marwan Barghouti, the number two member of the Fatah parliament after chief Palestinian negotiator Ahmed Queri, founded the Brigades along with Arafat. In 2004, an Israeli court convicted Barghouti, who has boasted of being an architect of the *intifada*, on five counts of murder. Number three on Fatah's parliament list is

Abu Ali Yata, sentenced by Israel in the 1980s for killing two Israelis, then released in a 2008 prisoner exchange.

Other Fatah parliament members who served in the Brigades include Nasser Jumaa, previously the well known chief of the al-Aqsa Martyrs Brigades in Nablus and accused by Israel of participating in dozens of terror attacks, and Jamal Tarawi, a top member of the Brigades in the Old City of Nablus, where, among other things, he led a series of attacks in 2000 against Israelis at Joseph's Tomb, Judaism's third holiest site. Also on Fatah's parliament list is Hassam Khader, who served eight years in an Israeli prison after he was found guilty of raising funds for the Brigades from Hezbollah and Iran; and Jamal Hweil, a leader of the Brigades in Jenin. I should mention Fatah holds only forty-five of 132 parliamentary seats, which means Fatah's legislative body is teeming with Brigades terrorists.

Brigades members serve in Fatah's official security forces as well, as chapter seven will detail. For this book, I was provided with a list of the fifty most senior Brigades leaders. I found that all of them—every single one—serve in various Fatah security forces. Abbas in early 2006 appointed senior al-Aqsa Martyrs Brigades leader Mahmoud Damra as commander of the Force 17 Palestinian security unit. Damra, arrested by Israel in November 2006, was on the Jewish state's most wanted list of terrorists.

It requires no serious investigative reporting to discover members of "mainstream" Fatah militias who are also members of the violent al-Aqsa Martyrs Brigades. Fatah does not attempt to hide its integration of the Brigades. "During our official service and during our job hours we are soldiers for Fatah. What we do in our free time is our business," Abu Yousuf, a Brigades chief in Ramallah who doubles as a Fatah security officer, explained to me in a 2007 interview. "Of course as members of Fatah, some of us are members in the Brigades and we take part in the defense and protection of our people and in the fight against the Israeli occupation."

I know through off-the-record conversations that Brigades leaders are in regular communication with several top Fatah officials, including at least one senior Palestinian negotiator who leads a team that conducts talks with the Israeli government.

Does the al-Aqsa Martyrs Brigades coordinate their terror attacks with Fatah's highest leadership? I have not found any conclusive "smoking gun" proof that the highest Fatah leaders, such as Mahmoud Abbas, give explicit instructions directly to the Brigades to carry out specific attacks, the way that Arafat was recorded ordering the murders of the American diplomats in Khartoum. Superficially, there appears to be at least a degree of separation, and therefore a façade of deniability, to the Abbas-Brigades connection.

I once asked a top Brigades terrorist if he had received instructions from Abbas or other senior Fatah officials when, in January 2007, the Brigades took responsibility for a series of rocket attacks from Gaza, some of which took place during the exact time Israeli and Palestinian leaders met for rounds of talks aimed at ceding territory to Fatah. A reporter for the Israel Resource News Agency asked Israeli Prime Minister Ehud Olmert's spokeswoman, Miri Eisin, whether she knew if the Brigades were coordinating their attacks with Fatah. Eisin replied that the Brigades militants firing the rockets from Gaza were not affiliated with Fatah and did not take orders from Abbas, who, she said, had repeatedly condemned the rocket attacks.[8]

In response to Eisin's statements, I interviewed Abu Ahmed, at the time the al-Aqsa Martyrs Brigades chief in the northern Gaza Strip. He told me his group, including the militants launching rockets, is loyal to Abbas and coordinates "resistance operations" with the Fatah party. "The al-Aqsa Brigades is the military wing of the Fatah and President Abu Mazen [Abbas] is the chairman of the movement. We are committed to our leadership, to Abu Mazen. All our activity is in accordance with the political line of Fatah, which consists of fighting the occupation until the creation of a Palestinian state. The rocket shooting is part of this vision," Abu Ahmed said.

Asked why Abbas had distanced himself from the Brigades's attacks, Abu Ahmed replied, "Listen, we are aware of our president's [Abbas's] declarations but we are also aware of the international political system that brings the president to adopt this position." The terrorist leader said that Abbas had never asked his group to halt the rocket fire: "We know what is Fatah's general political line and we act according to this line and I can say that we were never asked to stop shooting rockets. Therefore, the rocket shooting is not in any way harming our loyalty and our commitment to [Abbas] and his leadership."

Much of the Brigades's terrorism is strategic and very obviously promotes Fatah's agenda. The January rocket attacks, for instance, took place during a ceasefire that had been signed between Israel and Gaza-based terrorist groups three months earlier. During the period of the "truce," more than sixty rockets had been fired by Palestinians from Gaza, seriously injuring two Jewish teenagers and disrupting life in neighboring Israeli cities. The Brigades took "credit" for most of the attacks, in an obvious attempt to disrupt the truce. A ceasefire at the time would have favored Hamas, which had been consolidating power in Gaza and had engaged in repeated, intense clashes with Fatah. But Abbas's group did not want Hamas to be the deal makers and truce brokers in Gaza. So, due to Palestinian political infighting, Israel's "peace partner" fired rockets at Jewish homes.

FATAH GLORIFICATION OF TERRORISTS

Aside from maintaining a murderous group that terrorizes and kills Jewish citizens, Abbas and other senior Fatah officials do not shy away from publicly supporting and celebrating terrorism, as when Abbas held a meeting with one of the vilest of anti-Israel terrorists.

In August 2008, it was widely reported that Abbas had a sit-down in Beirut with Samir Kuntar, a notorious child-murdering terrorist. Israel had freed Kuntar a month earlier in a bitterly controversial prisoner exchange deal with the Lebanese Hezbollah terrorist group. That deal finally saw the return to Israel of the bodies of two Israeli soldiers abducted by Hezbollah in 2006, a kidnapping raid that led to full-scale war between Israel and Hezbollah in Lebanon.

Some twenty years earlier, on April 22, 1979, Kuntar had led a team of four terrorists who entered Israel from Lebanon by boat to carry out an attack. The four first murdered a policeman who discovered them when they entered Israeli territory. The raiding party then invaded an Israeli border town, breaking into an apartment and taking hostage twenty-eight-year-old Danny Haran along with his four-year-old daughter, Einat. Danny's wife, Smadar Haran, was able to hide in a crawl space above the bedroom with her two-year-old daughter, Yael, and a neighbor. Smadar, though, accidentally smothered her daughter to death while trying to mute her cries. Kuntar shot Danny Haran to death and then beat Haran's four-year-old daughter to death with his rifle.

Over the years, the baby killer Kuntar became a hero in Lebanon and in the Palestinian territories. When Abbas's 2008 meeting with Kuntar generated some Israeli criticism, the Palestinian leader claimed the meet-and-greet had been unplanned and that Kuntar had in fact invited himself. This prompted Kuntar to release his own statement to the news media asserting it was Abbas who had requested the meeting.[9]

Despite Abbas's public attempts to distance himself from Kuntar, Fatah's true opinion of the terrorist is well known. Just after Kuntar was released, Abbas, speaking from Malta, told the Arabic news media, "I congratulate the family of the hero [K]untar and the families of other prisoners to be released."[10] As far as I could find, I was the only English-language reporter to quote those remarks. One week later, after Kuntar had settled down in Lebanon, Fatah sent a full delegation to visit him, calling the child killer "beautiful," and a "pure and clean" hero. Palestinian Liberation Organization ambassador to Lebanon Abbas Zaki, a senior member of the Fatah Central Committee, led this delegation—which included other PLO and Fatah members—to visit Kuntar in Lebanon's Mount Druze village of Abayeh.

Zaki's office e-mailed me his in-person statements to Kuntar, which included this:

> These are great hours that we are celebrating a big victory represented by your being released.... You are a leader of Arab and Palestinian prisoners. I am proud that this delegation has you in our minds and hearts. Your beautiful image; your pure and clean person who dedicated his life since very young to Palestine and to Palestinian causes.

Kuntar's release was widely reported, but much less known was that in the same release deal Israel also exchanged the body of an infamous female terrorist, Dalal al-Mughrabi, glorified by Fatah and in the greater Palestinian terrorist community as one of their most significant martyred "heroes." In March 1978, Mughrabi planned and led a treacherous attack in which she and ten other Palestinians infiltrated Israel by sea, landed on a beach, killed an American photographer, and then hijacked a crowded bus. Israeli forces pursued the bus, sparking a long shooting battle in which the terrorists fired from bus windows at nearby passenger cars, killing several Israelis. Eventually, the terrorists blew up the bus in a suicide operation, killing themselves and a total of thirty-six civilians. It was one of the bloodiest attacks to strike the Jewish state.

Israel kept the remains of Mughrabi and her fellow assassins in part so that Palestinian society would not turn their burial places into shrines. But Fatah has long glorified Mughrabi as one of the most important "martyrs" in Palestinian society. Official Fatah institutions, such as Fatah-run girls' schools and police training camps, bear her name. Fatah-controlled television and radio routinely broadcast songs and poems in her honor. During the Palestinian *intifada*, Fatah's al-Aqsa Martyrs Brigades named a cell after Mughrabi. That cell, which is still active, perpetrates numerous shootings and suicide bombings. The Brigades routinely renames cells after infamous terrorists, such as George Habash, who was the leader of the Popular Front for the Liberation of Palestine. The Marxist-Leninist nationalist PFLP is the second-largest political and military grouping in the PLO.

The PFLP gained notoriety in 1970 for hijacking four Western airliners over the U.S., Europe, the Far East, and the Persian Gulf. The aircraft were blown up in the Middle East after passengers and crew disembarked. In 1972, the PFLP then gunned down twenty-seven people at Israel's Lod airport. It continues operating from Syria, Jordan, and the West Bank. More recent attacks include scores of deadly shootings against Israelis; the 2001 assassination of Rechavam Ze'evi, Israel's tourism minister; and suicide bombings on an Israeli highway and in Tel Aviv's popular Karmel Market.

Habash died of a heart attack in January 2008. After his death, Abbas declared three days of mourning while Fatah news media broadcast constant streams of footage memorializing Habash. According to Palestinian diplomatic sources I interviewed, Abbas personally received lines of mourners for Habash during the three mourning days, but he was interrupted by a meeting with Olmert during which the two discussed the peace process.

In fact, Fatah celebrates nearly every major bloody attack against Israel. On March 6, 2008, a gunman walked into the Mercaz Harav Yeshiva, a prominent boys' seminary located where the main highway enters Jerusalem, and fired hundreds of rounds at students studying sacred texts in the library, killing eight children and wounding about a dozen more.

Fatah's news media networks praised the bloody massacre as "heroic." It later turned out the attack was planned by a terrorist associated with Fatah, who moonlighted with Islamic Jihad and similar groups.

"In a heroic act of martyrdom, at least one hero infiltrated a Zionist school in occupied Jerusalem," stated the beginning of a news dispatch on Fatah's *Firas Press* Web site.[11] Another Fatah-affiliated news site that I browsed, *PalPress*, also used the term "heroic" to lionize the perpetrator of the *yeshiva* massacre.[12]

One week after the bloody shooting, the IDF carried out an arrest raid in which it killed Muhammad Shehadi, a Bethlehem-area operative identified by security officials as the planner of the *yeshiva* massacre. A few days before, Israeli forces had bulldozed Shehadi's home in retaliation for the attack.

Shehadi was a well known Fatah agent who also worked with other groups of assassins. He ran and lost in the 2006 Palestinian elections as a Fatah candidate. According to Palestinian security officials familiar with Shehadi, after losing his election bid as a Fatah leader, Shehadi worked for about six months for Islamic Jihad but then switched back to Fatah. A Palestinian security official, speaking just after Shehadi was killed, explained that Shehadi had continued to work with Islamic Jihad sporadically but he was more readily identified with Fatah. "He was Fatah," the security official told me. "In the last few weeks, he was working only with Fatah. Islamic Jihad might consider him among their men in Bethlehem, but it's absolutely wrong for [the Israeli media] to label him as the Islamic Jihad commander."

"He would go wherever the money was," said the Palestinian security official. "He thought he could get more money from Islamic Jihad, so he worked for them for a few months, but then switched back to Fatah because he didn't like his Islamic Jihad salary."

According to Israeli security officials I spoke with, Shehadi was killed after the Israeli military received intelligence that he planned to attend a secret Fatah congress planning meeting in Bethlehem. Shehadi was killed along with Ahmed Dalbul, a Bethlehem-area leader of the al-Aqsa Martyrs Brigades, Fatah's declared military wing.

ISRAELI MEDIA COVER-UP

All of Shehadi's Fatah connections are well established. Yet the Israeli media persisted in portraying him as an Islamic Jihad man. *Ynet,* the Web site affiliated with *Yediot Aharonot,* Israel's leading daily, identified Shehadi as "an Islamic Jihad operative" who planned the *yeshiva* shooting.[13] Israel's *Ha'aretz* newspaper reported Shehadi was "the commander of Islamic Jihad in the Bethlehem area," and was killed along with "two other Islamic Jihad members."[14] Israel's Channel 2 identified Shehadi as Islamic Jihad. None of the Israeli news media reports I read described Shehadi as working for Fatah.

It sometimes seems there is no "red line" Fatah can cross that would prompt the Israeli news media to brand the organization as extremist. Apparently, this includes Abbas himself calling for attacks against Israel in a speech before the international news media.

In one of the most absurd moments I have experienced as a reporter in Israel, in January 2007, it was widely reported that the U.S. had shipped assault rifles to arm Abbas's Fatah militias. Abbas gave a public speech in Ramallah in front of hundreds of Palestinians and the international and Israeli news media in which he urged Palestinians to use their assault rifles against Israel instead of the rival Hamas group.

"Shooting at your brother is forbidden. Raising rifles against the occupation is our legitimate right, but raising guns against each other is forbidden. We should put our internal fighting aside and raise our rifles only against the Israeli occupation," said Abbas during the speech, which I attended and which was part of a ceremony commemorating the forty-second anniversary of the founding of his Fatah party.

Abbas then cited Koranic verses to claim that Jews are corrupting the world. "The sons of Israel are mentioned as those who are corrupting humanity on Earth," Abbas said during a portion of his speech in which he criticized recent Israeli anti-terror raids in the northern West Bank.

But scores of Israeli and English-language articles reporting on the speech never quoted Abbas's anti-Semitic remarks or his call to arms against the Jewish state. Most of the articles, written by reporters in attendance, claimed that Abbas had given a talk about making peace with Israel. Some of the articles deliberately cut out Abbas's anti-Israel remarks. For example, a widely circulated Associated Press article entitled "Abbas calls for respect at Fatah rally" stated that Abbas had used his speech to call for rival factions to respect each other. The Associated Press quoted Abbas as saying, "Shooting at your brother is forbidden," but the article stops short of quoting the rest of Abbas's sentence in which he recommends Palestinians use their weapons against Israel.[15]

AMNESTY, SHAMNESTY

Five months after that speech, one of the most dangerous exposures of Fatah as less than moderate began playing itself out. In June 2007, Olmert announced he was granting amnesty to hundreds of al-Aqsa Martyrs Brigades terrorists as a gesture to bolster Fatah against Hamas. As part of an effort to help solidify its control of the West Bank following Hamas's seizure of Gaza, Fatah leaders had requested that Israel pardon members of its Brigades hit group so that Fatah would be better able to fight Hamas. All at once, this request and the resultant Israeli "gesture" exposed Fatah as supporting terror and negated the imaginary separation

15

between Fatah and the al-Aqsa Martyrs Brigades. The very request, that Fatah would need pardons for hundreds of terrorists to help bolster itself, contradicts the organization's image as moderate and as Israel's partner for peace.

The Israeli amnesty was supposedly conditioned on the Fatah terrorists' disarming, refraining from attacks against Israel, and spending three months in PA detention facilities and another three months confined to the West Bank city in which they resided. If the terrorists completed their side of the deal, Israel would grant them permanent amnesty, allowing the various killers freedom of movement in the West Bank and taking them off Israel's most wanted list to ensure they would not subsequently be arrested.

At first Olmert pardoned 178 Fatah terrorists. Then another forty-five received amnesty, then about fifty more. Then seventy-five more. Eventually, almost the entire al-Aqsa Martyrs Brigades obtained temporary amnesty, and about 45 percent won permanent amnesty, including much of the senior Brigades leadership, who maintain their amnesty under the new Israeli administration of Benjamin Netanyahu. But of course the pardoned Brigades members, including many terrorists who received permanent amnesty, never kept their side of the deal. Instead, the triggermen openly brandished their weapons and continued to attack Israel.

In the month of September 2007 alone, attacks by the Brigades included a series of shootings and the lobbing of grenades at IDF forces in the West Bank. In the same month, Palestinian gunmen ambushed three Israeli civilians, two women and a man, as they drove between the West Bank Jewish communities of Karnei Shomron and Kidumim. According to Brigades sources, Brigades snipers on the amnesty list carried out the attack. Ayad Frehat, a Brigades leader in the West Bank city of Jenin, told me that month that his group in the West Bank would neither disarm nor cease attacks on the Jewish state in spite of an amnesty. "We respect our leaders but will keep fighting until Israel withdraws completely from the West Bank. We are the resistance. We will keep fighting and never give up our weapons until Israel withdraws," said Frehat.

On many occasions, Israeli security forces caught pardoned Fatah terrorists red-handed plotting attacks. Just a few examples: the

IDF on September 16, 2007, arrested pardoned Brigades member Fadi al-Kene after catching him smuggling explosives into the West Bank city of Nablus. Al-Kene carried a small pistol at the time of his arrest. One month earlier, the IDF had caught two pardoned Brigades terrorists smuggling bullets from Jenin to the al-Badin checkpoint outside Nablus. The amnesty merely granted them the freedom of movement to attempt to transfer their munitions.

In April 2008, Israel released the information that it had captured two Palestinians from Nablus who worked illegally at the Grill Express, a restaurant in the city of Ramat Gan, a satellite of Tel Aviv. Upon interrogation, Aham Rial and Anas Salum, both twenty-one years old, confessed they planned to poison the restaurant food with a white, odorless, tasteless deadly poison that they said takes effect about five hours after it is ingested.[16] According to security officials I spoke to, there is specific information that Hani Caabe, a senior Brigades leader in the Old City of Nablus who had received a pardon from Israel, sent the two on their mission.

The sheer number of attacks and foiled plots involving pardoned Fatah terrorists are too numerous to list here. The threat to the citizens of Israel posed by the amnesty deal, pushed through as part of the illusion of a peace partnership, is clear and present.

"PEACE PARTNER" FUNDING, ARMING GLOBAL JIHAD?

In what might be the most outrageous example of the "moderate" Fatah supporting terror, off-the-record information from informed security officials indicates that about a year after Hamas took over Gaza, Fatah began supporting al-Qaida allies in the territory, including some of the most radical Islamist organizations. August and September 2008 saw a strange and marked rise in the boldness of fundamentalist Islamist organizations in Gaza, particularly three groups: Jihadiya Salafiya (the Jihad of Ancestors), Jaish al-Islam (Army of Islam), and the Islamist Doghmosh clan, a powerful Gaza family. The Doghmoshes lead Jaish al-Islam, but also act independently as a clan. They achieved notoriety for the March 2007 abduction of BBC reporter Alan Johnston.

Jihadiya Salafiya announced in August 2008 that it had established an armed wing, called the Damascus Soldiers, and it brandished weapons in a public display in Gaza. Suddenly, all three Islamist organizations—Salafiya, Jaish, and the Doghmosh clan—evidenced an infusion of weapons and began openly to challenge Hamas. These three Gazan Islamist organizations subscribe to a strict interpretation of the Koran, unlike other radical Islamic organizations such as Hamas and the Muslim Brotherhood, which have demonstrated "laxity" in some aspects of political life while still holding an Islamic worldview. The three groups openly identify with al-Qaida ideologically; they believe in jihad as the primary way to spread Islam around the world, including jihad against secular Muslim states.

Hamas had in the past worked with the al-Qaida-allied groups in Gaza. It took "credit" along with Jaish al-Islam for the kidnapping in June 2006 of Israeli soldier Gilad Shalit. But Jihadiya Salifiya and Jaish al-Islam later began attacking Hamas by publishing pamphlets labeling Hamas as "non-Muslim" since the actively homicidal group had run in the 2006 democratic elections, which the Islamist organizations viewed as an unacceptable expression of Western values. Since the elections, al-Qaida leaders outside of Israel have released audiotapes at a frequency of about six per year, blasting Hamas for participating in elections and in the democratic process. Hamas engaged in heavy fire clashes with the al-Qaida-oriented Islamist organizations in Gaza in September 2008 in which eleven were killed.

According to informed security officials, top members of Fatah funneled large quantities of cash to Jihadiya Salafiya, Jaish al-Islam, and the Doghmoshes in a bid to build up the Islamist groups at the expense of Hamas. These security officials denied any official decision within Fatah to bolster the Islamist radicals, saying that top Fatah officials acted independently. A perusal in August and September of official Fatah Web sites, including Fatah news sites, revealed a strange phenomenon—Fatah was publishing the anti-Hamas pamphlets of the three Islamist organizations in question and also providing the al-Qaida-linked groups a platform to espouse their ideology. Fatah news sites had previously shied away from promoting al-Qaida. A senior source in Hamas's Interior Ministry told me that Hamas had arrested a number of Fatah members in Gaza suspected of serving as links between the Islamist ultra-radicals and Fatah officials in the West Bank city of Ramallah.

Despite this, the U.S. and Israel continue to uphold Fatah as a partner in peace. Before long, the myth of a moderate Fatah may help to generate a crisis of unimaginable proportions, with President Barack Obama supporting negotiations in which Israel is committed to grant Fatah control of most of the West Bank and perhaps sections of eastern Jerusalem—areas bordering Israel's central population centers and within rocket distance of the country's international airport. And yet there seems to be little debate within Israeli society regarding the wisdom of evacuating strategic territory and handing it over to a Palestinian organization seeped in violence and terror and whose leadership, school system, and official media outlets celebrate Jewish death and make very clear that its goal is the total elimination of Israel.

CHAPTER TWO

HOW ISRAEL ALREADY DIVIDED JERUSALEM

It was a hot July day in the holy city. The elegant King David Hotel was preparing for the arrival within hours of then-U.S. presidential candidate Barack Obama, who was visiting Israel on a whirlwind tour of Europe and the Middle East.

Just down the street from the King David, a few hundred feet away on Keren Hayesod Street, a massive bulldozer rammed into pedestrians and oncoming traffic, injuring nineteen people, including a mother and her infant and a man whose leg was severed. The attack stopped only when an armed civilian and a border policeman shot the bulldozer terrorist dead. Twenty-two-year-old Hassan Abu Tir, an Israeli citizen living in an Arab eastern Jerusalem neighborhood, was later identified as the driver.[1]

The bloody rampage of July 22, 2008, was only the latest in a series of terrorist attacks in western, mostly Jewish, sections of Jerusalem carried out by Arabs living in neighborhoods of the eastern part of the city. The bulldozer attack mimicked a similar one earlier in July, when another Israeli Arab from eastern Jerusalem had stolen a bulldozer from a construction site and plowed into street traffic and unarmed pedestrians. In that attack, three civilians were killed before that savage driver also was shot by an armed Israeli.[2]

Four months earlier, on March 6, 2008, a thug infiltrated the Mercaz Harav boys' seminary in Jerusalem and shot to death eight *yeshiva* children and wounded many others. Scenes of the *yeshiva's* blood-soaked floors and of bodies being lined up outside the library soon flashed onto Israeli television. I arrived outside the *yeshiva* about an hour after the attack and watched as prayer books, Torah scrolls, and Talmud texts soaked with blood were carried from the building.

Living under the constant threat of terrorist attack, Israel maintains a full-time emergency squad of religiously trained workers whose job it is to clean up and properly bury usually unidentified body parts in the aftermath of these outrages. The head of this emergency service—known by its Hebrew acronym ZAKA— was among the first to arrive at the *yeshiva* following the attack. He described the scene inside as a "slaughterhouse."[3]

ISRAEL'S LEADERS JUSTIFY CAPITAL CONCESSIONS

Just days after the second bulldozer attack in July, Prime Minister Ehud Olmert used the terrorist rampage to propound the necessity of Israel ceding largely Arab eastern sections of Jerusalem to the Palestinians. "Whoever thinks it's possible to live with 270,000 Arabs in Jerusalem must take into account that there will be more bulldozers, more tractors, and more cars carrying out attacks," Olmert said.[4] At the time, Olmert was conducting intensive negotiations with the Palestinian Authority. Those talks grew out of the November 2007 U.S.-sponsored Annapolis conference, which sought to create a Palestinian state before President Bush departed office in 2009.

Olmert argued that there are too many Arabs in eastern Jerusalem, that their neighborhoods are increasingly fundamentalist and ungovernable, and that Israel must therefore separate itself from these parts of the city in any settlement of the Israeli-Palestinian conflict. To drive home the point, Olmert's vice premier, Haim Ramon, spelled it out in the Knesset, Israel's parliament. "One of the main reasons that the attack was carried out with such ease was because there are Palestinian villages that for some reason are called Jerusalem—Jebl Mukaber and Sur Bahir. They need to be treated as we treat Ramallah, Bethlehem, Jenin, and Nablus."[5] Ramon was referring to the peripheral eastern Jerusalem neighborhoods that were home to the perpetrators of the recent attacks, and he was arguing that these neighborhoods, as a bloc, should be treated as a separate Arab city.

Over the years, those densely populated Arab neighborhoods have truly come to resemble the various West Bank Arab cities. While these sections of Jerusalem are legally under Israel's jurisdiction, even Israeli police units stay off of their streets. Instead, Arab civilian patrol organizations closely affiliated with the PA carry out most police duties. The eastern Jerusalem areas have increasingly become home to Islamic radicals. According to Israeli security organizations, a significant terrorist apparatus is now based in eastern Jerusalem. Its clear aim is to keep up a steady stream of attacks on western Jerusalem neighborhoods in order to pressure Israel into ceding eastern Jerusalem—exactly what Olmert and Ramon and other believers in the "peace process" advocate. While it is not yet clear how far Prime Minister Benjamin Netanyahu is willing to go, President Barack Obama backs continuing Israeli-Palestinian negotiations where they were left off by Olmert, according to both Israeli and Palestinian diplomatic sources. Indeed, Secretary of State Hillary Clinton in March 2009 affirmed the U.S. would be "vigorously engaged in the pursuit of a two-state solution every step of the way."[6]

JEWISH POLICIES DRIVE ARAB GROWTH

The sad fact is that Israeli leaders and at least one major U.S. Jewish group are directly responsible for the rapid growth of Jerusalem's Arab enclaves. As I will document, they have allowed over one hundred thousand Arabs to occupy tens of thousands of illegally constructed housing units in eastern and northern Jerusalem—including on land purchased by Jews for the express purpose of Jewish construction; and these real estate quislings are unwilling to contest illegal Arab settlement while eastern Jerusalem communities became Arab-majority sanctuaries for terrorists.

During the 1967 Six Day War, Israel recaptured eastern Jerusalem—including Judaism's holiest site, the Temple Mount—from the Hashemite kingdom of Jordan. The Jordanians attacked Israel in 1948 and occupied Jerusalem illegally until 1967 when Jordan attacked Israel again but were repulsed, with the result, among other things, that Jerusalem returned to Jewish sovereignty. While Jews have maintained a presence in Jerusalem for three thousand years, there has been a constantly increasing Jewish majority in the city since at least since 1850, when about twelve thousand Jews lived there along with about five thousand Christians and about four thousand Muslims. Many Jews were violently expelled during deadly Arab revolts in 1929. Today, Jerusalem has an estimated total population of 724,000, of whom about two-thirds, or roughly half a million, are Jews, and about a third, or a quarter of a million, are Arabs, mostly Muslim, but also including many Arab Christians.[7]

The Palestinians have not always claimed eastern Jerusalem as a future capital. Despite Arab claims and propaganda to the contrary, Jerusalem was never "Islam's third holiest city," after Mecca and Medina, as I will document in chapter five. The traditional religious centrality that Jerusalem enjoys for Jews and Christians is absent in Muslim traditions. Instead, Arab and Muslim claims to the city emerged only in the twentieth century, in response to political Zionism.

The weakness of Arab and Muslim claims notwithstanding, major Jerusalem neighborhoods now seem slated for incorporation into the capital of a Palestinian state unless Israel gets strong new leadership. Included in the Palestinian capital are the present northeastern Jerusalem suburbs of Kalandiya, Kfar Akev, Samir Amis, and an area known as Shoafat adjacent to the northern Jewish neighborhoods of Neve Yaacov and Pisgat Ze'ev. All four neighborhoods, now occupied by large numbers of Arabs, are routinely referred to by Israeli leaders when floating plans regarding the cession of Jerusalem's territory.

"It is in Israel's interest that all the Jewish neighborhoods in Jerusalem receive international recognition, and that Arab neighborhoods like Shoafat are transferred to the Palestinians," Vice Premier Ramon told one meeting of the Israeli government's security cabinet.[8] Those neighborhoods, according to numerous informed sources, were also slated for forfeit to a Palestinian state by former Prime Minister Ehud Barak during the U.S.-brokered Camp David Accords in 2000, in which Barak offered the late Palestinian leader Yasser Arafat a state in most of the West Bank, Gaza, and eastern Jerusalem.

ARABS BUILD ON JEWISH LAND

After a considerable amount of journalistic excavation I discovered that some of the eastern Jerusalem land likely to be ceded—specifically 720 acres in Kalandiya and Kfar Akev and fifty acres in Shoafat—was actually purchased by a Jewish group for the explicit purpose of Jewish settlement, but instead was utilized for illegal Arab construction. This land, purchased by the Jewish National Fund, or JNF, remains under the management of the Israeli government in an agreement with the JNF. The JNF today sits in coalition with major American Jewish organizations, some of which in turn provide the JNF with crucial funding. The JNF solicits other funds from individual donors.

The land in question was legally purchased on behalf of the JNF using Jewish donations in the early 1900s, immediately after the organization's founding, with the specific charge of repurchasing and developing the land of Israel for Jewish settlement.

During a tour of Kalandiya and Kfar Akev I found dozens of Arab apartment complexes housing thousands of Arabs, a Palestinian refugee camp supported by the UN, and a UN school for Palestinians constructed on the Jewish-owned land. According to officials in Israel's Housing Ministry, Arabs first constructed a few facilities illegally in Kalandiya and Kfar Akev between 1948 and 1967, when the kingdom of Jordan controlled the land. Sections of Kalandiya, still owned by JNF, came under the management of the Israeli government's Land Authority in the late 1960s.

According to these officials, the vast majority of illegal Arab construction in Kalandiya and Kfar Akev has taken place in the last twenty years—under Israeli supervision—with construction of several new Arab apartment complexes still going on just prior to the publication of this book. Neither the Israeli government nor the JNF has taken any concrete measures to stop the illegal Arab building.

The JNF also purchased much of Jerusalem's Shoafat neighborhood in the early 1900s and placed it under the management of the Israel Land Authority about forty years ago. A good deal of the illegal Arab construction in Shoafat has taken place in the past fifteen years, with some apartment complexes still being built as of this writing. In Kalandiya, Kfar Akev, Samir Amis and

Shoafat, Israel has built a security fence that cordons off the "Arab sections" of the JNF land from the rest of Jewish Jerusalem—another sign that the neighborhoods are slated for Israeli forfeiture.

Some of the internal JNF documents I obtained describe illegal Arab construction on the Jewish-owned land. A survey of Kalandiya, for example, conducted in December 2000, summarized on JNF stationery and signed by a JNF employee, states: "In a lot of the plots I find Arabs are living and building illegally and also working the JNF land without permission." The JNF staffer goes on to document illegal construction of Arab apartment complexes and the UN school under the property management of Israel's Land Authority.

In an official clarification I received regarding the status of the Jewish-owned land, the JNF wrote: "The documents you obtained show clearly that the manager of these lands is the Israel Land Authority. It is evident that JNF is caring for these lands with inquiries, passing information and much more." The JNF charter, viewable on the organization's Web site, states: "Since the first land purchase in Eretz Israel in the early 1900s for and on behalf of the Jewish People, JNF has served as the Jewish People's trustee of the land, initiating and charting development work to enable Jewish settlement from the border in the north to the edge of the desert and Arava in the south."[9]

Following the initial publication of my findings, angry JNF donors apparently contacted the organization for clarification. But the JNF's response was misleading. The organization's CEO, Russell Robinson, sent letters stating that the Jewish-owned land that I investigated "was under Jordanian management prior to 1967."

"During that time the Jordanian government oversaw all activities, including the UN building. Under international law this makes matters pertaining to the land more complicated than what [Klein describes]," stated Robinson's letter to donors.

It is true that Jordan, together with other Arab countries, attacked Israel after its founding in 1948 and administered eastern sections of Jerusalem following an armistice agreement. The agreement lasted until Jordan attacked again and Israel liberated the entire city of Jerusalem in 1967. During the period of

Jordanian control, some new construction took place, including in areas previously purchased by Jews.

But a careful examination of certified Israeli government aerial photos that I obtained of the JNF sites which Robinson claimed were illegally built upon prior to 1967 while under Jordanian control, reveals a much different story. A photo taken in 1991 of one of the sites, Shoafat, shows the entire area was a forest—meaning all illegal Arab construction took place long after 1967, while the land was under Israeli control. An aerial photo taken in 1967 of the second site, Kalandiya, which is now a large Arab town, shows construction of a UN building, but few other sites, indicating the vast majority of Arab construction—dozens of large apartment complexes—occurred under JNF control. In other words, Russell's explanation that illegal Arab construction on his group's property took place during the Jordanian occupation is for the most part simply inaccurate.

ISRAEL BARS JEWISH OWNERS FROM JERUSALEM

Not all properties in eastern Jerusalem are owned by the JNF. Some land is owned by private Jewish landlords. In one case, the Israeli police barred the Jewish owner of a property in Shoafat from reclaiming his land.

In August 2008, dozens of activists flanked by two nationalist Knesset members attempted to enter Shoafat to reclaim a five-acre Jewish property on behalf of the site's owner, identified as a private Israeli citizen named Eliyahu Cohanim, who had given the group power of attorney over the site. Cohanim said that he had been dismayed to find Arabs building illegally on his land and that the PA was planning to construct in the area, including on his property.[10]

As the group congregated near Shoafat, policemen reached the area and prevented the Jewish activists from entering the neighborhood. The police announced that they had a court order barring Israeli Jews from entering the site without police coordination. It was the third time the police had blocked the group acting on behalf of Cohanim from exercising his right to reclaim his legally owned land. During the other attempts, the police charged the group with disturbing the peace.

"[The Israeli police] help the Arab criminals who build on Jewish land in Jerusalem and, instead of destroying the [illegal] Arab houses, they prevent the owner of the land in Jerusalem from going into the land," said National Union Party Knesset Member Aryeh Eldad.[11] Knesset Member Effie Eitam, also of the National Union party, participated in the attempts to reclaim the land. He accused the Israeli government of "dividing Jerusalem" by not allowing Jews into an Arab-occupied, largely Jewish-owned neighborhood.[12]

I found that some of the illegal Arab construction in numerous other eastern Jerusalem neighborhoods took place in the mid-1990s, while Olmert was still mayor of Jerusalem (from 1993 through 2003). At the time, Mayor Olmert famously made repeated public statements calling Jerusalem the "eternal and undivided capital" of Israel. According to current and former Jerusalem municipal workers interviewed for this book, however, during Olmert's tenure as mayor he instructed city workers not to take action against hundreds of illegal Arab building projects throughout eastern Jerusalem, giving housing to thousands of Arabs. "He did nothing about rampant illegal Arab construction in Jerusalem while the government cracked down on illegal Jewish construction in the West Bank," said one municipal employee who worked under Olmert. She spoke on condition of anonymity because she still works at the municipality. A former municipal worker during Olmert's mayoral tenure told me he had been transferred in 1999 to a different government posting after he tried to highlight the illegal Arab construction in eastern Jerusalem. This whistleblower also spoke on condition of anonymity, fearing for his current job.

The Jerusalem Forum is a nationalist activist organization that promotes Jewish construction in eastern Jerusalem. In 2007 it published an investigation that got a small amount of Israeli news coverage, claiming Olmert's city hall had deleted hundreds of files documenting illegal Arab building projects throughout Jerusalem's eastern sections.[13] The Forum's conveyed its findings to Israel's state comptroller for investigation. The report detailed cases in which Jerusalem municipal officials allegedly erased files revealing over three hundred cases of Arab construction in eastern Jerusalem deemed illegal, starting from 1999. The illegal buildings were reportedly constructed without permits and still stand. According to law, they should be demolished. A follow-up Israeli news report investigating the Forum's charges alleged that Ofir May, the head of Jerusalem's Department of Building Permits, erased the files with the specific intention of allowing the statute of limitations on enforcing the demolitions of the illegal construction to run out. The Jerusalem municipality never denied the charges. In response to the allegations it merely released a statement claiming that the threat of Arab violence had kept it from bulldozing the illegal buildings. "During the years of the *intifada*, the municipality had difficulty carrying out the necessary level of enforcement in the neighborhoods of eastern Jerusalem due to security constraints," the statement read. The Forum's report estimated that the deleted municipal files detailed more than twenty thousand illegal units in which an estimated one hundred thousand Arabs now reside.

PALESTINIAN CAPITAL IN THE MAKING

Meanwhile, even though eastern Jerusalem is entirely controlled by Israel and is officially part of the Jerusalem municipality, the Palestinian Authority has been expanding its official activities in those areas. According to Palestinian authorities, the PA can do this because it has the tacit approval of the Israeli government.

Just prior to the publication of this book, I conducted a second tour of Kfar Akev, Kalandiya, Shoafat, and Samir Amis, uncovering some surprising developments. Official PA logos and placards abounded, including one glaring red street sign at the entrance to the neighborhoods warning Israelis to keep out. Another official sign, this one in Kfar Akev in Jerusalem, reads in English, "Ramallah-Jerusalem Road. This project is a gift form [sic] the American people to the Palestinian people in cooperation with the Palestinian Authority and PECDAR. 2007." The sign bears the emblems of the American and PA governments and of the U.S. Agency for International Development, or USAID.

I found that some local schools in the Jerusalem neighborhoods are officially run by the PA—some in conjunction with the UN—with many teachers drawing PA salaries. Civil disputes are usually settled not in Israeli courts but by the PA judicial system, although at times Israeli courts are used depending on the matter.

Councils governed by PA President Mahmoud Abbas's Fatah organization oversee some municipal matters. USAID provides the PA funds for Jerusalem road and infrastructure projects.

Israeli security officials said the local Jerusalem police rarely operate in Kfar Akev, Kalandiya, and Samir Amis; instead security has been turned over to the Israel Defense Forces and Border Police, who work almost daily with PA security forces. The PA police operate in the Jerusalem neighborhoods in coordination with Israel. Shmulik Ben Ruby, a spokesman for the Jerusalem police, confirmed the arrangement. "If there are fights between some local families, sometimes we involve the PA police to make peace between the families," he told me. "Yes, the PA police can operate in these neighborhoods in coordination with the IDF and Border Police."

In June 2008, the PA held one of a series of official meetings in eastern Jerusalem to discuss dealing with expected Palestinian sovereignty over key sections of the city, participants informed me. Officials present included the PA's treasury minister, who drove in from Ramallah, passing through Israeli checkpoints. A spokesman for the Jerusalem section of Abbas's Fatah party, Dmitri Ziliani, told me the June planning meeting concerned the activities and structure of Fatah's local command in eastern Jerusalem neighborhoods. "We were covering the best ways to improve our performance on the street and how we can be of service to the community," Ziliani claimed. According to other participants in several recent PA meetings in Jerusalem, this "performance assessment" included extending an already existing network of Fatah community policing, as well as setting up local Fatah administrations, such as treasury and waste management.

The PA meetings in Jerusalem started immediately following the Annapolis Summit. According to Palestinian sources, PA officials urged the U.S. to support what they said was a key demand allowing the PA to open official institutions in Jerusalem. The U.S. took the request to the Israeli government. While Israel has not officially approved the PA's presence in Jerusalem, and it is unclear which stance Netanyahu's administration will take, Palestinian diplomatic sources claim there was an unwritten agreement in which Israel pledged not to interrupt certain PA activities in Jerusalem.

According to Israeli law, however, the PA cannot officially hold court in Jerusalem. The PA previously maintained a *de facto* headquarters near the Old City, in a building called Orient House, but the building was closed by Israel in 2001 following a series of suicide bombings. Israel said it had information indicating the PA used the House to plan and fund the attacks.[14] Thousands of documents and copies of bank certificates and checks Israel seized from Orient House reveal how the offices were used to finance terrorism, including direct payments to the al-Aqsa Martyrs Brigades's hatchet men. The Brigades ghoulishly takes responsibility for scores of deadly suicide bombings, shootings, and rocket attacks aimed at Jewish civilian population centers.

U.S. PLANS TO SPLIT JERUSALEM

In the battle over Jerusalem, the U.S., which provided the PA aid to rehabilitate sections of Jerusalem, is not an impartial bystander. According to informed Israeli officials, President Obama's administration is carefully monitoring Jewish construction in eastern Jerusalem and has already protested to the highest levels of Israeli government about evidence found of housing expansion in those areas. The officials, who spoke on condition that their names are withheld, said Obama's Mideast envoy, George Mitchell, oversaw the establishment of an apparatus based in the U.S. consulate in Jerusalem that closely monitors eastern Jerusalem neighborhoods, incorporating regular tours on a daily basis.

Said one Israeli official: "If the U.S. notices even one bulldozer on the region of E1, they immediately call us on the level of the prime minister and ask what that bulldozer is doing there and whether we are planning anything in Jerusalem." The official was referring to the Jewish neighborhood of Maale Adumim, located in eastern Jerusalem. The Israeli government previously approved the expansion of the community, but new construction largely has been halted.

According to Israeli and Palestinian officials I've spoken with, officials from the U.S. State Department in 2008 presented both negotiating sides with several proposals for consideration regarding the future status of Jerusalem—plans which were passed on to Obama's State Department. It was unclear whether or not any of the U.S. proposals was accepted.

One U.S. plan I obtained was divided into timed phases and, among other things, called for Israel eventually to consider forfeiting parts of the Temple Mount, Judaism's holiest site. According to the first stage of the U.S. proposal, Israel would initially give the PA partial municipal and security sovereignty over key Arab neighborhoods in eastern Jerusalem. The PA could then open official institutions in the city, elect a mayor for the Palestinian side, and deploy some kind of self-described basic security force to maintain law and order. The specifics of such a force were not detailed in the plan. The initial stage also called for the PA to operate more mundane municipal institutions, such as offices to oversee trash collection and the maintenance of roads.

After five years, if both sides kept specific commitments called for in a larger agreement of principles, the PA would earn full sovereignty over agreed-upon eastern Jerusalem neighborhoods, and discussions would be held regarding an arrangement for the Temple Mount. The plan doesn't specify which parts of the Temple Mount could be forfeited to the Palestinians or if an international force might be involved. The PA also could deploy official security forces in Jerusalem separate from a non-defined "basic force" after the five-year period and further could open up major governmental institutions, such as a president's office and offices for finance and foreign ministries.

The U.S. plan leaves Israel and the PA to negotiate which Jerusalem neighborhoods would become Palestinian. According to diplomatic sources, while specific neighborhoods were not officially listed, American officials recommended that sections of Jerusalem's Old City as well as certain largely Arab neighborhoods such as Jabal Mukabar, Beit Hanina, Abu Dis, and Abu Tur become part of the new Palestinian capital. Also recommended were Shoafat, Kfar Akev, Samir Amis, and Kalandiya, neighborhoods that the Jewish state and the JNF seem already to have abandoned.

CHAPTER THREE

PLOWSHARES BEATEN INTO SWORDS IN GAZA

O*nce it became clear* that Prime Minister Ariel Sharon would attempt an historic and complete withdrawal from Gaza and also from four northern West Bank communities, I felt the need to do my part to show the real situation in Gaza and the likely disasters resulting from an Israeli retreat from the territory. In February 2005, six months before Gaza's Jews were expelled by their own government, I packed my bags and relocated from the U.S. to an apartment in Jerusalem, taking out a second living quarters in Gaza's slate of Jewish communities then known as Gush Katif, in a tree-lined suburban-style neighborhood called Ganei Tal. Before Israel's withdrawal, nearly ten thousand Jewish residents, or 1,667 families, constituted Jewish Gaza.

Immediately upon entering Gush Katif I was struck by the natural beauty of the place. It looked like Orange County, California, transplanted to the Gazan desert. Many of Gush Katif's towns were dotted with beautiful homes featuring sea views and brimming with sun-splashed orchards and flower nurseries. I found well-appointed museums, architectural gems of synagogues, athletic facilities with pools and tennis courts, and even a seafront hotel once considered a prestigious resort, but later shut down after repeated attacks by Palestinians. Gush Katif even had one of the most beautiful beaches I've ever seen, called Palm Beach. Katif's seafront teemed with Jewish children playing in the sand, teenagers body surfing, and residents jogging with their dogs.

Gaza's Jews themselves were far from the extremist zealots that the international and Israeli news media seemed so fond of reviling.

Most, peaceful farmers, tended to the area's technologically advanced greenhouses, a model of Israel's simple-but-sophisticated agriculture that supplied much of the country's produce. As Israelis moved on to the sand dunes and built extensive greenhouses, they gladly hired local Palestinians to help grow and export the produce that at its high point generated a significant portion of Israeli foreign exchange. Jews and Arabs worked side by side, tending tiny green shoots and luxurious blooms of fragrant flowers, winter strawberries, and perfectly formed tiny tomatoes. Jobs in Jewish-owned greenhouses were much sought by Palestinians and by their impoverished neighbors, the local Bedouins.

Many Jews had moved to Katif in search of economic opportunity and cheap land. Most of them also were followers of the religious Zionist ideology, meaning they subscribed to the definition of Israel as a Jewish state not only by demography, but also by spiritual character and biblical heritage. For the "national religious" camp, Gaza is considered part of Greater Israel—the biblically and culturally important lands connected to the Jewish people and its history. The overwhelmingly peaceful outlook of these "religious settlers" would later be revealed to the whole country when they refrained from violence or bloodshed while Israeli soldiers and police forced them from their homes.

BUILT ON SAND DUNES

Long ago Gaza was a strategic regional trade center. It is part of the Torah's narrative. The biblical patriarchs Abraham and Isaac are said in Genesis 24 to have lived in Gerar, a Gaza town next to Gush Katif. The stories of Samson and Delilah unfolded in Gaza; it is also where King David was said to have slain Goliath. The books of Joshua and Judges relate how Gaza (or Azza in Hebrew) was captured by and later allotted to the tribe of Yehuda. Assyria held the territory in 732 BC, the Babylonians in 586 BC, the Persians in 525 BC, and later the Macedonian Greeks in 332 BC, until it was retaken by Jonathan the Hashmonean in 145 BC—all while Jews continuously lived there.

King Herod controlled Gaza for a short period, as did the Romans, and then the Byzantines, again all while Jews lived on the land. The Arabs conquered Gaza in the AD 630s, after a siege during which the Jewish population of Gaza defended the territory alongside the Byzantine army. The Crusaders briefly governed Gaza in the twelfth century. The Kurdish Muslim conqueror Saladin captured the territory for the Ayyubid Arab leaders in AD 1170, while Jews were prosperous there, mostly as farmers and winemakers. Contemporaneous records describe a synagogue and a chief rabbi there in 1488. The Ottomans ruled Gaza from 1517 until the First World War, with Jews there in the seventeenth century establishing renowned centers of Torah study. According to some accounts, Gaza's Jewish farmers kept the strict Jewish laws of working the land while Arab Gaza at the time was largely dominated by Egyptian culture. Napoleon occupied Gaza briefly in 1799, but afterward its fortunes began to decline and a number of Jewish families moved out. In the early twentieth century the Turks controlled Gaza. The British took over in 1917, with Jews staying in the area until countrywide Arab anti-Jewish riots forced the remaining Jews of Gaza to flee in 1929. Between the two world wars, the Gaza Strip was part of the British Mandate of Palestine under the authority of the League of Nations. Fearing more Arab riots, the British barred Jews from living in the area, though some Jews returned and in 1946 established the town of Kfar Darom near the Egyptian border. Kfar Darom later became a satellite of Gush Katif.

In 1948, Egypt and four other invading Arab armies attacked the newly formed Jewish state, threatening to annihilate it. Gaza served as the gateway for neighboring Egypt's invasion from the south. The Arabs lost the war, but the Egyptians occupied Gaza until they again used the territory to attack in the 1967 Six Day War, also aiming at destroying Israel. The Arabs lost again. But this time, Israel retained Gaza—incidentally, saturated with Jewish history—as a buffer against future Egyptian aggression. Following the capture of Gaza, successive Israeli governments over the years urged thousands of their citizens to move to the territory and build communities there, believing Israel needed to retain Gaza to ensure the country's defense. Ariel Sharon, who ran for office on an anti-withdrawal platform, was for most of his military and political career one of the most vocal proponents of strengthening Gush Katif. Several streets there were named for him.

Contrary to the news media's mantra—that Gush Katif was built on stolen Arab land—Gaza's Jewish communities were actually constructed on desolate sand dunes. Prior to Israel's retreat, I had the privilege of interviewing Sylvia Mandelbaum, a great-grandmother and one of the oldest residents of Gush Katif. Mandelbaum, by that time aged "none of your business," came to Gaza when it was nothing but endless mounds of sand. She helped turn the desert into a blooming paradise with much assistance from Sharon himself. Mandelbaum immigrated to Israel from New York in 1971. Speaking with a slight Brooklyn accent, she recalled her first days in Gush Katif in the early 1980s, when many of the territory's Jewish communities were being built: "It's funny the way the media says Jewish settlers are living in the middle of Palestinian towns. When I arrived, the whole thing was nothing but sand. Sand up to my doorsteps. No civilization. Then everything turned green.

"Back then, you came and built your own house. I came because of the beauty of the place and because I could build my own personal paradise. I oversaw construction of my house and built everything according to my own personal specifications." Working with contractors, Mandelbaum planted outside her house little fields of mangos, apples, clementines, figs, lemons, almonds, avocados, tomatoes, and assorted other fruits and vegetables.

"They said we were crazy to move to a desert. But look now. We made the desert bloom. We built one of the most beautiful, peaceful communities in the world. And now Sharon wants to take it all away," Mandelbaum said at the time, sitting in her living room in her soon-to-be-evacuated home while visibly holding back tears. Mandelbaum recounted how she built her house with personal encouragement from Sharon, who was minister of industry and trade from 1984 to 1990, and later was housing minister.

"Sharon came here and told me I was at the forefront of Israel, that building in Gush Katif is the Zionist dream," Mandelbaum stated. "He said our communities would last forever. He helped in the government to get us a lot of assistance. He told me this is my Israel. I wanted to say, 'Mr. Sharon, this is our Israel.' Even back

36

then, he was a little disconnected. I will never forgive him for this evacuation. For lying to me."

RAINING ROCKETS

While Israeli settlers built Gush Katif from scratch, several of its communities adjoin what became important Palestinian cities, providing the Israel Defense Forces with a crucial launch pad from which to carry out anti-terror operations in Gaza. After the Gaza retreat, however, when Hamas rockets landed with abandon on the nearby Israeli town of Sderot, IDF ground forces entered the territory from its border with the Negev desert, providing Gaza-based terrorists foreknowledge of operations and time to prepare traps for the Israeli army. Ironically, there was peace between Gaza's Jewish residents and local Palestinians prior to the signing of the Oslo peace accords in 1993, in which Israel first agreed to transfer strategic territory to the Palestinians. Many Gush Katif residents recalled days in the late '80s and early '90s when they securely shopped in Gaza City or Khan Yunis, which only after the "peace process" became terrorist hornets' nests. The Oslo process re-imported PLO leader Yasser Arafat from his exile in Tunisia, handing him authority over West Bank and Gaza Palestinians. Arafat turned the Palestinian territories against the Jewish state and directed the launch of an unprecedented campaign of killings. Following Arafat's rise to power, Gush Katif's Jews found themselves under increasing Palestinian fire, at first from mostly low-grade attacks. But these escalated dramatically during the deadly second *intifada* launched by Arafat after he turned down an Israeli offer of a Palestinian state during the 2000 U.S.-brokered Camp David Accords.

Following Israel's March 2004 announcement of its decision to withdraw from Gaza, an almost daily onslaught of Palestinian rocket attacks erupted that targeted Gush Katif, killing several Jews. I endured some of the daily rocket and mortar barrages alongside the Gush Katif residents. The barrages usually came in waves throughout the day. Early morning brought a particularly large volley of rockets, while children set off to school and adults ventured to work, mostly on a farm or in a greenhouse. The volleys would increase again toward sunset and would continue at a slower pace during the night.

At first, I ran away scared silly. During my first night in Gush Katif, at about three in the morning a rocket slammed into a community just outside Ganei Tal. I nearly had a heart attack. I heard a high-pitched buzzing sound and then a crash that sent jolts down my spine. Quickly grabbing some of my belongings, I scurried out of my apartment and into my trusty Land Rover and drove the one hour and thirty minutes back to Jerusalem, where I could sleep outside Palestinian rocket range. A few days later, I mustered the intestinal fortitude to return to Katif, where I again found myself under rocket attack. A volley of mortars landed just yards away from the place where I had been eating in the town center of Neve Dekalim, which was the largest of Gush Katif's communities. Neve Dekalim was considered the capital of Jewish Gaza. I took cover inside the restaurant and braved it out the rest of the day. Nightfall brought with it an inevitable rain of rockets, forcing me to stay up most of the night watching DVDs to distract myself. After a few days, I feared the rockets less and less. Two weeks into my reporting from Gush Katif I was sleeping through rocket attacks and going about my daily duties with little regard for the projectiles, just like most other Katif residents. Like a child living in a dysfunctional household, Jewish Gaza adapted to the constant terror of rocket barrages. And so had I.

The media regularly referred to Palestinian rockets as "homemade," as if they were cookies or cucumber salad, downplaying the significance of the rockets while stressing the enormity of Israeli military aircraft and Merkava tanks that operated against "militants" in Gaza. In actuality, "homemade" Palestinian rockets are quite deadly. Most rockets fired were Qassams, which are improvised steel rockets, about four feet in length, filled with explosives and fuel and packed with tiny nails and shards that fire out like bullets upon impact. At the time, Qassams could travel between one and four miles depending on the sophistication of the particular rocket. Palestinian button men are constantly improving the distance and effectiveness of their rockets, to the point where they can now reach quite far into Israel. Qassams lack a guidance system and are launched in an effort to use the rocket's trajectory and known travel distance to aim at a particular Jewish community. It is true that Qassams are homemade in the sense that Palestinian rocket factories are routinely hidden in civilian apartment complexes. The main point of using civilian homes and civilian commercial buildings is to complicate Israel's attempts to take out the terrorists' production facilities without harming civilians.

In all, eight Israelis were killed in Gush Katif by mortar fire and another seven from Qassam attacks. It was an absolute miracle defying all odds that more Jews were not killed. Every day brought with it amazing stories of close encounters with Palestinian rocket and mortar attacks.

As the date of Israel's Gaza withdrawal—August 15, 2005—swiftly approached, Palestinian rocket fire intensified dramatically, to make clear to all that the Jewish state was running away under fire. Also as the date approached, the IDF scaled back its anti-rocket operations, leaving some to charge that Israel was intentionally allowing attacks on Jews. According to a soldier I spoke to stationed at the Kissufim Crossing, a major checkpoint separating Gaza's mid-section from Khan Yunis: "It's politics. We want to defend [the Jewish communities of Gaza] and there is a lot that can be done about the Qassams, but we're not being allowed to."

Brigadier General Effie Eitam is a nationalist Knesset member who had also temporarily moved to Gush Katif. Eitam served on the Knesset's prestigious Foreign Affairs and Defense Committee at the time; he told me: "The IDF knows who is launching the mortars [and rockets], from where exactly and when. They have been instructed by the political echelon, by Sharon, to do nothing about the attacks. The goal is to make life as bad as possible so people will want to leave and not spoil the disengagement process. We see the military is indeed actually doing nothing. They are just watching the mortars and Qassams fall." Ami Shaked, chief security coordinator for Gush Katif, charged the "political leaders supporting the evacuation from Gaza have told the IDF not to stop the mortars and Qassams. I know this, but anyway it is obvious to everyone. The IDF are not even using 5 percent of their capabilities to stop the rockets," Shaked told me.

The constant rocket barrages allowed Hamas to claim total victory in Gaza even ahead of Israel's actual retreat. "The Zionist enemy is retreating with its tail between its legs while the Islamic resistance [Hamas] shoots rockets without any stopping. This is a victory for the Islamic resistance and must be recognized as a successful model to liberate all our sacred land," Abu Abdullah, a leader of Hamas's so-called military wing in Gaza, told me in a 2005 interview. "All our sacred land" is a reference to the entire state of Israel. Hamas, of course, had claimed victory immediately after Sharon announced his disengagement plan. Their leaders issued regular proclamations crediting the terror group's so-called resistance operations against the Zionist enemy as the impetus for the Israeli retreat and proof that violence works. As the Gaza evacuation drew closer, Hamas ramped up its public claims of victory.

ORANGE FEVER

The planned Gaza withdrawal, meanwhile, polarized the nation of Israel and galvanized the settlement establishment and its supporters. First the anti-withdrawal camp started a color war. The color orange spread like a fierce contagion. People wore it. Billboards shouted it. Kids distributed orange bands on the streets. Orange ribbons dangled from cars, buses, baby carriages, backpacks. Orange signified the citrus groves that grew bountifully in Jewish Gaza. The settler leaders' plan was to have as many Israelis as possible drape the country in orange to protest the evacuation and show solidarity with the Jews who would be forced to vacate their homes. Colors, however, could not stop the withdrawal. Next they tried protests. The settlement establishment was largely led by the Yesha Settler Council, the main body representing the Jewish communities of Gaza and the West Bank. The Yesha Council next organized a series of protests, each more massive and enterprising then the one before.

I reported from nearly every major anti-withdrawal protest. At Nativot, a Negev desert city several miles south of Gaza, nearly one hundred thousand people poured into a central meeting site on July 18, 2005, rallying against the evacuation. Afterwards, tens of thousands of protestors attempted to march inside Gaza to obstruct the evacuation, but were stopped by over ten thousand Israeli police and soldiers deployed to thwart the protest plans. I was tangled in the ensuing clashes that night when the protesting multitudes breached police lines and made it closer to Gaza. But Yesha leaders eventually led the marchers into a fortified farming community called Kfar Meimon, where Israeli forces easily surrounded them, besieging and tiring them out until the Yesha leadership was forced to concede.

In another massive protest, on August 2, an estimated sixty thousand Israelis congregated in Sderot, a Negev town less than two miles from Gaza that, following the Gaza withdrawal, became the front line of Hamas's rocket war against the Jewish state. Yesha leaders organized a large anti-withdrawal rally that culminated in yet another march to Gaza in hopes of halting the evacuation. But just minutes before the rally, which I attended, Yesha leaders struck a last-minute agreement with police declaring that they would march only from Sderot to Ofakim, which is about five miles south of Gaza but closer than Sderot to the Jewish communities of Gush Katif, and from Ofakim would plot their next move. Most at the rally had brought along sleeping bags and supplies and were intent on marching to Gaza. The next day, under blazing heat, tens of thousand of nationalist protestors camped out in a large field at the outskirts of Ofakim. Police easily deployed around Ofakim and set up dozens of heavily guarded checkpoints to keep the marchers away from Gaza. A few protestors broke through independently, but most eventually tired and grudgingly accepted instructions from Yesha leaders to board buses that would take them back to Jerusalem and Tel Aviv.

The protestors were highly motivated. I watched in amazement as tens of thousands of people of all ages, including entire families, braved hot weather, long marches, and prolonged camping in tents while eating rationed food, all in hopes of halting the evacuation. They foresaw that the Gaza retreat would have disastrous consequences for the Jewish state. Had they been utilized properly, the protestors could greatly have inhibited the Israeli government's ability to uproot Jews. In the end, the settlement establishment clearly made a strategic decision to surrender Gaza while tiring out the nationalist camp in aimless protests and marches that did nothing to halt the withdrawal.

JEW VERSUS JEW SHOWDOWN

Meanwhile, reporting from Gaza in the final countdown to the withdrawal, I found most residents of Gush Katif had not resigned themselves to the reality of their expulsion, believing something or someone would stop the government from carrying out its plan. A week or so before the scheduled retreat, news media outlets from around the world descended upon Jewish Gaza and hunkered down anywhere they could find space in Gush Katif, bracing themselves for a potential Jew-versus-Jew showdown. I met scores of reporters who for years had produced pieces covering Gaza, but had never once set foot in Gush Katif to see the situation for themselves. One reporter, a well-known correspondent for a cable news network, told me she was stunned upon finding that the Jews of Gush Katif were well mannered and peaceful, not a vulgar rabble of crazed fanatics.

Israel's evacuation from Gaza began officially at midnight on August 14, and reality finally set in for the Jewish residents. After a complete closure of the Jewish communities of the Gaza Strip, which the Israeli army and civil police units had barred all civilians from entering, residents had forty-eight hours to depart of their own accord. Anyone remaining faced forced removal from their homes. Thousands of Israeli evacuation forces built up inside and outside Gaza. The night before, I had moved from Ganei Tal to Neve Dekalim, using great-grandmother Sylvia Mandelbaum's home as my reporting base. Mandelbaum had left weeks earlier, but the majority of Gush Katif residents stayed. It was from Neve Dekalim that I experienced the start of the Gaza evacuation. The families of Neve Dekalim responded to the initial closure of Gaza by blocking army vehicles headed toward their community. Some threw themselves atop military convoys, begging soldiers to leave them alone. "Don't uproot us. Refuse orders," one woman screamed as she stood in front of an army jeep. Teenagers, including some nonresidents who had managed to infiltrate the area in the previous few weeks, gathered around two army trucks and began pounding at the windows. "Jews do not evacuate Jews," a crowd of about eighty children chanted as the army stood down.

The morning of the fifteenth, soldiers and police officers attempted to enter Neve Dekalim to distribute final eviction notices, warning residents they must depart. Hundreds of residents stalled the evacuation forces at the main town gate; the residents sat at the entrance and sang to the police—in stark contrast to the violent mobs anticipated by the news media. I watched in awe as the residents of Neve Dekalim chanted soft harmonies to forces in full battle gear amassed outside the city's entrance gate, fortified by army vehicles and horse-mounted policemen, all of whom arrived for the singular purpose of expelling fellow Israelis from their homes. After a two-hour standoff, police commanders at the front gate claimed they would leave, but a second police force infiltrated Neve Dekalim through a back gate at its industrial zone and tried to go from house to house to deliver eviction notices. Residents quickly made their way to the breached entrance and formed a line to block the police from invading. Following a few scuffles, the police decided to stand down, apparently after being ordered not to inflame tensions ahead of the next day's forced evictions. Instead, police handed the eviction notices to community leaders, who promptly discarded them. Throughout the day, several government-provided moving trucks rolled up and down the streets of Neve Dekalim and parked outside homes. With only twenty-four hours remaining before their legal and successful residence in Dekalim became illegal, only a handful of residents moved out. About two-thirds of the 467-family town remained, announcing they would not leave. About seventy families had departed in the weeks earlier, while more than one thousand protestors managed to infiltrate the neighborhood in hopes of stopping the withdrawal.

On Tuesday, August 16, I watched evacuation forces formally arrive at Neve Dekalim. Police and soldiers formed several human chains and attempted to advance slowly against hundreds of residents blocking the town entrance. A standoff between security forces and residents ensued, with both sides refusing to budge. Reacting to the large military buildup inside their community, residents of all ages congregated at Dekalim's city center and cried and pled with the forces to not expel them. "Please, please, don't take my home away from me," one woman cried. "How can you do this to us? This is where we live. Don't listen to your orders," a teenage boy beseeched. I saw a father and his children huddle together and weep for several minutes when they first saw the troop buildup. Several residents, crying, threw themselves onto soldiers.

Such confrontations prompted several soldiers, both men and women, to break down into tears themselves. Some of the crying soldiers took a break for several minutes, while others left entirely. Riot police dispatched to the scene with orders to push back the lines of residents to clear the way for moving trucks. A few activists from Brooklyn I had met earlier lit tires on fire and placed two large, burning garbage bins in the middle of the main road. I then watched in amazement as several news anchors broadcast live in front of the burning garbage bins and claimed settlers were violently resisting orders to evacuate, when in fact the opposite was true. Civilian resistance to the evacuation was almost entirely passive.

Five hours before the deadline to depart, at about 7 p.m. local time, evacuation forces split into teams of eight officers each and went house to house to warn the occupants to leave immediately. The troops, though, met singing families, each of whom started to sing in their private dining rooms. Loud songs flooded the streets of Neve Dekalim. Exuberant celebrations broke out inside and outside the Jewish homes. Not a single resident of Neve Dekalim departed. That night, at one of the town's main synagogues, hundreds of residents packed into the structure to celebrate the dedication of a new Torah scroll. Men of all ages swayed throughout the synagogue, singing "Am Yisrael Chai"—"the Nation of Israel lives on"—on the main floor while women sang on the upper balconies. Some congregants clapped and laughed; others broke down into tears, sobbing violently in each other's arms. I joined in the chorus and the dance, quickly finding myself flooded with the same emotions as just about everyone else there, while the sound of nearby rocket and mortar explosions boomed sporadically through the night. For many Dekalim residents I think this was the first collective outburst of mourning—the first communal realization that Gush Katif had fallen.

The next day, the deadline to vacate Jewish Gaza passed. Protests broke out in Neve Dekalim and other communities, with residents and foreign teenage protestors blocking buses brought in to haul off the remaining residents. Throughout the day, rumors persisted that Neve Dekalim would be the first Jewish community evacuated from

Gaza, and indeed it was. At noon, Israeli officers began escorting residents onto buses that swiftly separated them from homes in which many of them had lived for upwards of thirty years. Some of the residents were carried away kicking and screaming. All day, local settlement leaders held negotiations with police forces to ensure there would be no violence. These negotiations ended with the leaders calling on Dekalim residents to leave peacefully. Soldiers then formed groups of twenty men and women each and went door to door to remove residents from their homes. Members of one Dekalim family, the Friedmans, were dragged in front of me kicking and screaming and forced onto a waiting bus. "My home! My home! Please, my home," Mrs. Friedman yelled. Another family stood on their balcony for more than eight hours straight, singing and waving Israeli flags. I returned to that home almost every hour and was surprised to see the family still in position singing on their balcony, until Israeli troops finally surrounded the house and physically dragged them out. Both the troops and the family were crying in an image that will forever be branded on my mind. I remember one soldier leaving the scene prematurely, telling his comrades that he "just couldn't take it."

Before departing, some Dekalim residents, many with tears streaming down their faces, smashed the insides of their homes to bits; other lit their houses on fire, refusing to leave any property to the Palestinians.

The next day, the remaining Dekalim residents faced evacuation. As a member of the news media, I had the eerie opportunity to remain in Neve Dekalim for twenty-four hours following the evacuation. The place was a ghost town. Rows of houses that had once contained 467 Jewish families lay deserted, debris strewn across lawns and along the sidewalks. Many front doors stayed wide open, windows smashed through. Inside evacuated homes, kitchen counters, closets, and bathrooms lay in ruins, broken to pieces by the departing Jewish residents.

A tour through Dekalim's town center showed restaurants and stores abandoned. The shelves and counters inside the main food shop I had frequented sat empty. The city's recreation and community center stood abandoned. The municipal building, which housed city offices and some area businesses, was locked shut. Similar scenes unfolded in other towns of Gush Katif, culminating in the final Gaza Jewish city's evacuation on August 22.

Then on the twenty-third, a completely pointless evacuation occurred in four small communities in the northern West Bank. Israel's 2005 disengagement was not limited to Gaza alone; a forced evacuation of the northern West Bank Jewish towns of Ganim, Kadim, Sa-Nur, and Homesh took place as well. But unlike in the Gaza Strip, from which Israel entirely disengaged, the Israeli military continues to operate in the northern West Bank. The reasoning behind the uprooting of these tiny communities was clearly to send a message to West Bank Jews that they are next on the chopping block.

HAMAS'S HAPPINESS

Early in the morning on September 12, terrorists celebrated as the IDF lowered the last Israeli flag from the military's divisional headquarters in Gaza.[1] In the following hours the remaining Israeli soldiers pulled out of the strip, with the last one departing the following morning, thus completing Israel's retreat under heavy rocket fire. The terrorists wasted no time taking over. Hours after the final Israeli troops departed, Palestinians mobs destroyed most of Gush Katif's synagogues, with Hamas leaders that day holding Muslim prayer services in the former Jewish holy sites.[2]

In the weeks preceding Israel's retreat, leading rabbis had ruled that Jews could not destroy Gaza's twenty-two synagogues during the evacuation. Rabbi Shear-Yashuv Cohen, a member of the Chief Rabbinate, explained to me that according to Jewish law, Jews cannot destroy synagogues unless new ones are already built, and even then, the issues are complicated. The rabbis also feared that Jews in other parts of the world might interpret the bulldozing of Gazan synagogues as precedent to destroy other abandoned holy structures.

In front of international camera crews, gangs of Palestinians, mostly youth, ripped off aluminum window frames and metal ceiling fixtures from the Gush Katif synagogues. Militants flew the Palestinian and Hamas flags from Neve Dekalim's two main synagogues before mobs burned those down completely.[3]

A spokesman for the Popular Resistance Committees terrorist organization, Muhammad Abdel-Al (also known as Abu Abir), described to me the "great joy" of looting and burning the Jewish structures. "There was no intention to desecrate them but this was part of the great joy the young men had when they destroyed everything that could remind us of the occupation. It was in an unplanned expression of happiness that these synagogues were destroyed," he said.

The Hamas chief in Gaza, Mahmoud al-Zahar, arrived at the ruins of one synagogue in Kfar Darom and held a Muslim prayer session at the site with other top Hamas officials. Another senior figure in Hamas, Ahmad Jabari, announced victory and said his band would continue to attack Israel. "The withdrawal proves that the resistance is the only legitimate weapon. We will strike at any hand that reaches for our weapons," said Jabari.[4]

Abdel-Al announced that Hamas would use the Neve Dekalim synagogue, as well as the rest of the city's ruins, as launch pads to fire rockets into Israel and to train for attacks: "We are proud to turn these lands, especially these parts that were for a long time the symbol of occupation and injustice, like the synagogue, into a military base and source of fire against the Zionists and the Zionist entity," Adel-Al told me.

And that is just what happened. The Palestinians converted Gush Katif and the rest of Gaza into the terrorism capital of the Middle East, divided into cantons by gangs of thugs and murderers. Some of the gangs are merely predators, while others are doctrinally allied with the global jihad. Rockets launched from Gaza into nearby Jewish communities routinely come from Gush Katif. Islamic University, a Hamas-affiliated institution with a history of involvement in terrorist activity, quickly opened a branch in Nitzarim, a former Jewish community, building on the foundations of evacuated Jewish structures.[5] Other Gush Katif towns became advanced paramilitary training centers. In March 2007, when the IDF learned of loud explosions coming from the former Gush Katif coastal towns of Eli Sinai and Dagit, a senior member of Hamas's so-called military wing, Abu Abdullah, claimed to me that the communities were used for "physical shape exercises; use of weapons training; practice lands for ambushes of Israeli forces; courses for the reading of maps and [production and use of] explosives and many other trainings; military techniques, fighting in open fields and in built and populated areas; and rockets shooting." At around the same time, Hamas announced it used Neve Dekalim to test new rockets and explosives.[6]

As late as August 2008, terrorists paraded their capabilities in Gush Katif. A senior Gaza-based leader of the Islamic Jihad terrorist organization, Abu Muhammad, told me his group held drills that stressed Hezbollah-like guerilla operations, such as raiding Israel's border with Gaza and kidnapping Israeli troops, shooting practice using automatic rifles and rocket-propelled grenades, and explosives testing. "The old (Jewish) settlements gave the Palestinian resistance enough space to have big trainings. We never had this space and these possibilities when the Zionists were in Gaza," Abu Muhammad explained. Also that month, Abdel-Al's Popular Resistance Committees showcased its own training in the evacuated Gaza Jewish town of Kfar Darom. A sad fact about the Committees's training was that it reportedly included dozens of boys between the ages of nine and twelve, according to the Committees's own leaders.

JEWISH REFUGEES

As I will detail in chapter nine, Israel's Gaza evacuation led directly to Hamas's ascent to power and its complete takeover of the territory two years later, from which the massacre fellowship threatens not only Israel but also neighboring Egypt. In Israel's retreat, the country's enemies—including Hezbollah, Syria, and Lebanon—smelled Jewish weakness and pounced.

And while the terrorists fared quite well, the expelled Jews of Gaza have known mostly displacement and its attendant suffering. As of the writing of this book—more than three years after the Gaza withdrawal—the vast majority of the Jewish refugees, 81 percent out of 1,667 evacuated families, live in temporary homes, mostly in the Israeli Negev desert, many in small, government-built, prefabricated "trailer villas."[7] About 10 percent of the uprooted Jews have set out on their own to begin building houses, fed up with waiting for the fulfillment of Israeli government pledges to find permanent housing solutions. In the Negev refugee trailer communities, residents in many cases lack enough bedroom space to accommodate their families. Some use shipping containers as improvised additional bedroom space. "You can punch through my wall," a resident of Nitzan, the largest of about a dozen ex-Gush Katif trailer communities, told me upon a 2007 visit. "My friends come to visit me in coffee shops because there's not enough room in my living room."

Prior to the evacuation, the Gush Katif unemployment rate was less than 1 percent. Three years later, a July 2008 survey led by Israel's respected Maagar Mohot Institute found that 50 percent of the uprooted Jews remained jobless.[8] A study from August 2007 by an Israeli municipality—the Ashkelon Regional Health Bureau in conjunction with a local hospital—showed the uprooted youth not faring well, either.[9] Young refugees live "in a reality of constant uncertainty and in a situation of educational, family, social, and community instability. This influences the youth and causes many to enter a state of worry and fear," stated the report. The report found many evacuee students had to switch schools numerous times due to the government's failure to find the refugees permanent homes and that the instability caused difficulty in concentrating on studies.

The Forum for Israel, a nonprofit group working with Gush Katif refugees, in 2007 outlined for the Knesset major problems facing Gush Katif refugee teenagers. The group pointed to an elevation in suicidal thoughts and eating disorders.[10] The report also said 30 percent of former Gush Katif teens either failed to integrate into new schools or failed their final exams. Social workers said the expelled youth found it difficult to develop relationships and increasingly abused alcohol and drugs. Some entered psychiatric hospitals. "The situation is extremely grave," said Dror Vanunu, a former Gaza resident and the international coordinator for the Gush Katif Committee. Survey data from the Maagar Mohot Institute indicated that 96 percent of Gush Katif evacuees were hurt and disappointed at what they characterized as Israeli politicians' "indifferent" attitudes toward their pleas.

While the settlement movement and religious Zionism have been gravely wounded by the Gaza retreat and by attempts to minimize the movement's influence, they are by no means defeated. Yesha leaders faced a profound dilemma in the run-up to the Gaza crisis. They could have attempted to stop the withdrawal by advocating the use of force, but that would have undoubtedly resulted in Jew-on-Jew violence and death in the face of an overwhelming number of Israeli evacuation forces. Instead, the nationalist leadership clearly chose to forfeit Gaza and tire out the masses in ultimately fruitless massive peaceful protests against the evacuation.

But while they lost Gaza, the settlement movement won over the hearts of an untold numbers of Israelis in the process. Demonized for years by the mainstream Israeli news media (as well as in the international press) as Arab-hating, violent extremists, the almost entirely peaceful resistance of Gaza's Jewish settlers opened the eyes of the country. When the Israeli and international news media broadcast scenes of peaceful Jewish farmers torn from their homes by Israeli forces, it became nearly impossible not to sympathize with Gaza's Jews. That a country could uproot nearly ten thousand citizens from their homes, some taken by force, without a single death or major violent incident at the very least testifies to the ultimate humanity of the settlement camp (as well as of the army). In no other country can one imagine such an eviction carried out nonviolently. The myth of the extremist settler deconstructed in one humid, tear-jerking week in August.

Now, the news media and various politicians in Israel claim there is a difference between Gaza's peaceful Jews and the Jewish settlers in the West Bank, who, we are told, are truly extremist and dangerous. It remains to be seen whether or not the Israeli public buys into this. The IDF and the country's police forces, though, had a cathartic moment during their expulsion of their fellow Jews from Gaza. Soldiers and Gush Katif residents cried on each other's shoulders. I believe many of the Israeli soldiers were as surprised as the Israeli public when confronted with the reality of the Gaza retreat. And now, after Gaza has become a Taliban-style mini-state and Hamas terrorist breeding ground, as predicted, at least some in the Israeli army and police must be rethinking the logic of the eviction orders they carried out.

It is also worth noting that in August 2007, when then-Prime Minister Ehud Olmert ordered a small series of Jewish evictions in the southern West Bank city of Hebron, thirty IDF infantry troops and two commanders refused to participate. Parents of the protesting soldiers showed up at their children's army bases in solidarity with their sons. One father, named Moshe Rosenfeld, said in an interview with Israel's Army Radio, "My son didn't join the army to expel Jews, but to defend them."[11] In November 2008, a Maagar Mohot poll found a surprising one-third of Israelis thinks it legitimate for soldiers to refuse orders to remove settlements from the Golan Heights, the strategic mountainous territory that borders Syria and looks down into Israeli population centers.[12]

Meanwhile, U.S. policy appears to be moving toward pressing an Israeli retreat from the vast majority of the strategic West Bank and from eastern sections of Jerusalem, in line with U.S.-brokered negotiations that President Barack Obama has pledged to continue. I believe Israel's current leadership favors some sort of West Bank evacuation. This in spite of the traumatic fiasco of the Gaza withdrawal: a failure rarely mentioned, much less debated, in Israeli political, military, or general public discourse.

CHAPTER FOUR

ISRAEL'S WAR AGAINST THE JEWS

The whole world could see that Israel's retreat under fire from the Gaza Strip was a clumsy, improvised answer to its struggle with the Palestinians. Prime Minister Ariel Sharon claimed that since the Palestinian Authority was unwilling or unable to make peace, Israel would therefore withdraw unilaterally to "defensible borders." That would disengage Israel from a million Palestinians, even though Hamas proudly announced it would use the evacuation of Jewish civilians and soldiers from Gaza to stage attacks against the Jewish state and to further its goal of Israel's annihilation.

Puzzled, some looked for deeper explanations. They chalked up the Gaza evacuation to relentless international pressure against Israel. Some said it was part of an Israeli-U.S. deal regarding the war in Iraq, or the price of U.S. support for Israeli action against Iran. Most seem to miss how Israel's withdrawal from Gaza, and its policy of evacuating still more territory, are deeply tied to internal factors within Israel, a beneath-the-surface but very real war being waged within Israeli society. This is the battle of Labor Zionism attempting to minimize Israel's religious Zionist or Jewish nationalist camp, an internal war to determine Israel's future.

Zionism refers to the modern political movement for a Jewish state in the ancestral homeland of the Jewish people. Though this land has been known by various names over the centuries—Canaan, Israel, Zion, Judea and Samaria, Palestine, the Holy Land, Byzantium, Greater Turkey, Greater Syria, the Vilayet of Damascus, again Palestine, and again Israel—it has, since about the fifteenth century BC, over thirty-five hundred years, always remained the homeland of the Jews. Throughout the centuries and millennia of Jewish exile, while wandering (often fleeing) from one place to another, Jews never gave up on eventually returning to the land of our forefathers. The foundation of the modern state of Israel in 1948, following over twenty-seven hundred years of Jewish exile and persecution, was for most a miraculous dream come true. But after so many years of Jewish powerlessness there raged from the beginning a debate within modern Zionist circles as to which elements of national identity the Israeli state should assume—an argument that today still colors all levels of Israeli society.

Broadly speaking, Labor Zionism aims for Israel to grow into a secular, socialist, European-style country. Adherents to this ideology believe that many of the problems Jews faced throughout history were precipitated largely by our being perceived as different. Labor Zionists want Israel to have a national spirit but not a religious identity, hoping that the world will more readily accept a secular, assimilated, Europeanized, Jewish-majority Israel.

Religious Zionism, on the other hand, believes Israel should adopt a religiously oriented Jewish national identity. The religious Zionist camp also advocates Jewish power and argues that only Jews can be trusted to protect the Jewish state and Jewish lives. In recent years some Israelis have framed this as a debate over whether they want "a state of the Jews" or "a Jewish state."

ROOTS OF THE JEWISH CONFLICT

Labor Zionism took its original line in the early 1900s from the movement's main ideologues, including socialist Zionist pioneers Moses Hess, Ber Borochov, and Aaron David Gordon, as well as David Ben-Gurion, Israel's first prime minister, and historian and intellectual Berl Katznelson. These early leaders began organizing a socialist society of Jewish workers and peasants in Ottoman and then British Mandatory Palestine. They formed the *kibbutz* movement of collective farms, where members lived communally and shared the farms' labor and rewards. These socialist Zionists generally saw their communes as contributing to Jewish self-defense in the settlement period and to eventual Jewish statehood once the British departed.

Labor Zionism later transformed itself, along with the changing winds of political liberalism worldwide, from purely socialist principles to social democratic movements and parties, such as the British Labour Party. But to this day, the international workers' holiday of May Day is still widely celebrated in Israel, with red flags flying and the singing of the *Internationale.* In Israel, instead of focusing solely on the working class and the economy, Labor Zionists took the lead on what is today referred to as "the peace process," that is, attempting to have amicable relations with the Palestinians and with neighboring Arab states, even at the sacrifice of traditional Jewish lands or long-term strategic interests. While the movement went through various complicated makeovers over the years, Labor Zionism today retains its anti-religious attitudes, its ideal of a Europeanized Israel, and its almost pathological desire to sacrifice for peace even with the most implacable of enemies.

Religious Zionism as a political movement goes back to a number of late nineteenth and early twentieth century ideologues. These leaders helped stake out a middle position between the anti-religious outlook of the socialist Zionists and the anti-Zionist attitude of religious traditionalists. In the pre-state period, the most notable of these was Rabbi Abraham Isaac HaCohen Kook, who later became the first *Ashkenazi* (European) chief rabbi of the British Mandate. Rabbi Kook (pronounced "Cook") founded the flagship religious Zionist seminary, the Mercaz HaRav *yeshiva* (discussed in chapter one because of the 2008 terrorist massacre in the *yeshiva's* library). He viewed political Zionism as part of a larger blueprint from the Torah that prophesied the return of the Jewish people to their homeland, as promised to them by God. Kook's ideas and those of other early founders, notably the German Orthodox Rabbi Zvi Hirsch Kalischer, took form in 1902 in the foundation of the Mizrachi (National Religious) Zionist organization, which eventually became today's National Religious Party, or NRP.

Mizrachi viewed Jewish nationalism as a tool for religious objectives—Zionism promoted Jewish identity and awareness while restoring the Jewish people to God's promised land. Mizrachi, which saw political Zionism as a part of the promised messianic redemption, had a mostly marginal role in Israeli politics until the revolutionary 1977 election of Menachem Begin to prime minister. Though Begin was an old-style leader, his center-right Likud Party famously forged a coalition between several Jewish religious parties and the large number of socially disadvantaged oriental (Sephardic) Jews to create a durable conservative coalition. Begin changed the political landscape in Israel by motivating large numbers of Sephardic Jews to vote for Likud, seemingly moving his party more toward the right and toward religious Zionist ideology. Of course, Begin also later signed a peace treaty with Egypt whereby the Jewish state evacuated settlements it had built in the Sinai desert, and he oversaw a liberal economic agenda.

During six days of war in June of 1967, the nineteen-year-old Jewish state humiliated the armies of Egypt, Syria, and Jordan, and captured territories in which the Torah and thirty-five hundred years of Jewish history unfolded—the Old City of Jerusalem, the Gaza Strip, and Judea and Samaria (the West Bank), as well as the Sinai Peninsula from Egypt and the Golan Heights from Syria. The Labor Zionist government immediately declared that it considered these lands mainly as "bargaining chips" to be returned to Israel's Arab neighbors in the context of final peace agreements. This government quickly returned the Temple Mount to Muslim custodianship, inviting an avalanche of problems.

Religious Zionists led the charge to retain these areas and fill them with Jewish settlements. These territories are the heart and soul of religious Zionism. Eastern Jerusalem contains the Temple Mount— the holiest site in Judaism—as well as scores of other holy sites and religious Zionist institutions. The other territories are mentioned throughout the Torah and the Talmud. The book of Genesis relates how the patriarch Abraham entered Israel at Shechem, or modern day Nablus in the northern West Bank, and received God's promise of land for his offspring at the nearby West Bank town of Beit El. Abraham and Sarah were later buried in Hebron, in the southern West Bank. Beit El, or Bethel, meaning "house of God," is where Scripture says the patriarch Jacob slept on a stone pillow and dreamt of angels ascending and descending a stairway to heaven. In that dream, God spoke directly to Jacob and reaffirmed the promise of land. According to the book of Exodus, the Holy Tabernacle rested for 350 years in Shiloh, north of Beit El. Shiloh is believed to be the first area the ancient Israelites settled after fleeing Egypt, and served as the religious capital of Israel during the time of the Judges.

The excitement of religious Zionism over the Likud party reawakened in 2001 with the election of Ariel Sharon. First a heroic military figure, Sharon became a hero to the religious Zionist camp. Then, as a politician in Begin's government, later as minister of industry and trade from 1984 to 1990, and finally as housing minister, Sharon personally oversaw the massive growth of Jewish communities in the West Bank, eastern Jerusalem, and Gaza. He was the political patron of the settlement movement. After his election in 2001, he made great strides in suppressing Arab terrorism and in restoring Israel's deterrence posture. Therefore, when he abruptly switched course in 2004 and announced his intention to evacuate Gaza, the religious Zionist camp viewed his actions as the ultimate betrayal. Sharon's about-face fractured the whole Likud-led coalition and left the religious Zionist camp isolated. Sharon's turnabout also restored Labor Zionists to dominance in Israel.

LEFT IN CONTROL

Labor-oriented figures constitute most of the Israeli government and judicial system, including the top army brass and the Foreign Service; and they exert enormous influence over six of Israel's seven universities, all of its major think tanks and cultural institutions, and the editorial rooms of the vast majority of major news media outlets, including radio, television, and the Internet. In fact, every major media outlet in Israel toes the Labor Zionist line of evacuating territory in exchange for vague promises from the Palestinians. Following a series of Israeli government closures under questionable circumstances discussed later, currently no religious Zionist media outlets reach a significant portion of the Israeli population beyond a religious Zionist audience.

The religious Zionist members of Israel's parliament, the Knesset, wield little real power. The nationalist camp's power base lies in the grassroots—in religious Zionist communities, synagogues, nationalist organizations, and what are known as *Hesder yeshivas*. These are highly effective five-year seminary programs combining Torah learning with military service. *Hesder* students form the backbone of the Israel Defense Force's mid-level officer corps and its elite combat units. The whole country admires their bravery and dedication, though the Left is unhappy they have come to play so prominent a role.

The struggle of Laborites versus the national religious at times feels palpable on the streets of Israel, where it occasionally translates into enmity between religious and secular. It can be gauged in the disdainful gaze a scantily clad, beach-bound Tel Avivan gives to an orange-band wearing, head-covered national religious woman crossing the street with her baby stroller and four children. It's in the acrimonious look I have personally witnessed on the faces of secular security men who use force to quell a legal, non-violent religious Zionist protest.

It must be understood, though, that the war of Labor Zionists versus religious Zionists is by no means black and white. Not all secular Israelis are left-wing. And not all religious Zionist leaders, including a few Knesset members, are religiously observant. Many religious Israelis disdain the religious Zionist ideology. The *haredi* (ultra-religious) Shas party, which has hundreds of thousands of followers, has drawn fire in recent years for remaining in several Israeli government coalitions that carried out clearly anti-religious Zionistic actions.

The struggle, though, is most visceral on the national level, where the more elite Labor Zionist secularists routinely use their positions in the government and media to push their causes and to harass religious Zionists as best they can, including, at the expense of the country's security, targeting religious army combat units or uprooting religious Zionist Jews from their homes.

Jerusalem Post deputy managing editor Caroline Glick pointed out in a May 2008 column that Labor Zionists enthusiastically viewed Israel's evacuation of Gush Katif in Gaza as a stab in the heart of religious Zionism. "The subtext of the withdrawal—telegraphed to both Israelis and the international community—was that the withdrawal would cause the demise of religious Zionism at the hands of the leftist progeny of Labor Zionists. That is, the [Gaza withdrawal] operation wasn't about peace with the Arabs. It was about cultural supremacy within Israel," Glick wrote.[1] Indeed, the openly Labor-aligned *Ha'aretz* newspaper editorialized six weeks before the Gaza retreat that the disengagement "of Israeli policy from its religious fuel is the real disengagement currently on the agenda."

"On the day after the disengagement, religious Zionism's status will be different. The real question is not how many mortar shells will fall, or who will guard the Philadelphi route [connecting Gaza with Egypt], or whether the Palestinians will dance on the roofs of Ganei Tal [a Gush Katif community]. The real question is who sets [Israel's] national agenda."

THE PUBLIC RELATIONS ASSAULT

In the months leading up to the Gaza withdrawal, the Israeli government and the news media launched a vigorous public relations campaign against religious Zionism in general and the Jews of Gush Katif in particular. The campaign painted the settlers as extremist elements needing to be excised like cancers, even though Gaza's Jews were mostly peaceful farmers, who, when the time came, put up only passive resistance to Israel's evacuation forces. Just prior to the Gaza retreat, Israeli authorities blamed a series of extremist acts on the Jews of Gush Katif. Israeli news media and politicians complained about "violent settlers," but it turned out many of the acts in question were actually carried out by extremist outside organizations with no connections to the Jews of Gush Katif or the larger settler movement.

A case in point: extremist protestors from the outside based at the Palm Beach Hotel, a rundown former Jewish beachside resort on the Gaza shore, used the structure as a staging ground for rowdy confrontations with Israeli forces and with local Arabs. I visited the hotel protestors several times. Some of them were hooligans. They were led by individuals I believe have questionable allegiances. I knew the hotel occupants would cause problems. The Jewish residents of Gaza distanced themselves from the extremist hotel protestors. And yet the Israeli and international news media largely did not distinguish Gaza's Jews from the outside provocateurs holed up in the hotel.

In another instance prior to the Gaza retreat, a nineteen-year-old connected to fringe Jewish extremist elements, Eden Natan Zada, shot at Arab passengers on a public bus in the northern Arab town of Shfaram, killing four and wounding more than twelve others, some seriously.[2] A mob of angry Arab bystanders and witnesses assaulted and killed Zada. The teenager had lived in the town of Kfar Tapuach in Samaria (the West Bank) and was involved there with leaders of several organizations that claim to follow the legacy of assassinated Israeli religious Zionist icon Rabbi Meir Kahane. In my opinion, these organizations and their leaders not only act against religious Zionism, but Kahane would probably disavow them were he alive.

As an IDF soldier, Zada received jail time for refusing orders related to the Gaza evacuation. Police officials say Zada left behind at his basic training installation letters and other paraphernalia containing anti-Gaza withdrawal slogans. Politicians, security officials, and pundits seized on his terrorist act, along with scores of other extremist acts carried out by similarly dubious forces, as proof of a general settler threat to Israeli security—as though an average settler were likely to enter a bus and start shooting passengers. Such an alleged extremist threat was cited as legal cause prior to the Gaza retreat to arrest settler leaders who had committed no crime and to place them in administrative detention. Most settler leaders were released without charges following the Gaza expulsion. The issue of how the Israeli government treated Gaza's Jews after their evacuation continues to fester, as well.

JEWS TARGETED IN OLDEST JEWISH CITY

Aside from Gaza, other recent, though lesser known, evacuations illustrate how Israel's withdrawal policy demoralizes the religious Zionist camp. Take Hebron. Located in the biblical heartland of Judea on the West Bank, Hebron is the oldest Jewish community in the world. Jews have lived there almost continuously for over thirty-five hundred years. The city is home to the Tomb of the Patriarchs, the second holiest site in Judaism, believed to be the resting place of the biblical patriarchs and matriarchs Abraham, Isaac, Jacob, Sarah, Rebecca, and Leah. King David, progenitor of the eventual Jewish messiah, was anointed in Hebron, where he reigned for seven years. Ten centuries later, during the first Jewish revolt against the Romans, Hebron was the scene of extensive fighting where many Jews were killed. Throughout the Byzantine, Arab, Mameluke, and Ottoman periods, there are accounts of the trials of Hebron's Jewish community. In 1929, after an Arab attack left sixty-seven Jews dead, the entire Jewish community fled the city, with Hebron becoming temporarily devoid of Jews. Jews returned when Israel recaptured the area in the 1967 Six Day War.

Hebron is a major stronghold of religious Zionist identity. About nine hundred Jews, including 250 students, live in a ghettoized area, surrounded by some one hundred and thirty thousand Palestinian Arabs. To live under such circumstances requires of Hebron's Jews the most profound awareness of the city's rich biblical legacy and the desire to hold on to the most ancient chain of Jewish connection to Judaism's second holiest city.

At times the Israeli government has made life difficult for the Jews of Hebron, as if constant danger of terrorist attack were not burden enough. In August 2007, for example, Prime Minister Ehud Olmert carried out a series of evacuations that did not seem to have any purpose beyond intimidating religious Zionist Jews. At the time, Olmert pledged to Secretary of State Condoleezza Rice that he would bulldoze a series of West Bank "illegal outposts," a term used to refer to Jewish structures in the West Bank or eastern Jerusalem built without Israeli government permission. Olmert's pledge was reportedly a confidence-building gesture aimed at appeasing PA President Mahmoud Abbas.

Whereas construction in West Bank Arab cities remains largely unregulated, the Israeli government strictly enforces construction regulations in West Bank Jewish neighborhoods. Permits to build in Jewish Hebron, for example, are rarely issued. The Palestinians routinely complain about Jewish structures they claim sit on their territory. They say the structures impede their mobility and block the contiguous nature of Palestinian cities and towns. As part of his promise to Rice, it would have made more sense for Olmert to target the multiple Jewish "illegal outposts" constructed alongside several Palestinian villages. Instead, Olmert chose Hebron. On August 3, I was present as he sent in large numbers of security forces to demolish structures within Hebron's Jewish community and evict residents from a Jewish-owned former market place. The evictions and bulldozings had no practical purpose for the Palestinians whatsoever, since the target was within the confines of Hebron's tiny Jewish community, in structures where there were no Palestinians. Olmert sent a reported three thousand soldiers and police officers to expel two Jewish families from the former market. Authorities claimed the families' residence in Hebron was illegal, since their arrival hadn't been coordinated with the Israeli military. The families told reporters they moved in only after the military reneged on an agreement to allow them to live in the structure.

The former market in question, converted to small, two-story apartments, was built in 1929 after Arab riots temporarily forced Jews out of Hebron. For more than thirty years, a sign posted on the market boasted in Arabic that the structure was built on stolen Jewish property. Arab merchants illegally set up shop at the market but the IDF asked them to leave after a series of clashes broke out in the mid-1990s. Even though the market was stolen from Jews, Hebron's Jewish community "re-purchased" the market from its original Arab occupants in 2001, in hopes of avoiding any possible conflict with the Palestinians.

In January 2006, Jewish families took up occupancy in the former market to strengthen Jewish ties to the area. The structure is located yards from an infamous spot where five years earlier a Palestinian sniper murdered a ten-month-old Hebron girl, Shalhevet Pass. The former market, integrated within the Hebron Jewish community, sits adjacent to several Jewish apartments and Jewish municipal buildings. The original property owners had signed over the market to Hebron's Jewish community, and even the Israeli Supreme Court had ruled that the structure was Jewish-owned. Nevertheless, the Olmert government deemed the Jewish occupancy of the former market illegal, and decided to make an example of the families.

Following a standoff with the army in 2006, the Jews who had moved into the structure decided to leave, but only after reportedly receiving promises from military officials that they could return a few months later. But Israel's attorney general overturned the Supreme Court's decision and declared that the residents could not move in—two of the Jewish families moved back anyway, prompting Olmert immediately to order that they be kicked out. Outnumbered by the ridiculously massive call-up of security forces, and even threatened that they would need to reimburse the IDF for the costs of their evacuation, the two families had no choice but to go.

The forced evacuations in Hebron did not end there. On August 7, Israeli forces, acting again on orders from Olmert, bulldozed a Hebron synagogue built in memory of Pass, because it was constructed without a permit. The synagogue also doubled as a *yeshiva* for soldiers who served as part of a first-response team for attempted terror attacks against Hebron. Hebron community spokesman David Wilder expressed to me "shock and outrage" that Israel had demolished the synagogue.

Israeli forces then handed an eviction notice to a Hebron-based rabbi who had been using a mobile housing unit for a *yeshiva*. Rabbi Danny Cohen, an emissary to Hebron for the Chabad Lubavitch worldwide Jewish outreach movement, said he was surprised he received the notice, which demanded he remove his mobile structure from the city.[3]

Cohen taught the Torah and organized prayer quorums for Hebron residents from his trailer headquarters, which he parked in Hebron's Jewish neighborhood. The rabbi said he was forced to set up shop in the trailer because of extreme Israeli government regulations against building new Jewish structures in Hebron. Cohen felt his eviction notice demonstrated anti-Jewish policy on behalf of the Israeli government. "In Hebron one can witness outright discrimination. While Arabs have been building as much as they want, Jews are forbidden to build even the smallest structure. This mobile unit is not a permanent building and still the authorities ordered the emissaries not to use it in the city," Cohen said.[4]

VIOLENT JEW-ON-JEW CONFRONTATIONS

The bulldozing of Jewish structures is routine for Hebron and for Jewish communities throughout the West Bank. Local Jews usually peacefully protest the bulldozings, which eventually are carried out with little interference. One notable exception was the case of Amona. In probably the most heated exchange between the Labor and religious Zionist camps to date and perhaps a foreshadow of what is yet to come should Israel attempt more evacuations of Jews, Israeli forces on February 1, 2006, brutalized religious demonstrators protesting the demolition of nine homes in the small northern West Bank hilltop community of Amona. Numerous reports surfaced of excessive use of force against the protestors, many of whom suffered severe injuries.

More than fifteen hundred Israeli Defense Force soldiers and Israeli police officers had been called up to demolish the nine homes, after the court system ruled the houses had been constructed without permits. The government said the homes could be rebuilt at a later date in the same community if the construction was coordinated with the Ministry of Defense. The homes were located within the confines of a Jewish-only community, meaning their construction did not impede the mobility of any Palestinians.

Olmert ordered the demolitions carried out immediately and instructed the military to use "all force necessary."[5] The eviction was the first significant evacuation of Jews since Israel's 2005 Gaza retreat. The religious Zionist camp regarded the Amona evictions as a sign of more withdrawals to come and decided to put up a major protest, fearing that if the Amona evictions were carried out, Olmert would march on to remove Jews from more West Bank communities. In a statement, the Rabbis Settlement Council announced the Amona evictions had "the goal of destroying the religious Zionist public."[6]

Horse-mounted police officers, water cannons, and specially trained riot officers faced off in Amona against hundreds of protestors, who mainly attempted physically to block the Israeli eviction forces from carrying out their duties. A few Jewish protestors lobbed paint and other liquids at police officers. There were reports that a small number of protestors threw stones at the

Israeli forces. Israeli television broadcast live footage of demonstrators, including women and children, dragged and beaten by soldiers. Teenagers with bloody noses and head wounds were shown being taken from the scene. Police used batons and gas canisters to clear the area of demonstrators.

Emergency personnel treated more than three hundred protestors in makeshift first aid tents and evacuated at least seventy with moderate-to-serious injuries to Jerusalem hospitals. Three Israeli nationalist lawmakers, Effie Eitam, Benny Elon, and Aryeh Eldad, received wounds in the clashes. Eitam suffered a head injury after soldiers pushed him. He told me he went to a Jerusalem hospital for neurological tests. Elon was injured after reportedly being pushed off a bulldozer by troops. Eldad sustained an arm fracture after police shoved him to the ground. The clashes also resulted in wounds to dozens of police officers and the arrests of more than eighty protestors. After three hours of confrontation, the soldiers cleared the area and razed the nine Amona homes.

Many wounded demonstrators later attempted to file criminal charges against Israeli police forces but had trouble identifying the offending officers. In July 2008, the Jerusalem Magistrate's Court convicted one police officer of brutality for assaulting a young demonstrator.[7] Video footage caught the officer in full battle gear head-butting protestor David Ladwin with his helmet. Ladwin suffered serious injuries. The court ruled that the police officer acted "without any provocation on the youth's part, and without the youth having assaulted him."[8] Several more criminal cases of police brutality at Amona are pending after video footage helped witnesses to identify some of the assailants.

WAR INTENSIFIES

As the U.S. continues brokering negotiations aimed at an eventual evacuation from most of the West Bank and perhaps eastern sections of Jerusalem, the war against the religious Zionist camp intensifies. Israel's government, aided by the news media, has launched a campaign to disenfranchise the nearly 270,000 Jewish settlers who live in the West Bank. As always, they are painted as violent, extremist elements who threaten Israeli democracy and must therefore be removed.

During the writing of this book, reports of "extremist" West Bank settlers engaged in violence against Palestinians and Israeli troops have dominated the news in Israel. In one of many examples, the Israeli news media reported in September 2008 on settlers accused of shooting to death an eighteen-year-old Palestinian shepherd. The reports were based on Palestinian claims, but completely ignored settler investigations that showed it was extremely unlikely a Jew was involved in the death. Both pundits and Israeli politicians used the accusation to petition for harsher punishments against "extremist settlers." Finally, an official police investigation determined no settler had shot the shepherd.[9] Forensic experts found shrapnel had killed him after he picked up an unexploded shell that detonated in his hands.

In another incident, in late September 2008, a pipe bomb exploded outside the house of a leading Labor Zionist professor, Zeev Sternhell, a prominent proponent of expelling Jews from the West Bank. With little information on who was behind the blast, the Israeli media and politicians immediately pointed to settler elements. Olmert went so far as to claim a "direct link" between the attack on Sternhell and the assassination of Yitzhak Rabin. The former premier's murder in 1995 has become Israel's template for blaming the whole religious Zionist camp for the act of one Jewish nationalist extremist.

"An evil wind of extremism, of hatred, of malice, of violence, of lawlessness is blowing through certain sections of the Israeli public and threatens Israeli democracy," Olmert told the Knesset, in a clear reference to West Bank settlers.[10]

Putting an even finer point to it, then-Defense Minister Ehud Barak urged the Knesset to adopt a tougher stance on punishing West Bank settlers for "unruly" behavior.[11] Addressing the Knesset himself, Sternhell called on the government to rein in "extremist settlers," even though it was not even known who was behind the attack against him.[12]

Ironically, the tendency of framing the entire settler movement for the acts of fringe elements runs contrary to everything Sternhell and his Labor Zionist colleagues claim they stand for. They routinely argue that acts of terrorism by Palestinians are not indicative of the general Palestinian population and should not be used to indict all of Palestinian society.

During the Sternhell affair, the nationalist Knesset member David Rotem lamented, "for days now, people have been casting aspersions on the settler population saying that it was guilty, but does anybody know who did it?"[13]

WHO'S BEHIND "VIOLENT" SETTLERS?

Settler leader Daniella Weiss, who has had some run-ins with the police herself, took it one step further and accused Israel's Shin Bet Security Services of orchestrating the Sternhell attack and then using it to demonize West Bank Jews ahead of an expected evacuation of the territory.[14] "A settler would never have done a thing like that," Weiss said. "It's in Shin Bet's best interest to create this provocation, in order to libel the settlers and thereby pave the way to settlement evacuation." I must say that, after four years of on the ground reporting, including conversations with scores of security officials, I find Weiss's charges of Shin Bet involvement entirely credible.

Settlers in 2008 had been accused of an increasing number of attacks on Israel Defense Forces soldiers stationed near settlements, particularly near two communities—Yitzhar and Kfar Tapuach. Some residents of these two towns have connections to the same dubious, extremist fringe organizations that sent Zada to murder Arabs. These fringe groups, which seem to act against the settlement establishment, are widely condemned by the vast majority of the West Bank's Jewish communities and are not representative of the settlement movement.

This fact has not stopped the news media, including the international press, from using the Yitzhar and Kfar Tapuach attacks to tar the entire settlement movement. A *New York Times* article from September 2008, reporting from Yitzhar, is entitled "Radical Settlers Take on Israel" and depicts the situation in the West Bank as if Yitzhar represents the wider settler movement.[15]

The *Times* interviewed some of the most radical settlers in Yitzhar who are not respected by the settler community.

In an eerie flashback to the days of administrative detention just before the Gaza retreat, Israel's court system in 2008 placed bans on several West Bank Jews from returning to their homes, claiming they might incite violence.

TARGETING RELIGIOUS SOLDIERS

The war of Labor Zionism against its religious foes is by no means limited to withdrawals from territory. Secularists use other means to intimidate the religious Zionist camp, even when doing so means shooting the country in the foot.

The *Hesder yeshivas*, which combine Torah study with IDF service, are central to the security of the Jewish state. The five-year program, of which sixteen months to two years focuses on army service, comprises both training and active duty. *Hesder* students are highly motivated to defend the Jewish state. By choice, almost all *Hesder* students serve in the army as combat soldiers—an average of 88 percent sign up for combat as opposed to the national average of less than 30 percent. *Hesder* students routinely put their lives on the line on risky missions in the West Bank and Gaza. Their ranks have been central to all major Israeli operations during the past ten years, including Israel's twenty-two-day campaign against Hamas in Gaza that ended in January 2009, the Second Lebanon War in 2006, and Israel's anti-terror campaigns in the West Bank in 2002, in which troops went from house to house, often in fierce combat with terrorist groups.

The prevalence of *Hesder* men in combat units has prompted major concern within Labor Zionist circles that one day a significant portion of the IDF may refuse to uproot religious Zionist Jews from their homes. On this basis, the Israeli government has led a silent campaign to demoralize *Hesder* students. Just prior to the 2005 Gaza evacuation, the IDF curiously announced a decision to disband some *Hesder* special units and integrate religious soldiers into secular units, a decision that would make army service uncomfortable for many religious soldiers. Major General Elazar Stern explained to Israel

Army Radio that integrating the observant soldiers into regular units would help to moderate soldiers who might refuse to carry out orders.[16] "We in the army don't ever want units based on ideology, because we don't want to choose missions according to the ideological character of the units," Stern said. "We are using the same logic regarding the mission of the [Gaza] evacuation." The threats to disband the *Hesder* units, however, were never implemented.

In 2007, a government-appointed special committee on the army, headed by Major General Yehuda Segev, recommended the incorporation of women into combat units, a commendable achievement for Israeli feminists.[17] Israeli officials want to ensure the integration of women into *all* units, including *Hesder*-dominated religious combat units. This would pose a problem for *Hesder* students, who subscribe to traditional Jewish values on modesty that would bar men from serving so closely with women.

The government has also ordered the army to carry out certain operations that have directly insulted the *Hesder* units, such as the forced removal of Jews on the Sabbath from a tiny structure at a small outpost called Maon Farm, about eight miles south of Hebron.

Hesder leaders have read the tea leaves. Rabbi Yuval Cherlow, who leads a *Hesder yeshiva* in the city of Petach Tivkah, commented on the accumulation of issues antagonizing religious soldiers: "The question is whether it's a purposeful campaign against us, or is just coincidental, a process that happens to be under way. Everyone can interpret it as he sees fit; I choose to interpret it as a process that the state of Israel is undergoing that tramples on the issues that are important to us."[18]

SILENCING THE RELIGIOUS ZIONISTS

As mentioned, nearly all major Israeli television, radio, and print news outlets are aligned with Labor Zionism. Nonetheless, the government closed down the few religious Zionist voices on the airwaves, most notably the Arutz Sheva media network. Arutz Sheva, or Israel Channel Seven, was established in the West Bank Jewish city of Beit-El and began radio broadcasts in October 1988 from a ship anchored off the Mediterranean coast. The network featured religious-oriented Jewish music and programming and was the only major news media outlet in Israel to openly oppose the 1993 Oslo Accords, which granted Palestinian leader Yasser Arafat territory in the West Bank.

In 1994, the Israeli government moved to shut down Arutz Sheva by denying the company a broadcast license, thus driving the station to broadcast from further out at sea, beyond Israel's territorial waters. In 1995, when the Arutz Sheva transmitter ship docked at Israel's Ashdod port for annual repairs, communications minister Shulamit Aloni, of the leftist Meretz Party, ordered the police and ministry inspectors to raid the vessel during the nine days preceding the Jewish mourning day of Tisha B'Av—a time when Jewish tradition calls for refraining from listening to music, in accord with the solemnity of the period. The official pretext for the raid was that the ship broadcasted from Israeli territorial waters and that its transmissions interfered with planes landing at Israel's Ben-Gurion International Airport. In actuality, Arutz Sheva had shut down its radio broadcasts for the entire nine-day mourning period, since a good deal of its programming consisted of music. In other words, not only was the religious station not interfering with air traffic, it wasn't broadcasting at all. Still, Israeli police raided the Arutz Sheva ship and confiscated hundreds of thousands of dollars of broadcasting equipment, dealing the network a major blow.

The war against the independent radio station continued with the Israeli government's sudden increase of the range of what it considered territorial waters. This drove the Arutz Sheva ship even further out to sea. Accusing the group of continuing illegal broadcasts, Israel's attorney general then ordered a probe that included an investigation of companies that advertised on Arutz Sheva, causing the station to lose massive advertising revenue, according to Arutz Sheva staff interviewed for this book. Eventually, Arutz Sheva's operators were indicted and then convicted for illegally broadcasting in Israeli territory, bringing an end to the station's terrestrial radio broadcasts. The government witch hunt cost Israeli taxpayers a staggering $10 million, according to sources close to the investigation. Arutz Sheva continues its broadcasts today on the Internet, but the closure of its radio broadcasting irrevocably damaged the network.

Labor Zionists also work diligently to impose their ideology on Israel's public education system. That point was driven home for many in the religious Zionist community in 2006, when Olmert appointed Yuli Tamir, a member of the Labor party, as education minister. Tamir founded the radical European-funded Peace Now movement. The organization calls for Israel to withdraw from the entire West Bank, eastern Jerusalem—including the Temple Mount— and the strategic Golan Heights.

As soon as she obtained the education portfolio, Tamir went to work reforming Israel's education system to toe the Labor line. In one of her first acts, she ordered that all maps of Israel in school textbooks demarcate the 1949 armistice lines, or present a map of Israel minus eastern Jerusalem, the West Bank, and the Golan Heights. Tamir drew fury from religious circles when she approved a textbook for Israeli Arab schoolchildren that taught the Palestinian *Nakba* (Disaster) perspective of Israel's founding in 1948, which portrays Israel's War of Independence as an act of Jewish aggression.

Tamir in 2007 decided to cut by 50 percent the number of religious Orthodox females employed as Jewish and Zionist studies teachers in elementary schools through National Service institutions. The National Service allows women to perform alternative service to military enlistment through teaching and social services. Officials from Tamir's education ministry, speaking to Israel's *Yediot Aharonot* newspaper, called the Orthodox female teachers "too right-wing." Tamir also announced a number of cutbacks to Zionist and Jewish education studies, all the while expressing support for a program that would make Islamic religion and culture a required state-funded subject for Israeli Arabs.

And so the religious Zionist camp soldiers on, worn down by a long war that has left the ideology wounded but far from defeated. It remains to be seen if the new Netanyahu administration will pursue its predecessors' practices of targeting religious Zionism, while the media and cultural elite continue their collateral assault on the national religious establishment. Regardless, the Jewish state's policies against the national religious have already done the country great harm and threaten to wither the Zionist dream.

CHAPTER FIVE

ABANDONING THE TEMPLE MOUNT

Jews declared they dug and dug for proof that their imaginary Temples existed and they didn't find any sign. Nothing. We don't want to throw you into the sea but we say you are making us [Muslims] very upset with these lies about your Temples," said Sheikh Taysir Tamimi, the Palestinian Chief Justice and one of the most influential Muslim clerics in the Middle East. The prominent sheikh explained to me very sternly that the Jews have no historic connection whatsoever to the Temple Mount or Jerusalem. A Zionist conspiracy created the Jewish Temples. Muhammad used the Western Wall as a tying post for his horse. And Allah's angels built Islam's so-called third holiest site, the al-Aqsa Mosque.

I met Tamimi at his luxurious, well-decorated office in a poor Arab neighborhood on the outskirts of Jerusalem. Tamimi is considered the second most important Palestinian cleric after Muhammad Ahmad Hussein, the Jordanian-allied Grand Mufti of Jerusalem. Tamimi regularly preaches from the al-Aqsa Mosque. He represents mainstream Islamic thinking in the Palestinian territories.

"Israel started since 1967 making archeological digs to show Jewish signs to prove the relationship between Judaism and the [Temple Mount] and they found nothing," Tamimi told me.

He brushed off evidence accepted by respected archeologists worldwide verifying the existence of the Jewish Temples, including the discovery of Temple-era artifacts linked to worship, work areas where Temple stones were carved, key tunnels that snake under the Temple Mount, and over one hundred ritual immersion pools believed to have been used by Jewish priests to cleanse themselves before services. The cleansing process is related in detail in the Torah.

The Temple Mount is Judaism's holiest site. To deny its reality negates many of Judaism's core beliefs, to say nothing of Zionism. King Solomon built the First Temple in the tenth century BC. The Babylonians destroyed it in 586 BC. The Jews built the Second Temple in 515 BC after Jerusalem was freed from Babylonian captivity. The Romans destroyed the Second Temple in AD 70. The First Temple stood for about four hundred years, the second for almost six hundred. Both Temples served as the center of religious worship for the whole Jewish nation. They housed the Holy of Holies, the temple's inner sanctum containing both the Ark of the Covenant and the area upon which God's *shechina* or "presence" dwelt. All Jewish holidays centered on worship at the Temple—the central location for the offering of sacrifices and the main gathering place for the Jewish people.

According to the Talmud, God created the world from the foundation stone of the Temple Mount. The site is believed to be the Biblical Mount Moriah, where Abraham fulfilled God's test of faith by demonstrating his willingness to sacrifice his son Isaac. Jewish tradition also holds that *Mashiach*—literally "the anointed one," the Jewish Messiah—will come and rebuild the third and final Temple on the Mount in Jerusalem and bring redemption to the entire world.

The Western Wall is called the *Kotel* in Hebrew. It is the one part of the Temple Mount that survived the Roman destruction of the Second Temple and stands to this day in Jerusalem. The Temple Mount has remained a focal point for Jewish services for thousands of years. Prayers for a return to Jerusalem and the rebuilding of the Jewish Temple have been uttered three times daily by religious Jews since the destruction of the Second Temple. Throughout all the centuries of Jewish exile from their land, thorough documentation shows the Jews never gave up their hope of returning to Jerusalem and reestablishing their Temple. To this day Jews worldwide pray facing the Western Wall, while Muslims turn their backs away from the Temple Mount and pray toward Mecca.

According to Tamimi, the Western Wall, which predates the al-Aqsa Mosque by more than a thousand years, is actually part of the al-Aqsa Mosque. "The Western Wall is the western wall of the al-Aqsa Mosque," Tamimi told me. He said the Western Wall is properly called the Al-Boraq Wall, which he said was where Muhammad tied his horse, named Boraq, before ascending to heaven. "It's where Prophet Muhammad tied his animal which took him from Mecca to Jerusalem to receive the revelations of Allah," Tamimi told me. I asked the chief Palestinian Justice why the Koran does not mention Jerusalem once. "Jerusalem is in the Koran. It's mentioned in the first *sura* of the Koran," he stated falsely. As to Jerusalem being mentioned by name 622 times in the Torah, Tamimi said the Hebrew Bible was "falsified by the Jews. We don't believe in all your versions. The Torah as revealed to our Prophet Moses never once mentioned the Temple or Jerusalem."

Muslims constructed the al-Aqsa Mosque around AD 709 to serve as a place of worship near a famous shrine, the gleaming Dome of the Rock, built by an Islamic *caliph*, or supreme ruler. About one hundred years ago, Muslims began to associate al-Aqsa in Jerusalem with the place Muhammad ascended to heaven. Islamic tradition states Muhammad took a journey in a single night from "a sacred mosque"—believed to be in Mecca in southern Saudi Arabia—to "the farthest mosque," and from a rock there ascended to heaven to receive revelations from Allah that became part of the Koran.

While Palestinians and many Muslim countries claim exclusivity over the Mount, and while their leaders strenuously deny the Jewish historic connection to the site, things weren't always this way. In fact, historically, Muslims never claimed the al-Aqsa Mosque as their "third holiest site" and always recognized the existence of the Jewish Temples. According to an Israeli attorney, Dr. Shmuel Berkovits, Islamic tradition mostly disregarded Jerusalem. He points out in his book *How Dreadful is this Place!* that Muhammad was said to loathe Jerusalem and what it stood for to the other monotheistic faiths. Muhammad also made a point of eliminating pagan sites of worship and sanctifying only one place—the Kaaba in Mecca—to signify the unity of Allah.[1]

As late as the fourteenth century, Islamic scholar Taqi al-Din Ibn Taymiyya, whose writings later influenced the ultra-conservative Wahhabi movement in Arabia, ruled that sacred

Islamic sites exist only on the Arabian Peninsula, and that "in Jerusalem, there is not a place one calls sacred, and the same holds true for the tombs of Hebron."[2] Not until the late nineteenth century—when Jews started immigrating to Palestine—did Muslim scholars claim that Muhammad tied his horse to the Western Wall and associate Muhammad's purported night journey with the Temple Mount.[3]

MUSLIMS SHIFT POSITION ON TEMPLE MOUNT

A guide to the Temple Mount by the Supreme Muslim Council in Jerusalem, published in 1925, listed the Mount as the site of King Solomon's Temple. The Temple Institute, a Temple Mount activist group, acquired a copy of the official 1925 *Guide Book to Al-Haram Al-Sharif*, which states on page four, "Its identity with the site of Solomon's Temple is beyond dispute. This, too, is the spot, according to universal belief, on which 'David built there an altar unto the Lord...'" citing 2 Samuel 24:25.

But Tamimi calls the well-documented Jewish ties to the Mount and to Jerusalem falsehoods. "There was no Jewish civilization in Jerusalem," exclaimed the leading Palestinian cleric. "Many people lived here throughout the ages and they left some artifacts, but so what? There is no proof of any Jews being here. Jews came to the [Temple area] in 1967 and not before."

Tamimi's charges dance in tune to the ideology of the Palestinian leadership. The official Palestinian Authority Web site labels the Temple Mount as Muslim property. At U.S.-brokered Israeli-Palestinian peace negotiations in 2000, Palestinian leader Yasser Arafat reportedly astonished President Clinton when he repeatedly denied any Jewish connection to the Temple Mount.[4] Arafat demanded total Palestinian control over the holy site, participants later recounted.

As late as November 2008, Ahmed Qurei, the chief Palestinian negotiator—meaning the Palestinian Authority official leading all peace talks with the Jewish state—asserted that the Jewish Temples never existed and that Israel has been working to "invent" a Jewish historical connection to Jerusalem. In a press briefing I personally attended, Qurei said, "Israeli occupation authorities are trying to find a so-called Jewish historical connection" between Jerusalem and the Temple Mount, "but all these attempts will fail. The [Temple Mount] is 100 percent Muslim."[5]

"There is nothing Jewish about the al-Aqsa Mosque. There was no so-called Jewish Temple. It's imaginary. Jerusalem is 100 percent Muslim," he added.

Besides verbal denials, Palestinians erase physical evidence of Jewish history on the Temple Mount, at times seemingly with aid from the Israeli government. In one glaring episode I recently reported on, the Israeli government and the state's Antiquities Authority barred Israeli archaeologists from surveying massive damage that Islamic authorities were accused of causing to the holy site's antiquities. Israeli archaeologists were also blocked from viewing what might have been an historic Jewish Temple find on the Mount.

Then, in the summer of 2007, Prime Minister Olmert and the Antiquities Authority agreed to allow the Waqf—the Mount's Muslim custodians—to use bulldozers and other heavy equipment to dig a massive trench on the Temple Mount that the Waqf claimed was necessary to replace electrical cables outside mosques on the site. The Israeli police protected the dig, which extended to most of the periphery of the Temple Mount, and the Israeli government's Antiquities Authority supervised. Allowing the use of bulldozers at any sensitive archaeological site is extremely unusual, but particularly at a site such as the Temple Mount, which experts say contains sealed layers of artifacts as shallow as two to three feet below the surface. Israel has long barred Israeli archaeologists from excavating any area of the site, so no one has ever properly excavated the site. Heavy equipment such as bulldozers could easily damage existing artifacts, say experts, who assert the area should be excavated slowly and carefully by hand.

BULLDOZING JEWISH HISTORY

In September 2007, while bulldozers dug a trench thirteen hundred feet long and five feet deep, the Muslim diggers reportedly came across what may have been remnants of a wall Israeli archaeologists believed could be remains of an area of the Second Jewish Temple known as the women's courtyard. It would have been the first time an actual Temple wall was discovered on the Mount. However, Israeli police blocked leading archeologists from surveying the purported wall or viewing massive damage that Islamic authorities purportedly caused to the area during their dig.[6]

Jewish visitors went up to the Mount during the several hours on weekdays when the Mount is open to Jews, but both the Wafq and Israeli police tried to keep the visitors from the area of the digging.

Jews and Christians can visit the Temple Mount only on Sundays through Thursdays from 7:30 a.m. to 10:00 a.m. and from 12:30 p.m. to 1:30 p.m. It is closed to non-Muslims on all Christian, Jewish, or Muslim holidays or other days considered "sensitive" by the Muslim Waqf custodians. But to Muslims it is open nearly 24-7. Non-Muslim visitors to the Mount must enter from a particular gate, usually with a guided tour. Visitors pass a set of guidelines written in Hebrew and English on a large blue sign. These Israeli-enforced rules state, "Holy objects not permitted." The rules dictate that non-Muslims may not pray on the Mount. Non-Muslim visitors may not enter any of the mosques without direct Waqf permission. Waqf agents, who watch tours closely and alert nearby Israeli police to any violation of their guidelines, diligently enforce the rules. Israeli police units also screen visitors going up.

A third-generation Temple archaeologist, Dr. Eilat Mazar, told me that the Antiquities Authority refused repeated requests for her and other top experts to inspect the trench dug by the Waqf. Islamic authorities completely sealed the trench by the end of September.

"The Antiquities Authority told us to coordinate with the police. The police sent us back to the Antiquities Authority...they refused to allow us to inspect what the Muslims found," said Mazar, a senior fellow at Israel's Shalem Center and a member of the Public Committee for Prevention of the Destruction of Antiquities on the Temple Mount. Mazar also is a discoverer and lead archaeologist of a dig of Israel's City of David, an area just outside the Temple Mount believed to be an important site associated with the biblical King David, the second leader of a united kingdom of Israel, who ruled from around 1005 to 965 BC. "It's crucial this wall be inspected. The Temple Mount ground level is only slightly above the original Temple Mount platform, meaning anything found is likely from the Temple itself," the archaeologist said of the find.

Pictures smuggled off the Temple Mount from the area of the Wafq dig clearly showed what look like chopped-up antiquities. One picture I obtained showed concrete slabs broken by Waqf bulldozers—including a possible carved stone from Jewish Temple-era antiquity. "It certainly looks like Second Temple antiquity and could very well be part of a Second Temple courtyard wall," said Mazar, upon inspection of the picture. She said that in order to certify the stone in the photo in question, she would need to inspect it personally. But it is unlikely the government of Israel will allow Dr. Mazar, or anyone else from the Israeli side, to do so.

At one point toward the end of the dig, after Israeli police had repeatedly denied them permission to view the site, Dr. Mazar and other top archaeologists unilaterally ascended the Mount to hold a news conference and inspect the massive Muslim dig site. Again Israeli police blocked them from getting close to the trench.

Rabbi Chaim Richman directs the international department at Israel's Temple Institute. He visited the Mount with Mazar, and told me that when he attempted to take pictures of the damage, Israeli police confiscated his digital camera at the behest of Waqf officials.

Hearing this, I quickly assembled a camera crew myself and ascended the Mount to obtain footage of the Muslim dig. Using a film crew from InfoLive.tv, a new Internet television network focusing on the Middle East, I entered the Mount on September 6, 2007, but was barred from inspecting or filming the massive trench in a confrontation caught on tape. "I would like to see the dig and the bulldozers," I said to a Waqf official during a filmed conversation. But a Waqf guard directed the crew and me to closed areas of the trench instead of open areas where I could perhaps have seen any of the purported damage to the antiquities. The Waqf was moving to close most of the trench they had dug, following protests regarding the dig from Mazar and other top archaeologists, but some sections were still open. I persisted: "It's already covered up over there. I can't see it from there.... I want to see the dig." One

Waqf guard asked the InfoLive crew to shut off their camera. The guard can then be heard in the audio directing the crew and me to immediately vacate the Temple Mount. The Waqf and an Israeli policeman escorted us from the site.

Mazar asserts the Waqf is "trying to erase Jewish vestiges from the Temple Mount." The last time the Waqf conducted a large dig on the Mount—during construction in 1996 and 1997 of a massive mosque at an area referred to as Solomon's Stables—the site's Islamic custodians reportedly disposed of truckloads of dirt containing Jewish artifacts from the First and Second Temple periods.[7] The Waqf was widely accused of attempting to hide evidence of the existence of the Jewish Temples.

After Israeli news media reported on the disposals, authorities froze the construction permit given to the Waqf and a team of Israeli archeologists analyzed the dirt. The team, led by Bar-Ilan University's Gabriel Barkai, found thousands of Jewish Temple relics in the nearly-discarded dirt, including coins with Hebrew writing referencing the Temple, part of a Hasmonean (second century BC) lamp, several other Second Temple lamps, Temple-period pottery with Jewish markings, a marble pillar shaft, and other Temple-period artifacts.[8] Also found in the soil was an arrowhead with a shaft believed to have been used by the Roman legions during the siege of the Second Temple in AD 70.

Another priceless find was a First Temple-period *bulla*, or seal impression, containing ancient Hebrew writing, which may have belonged to a well-known family of priests mentioned in the book of Jeremiah (seventh century BC). "It bears the name Gedalyahu Ben Immer Ha-Cohen, suggesting that the owner may have been a brother of Pashur Ben Immer, described in the Bible as a priest and temple official." Barkai said.[9] The verse Barkai referred to is Jeremiah 20:1: "Pashur, the son of Immer the priest, who was also chief governor in the House of the Lord, heard that Jeremiah prophesied these things."

JORDANIANS SOLIDIFY THEIR CONTROL

The Palestinians and the Arab countries seem confident Israel will one day transfer full control of the Temple Mount to Muslims or to an international force. Already, the Mount is home to scores of mosques and Islamic institutions. Arab states fight for influence over the Temple Mount, though Jordan clearly leads the pack. From 1948 until Israel recaptured the site in the 1967 Six Day War, Jordan controlled all of eastern Jerusalem, including the Temple Mount. During the period of Jordanian control, Jews could not enter the Temple Mount or visit the Western Wall. Two days after conquering Jerusalem's Jewish Quarter, the Jordanians dynamited the Hurva Synagogue—the most prominent synagogue in Jerusalem for over three hundred years—and destroyed hundreds of synagogues in eastern Jerusalem. Jordan constructed a road that stretched across the Mount of Olives, adjacent to the Temple Mount, bulldozing hundreds of Jewish gravestones in the process and using them to build latrines for Jordanian troops.

Following the Six Day War, General Moshe Dayan, then chief of staff of the Israel Defense Forces, assured the Jordanian-allied Mufti of Jerusalem, Abd al-Hamid A Saih, that the holy site would remain under Islamic custodianship. Adding insult to injury, Dayan later also notoriously ordered an Israeli flag removed from the Dome of the Rock.

Today, Jordan maintains major influence over the Mount. Sheik Azzam Khateeb, installed in February 2007 as the new director of the Waqf, is known to be close to the Jordanian monarchy. The previous Waqf manager, Sheik Adnon Husseini, was loyal to the Palestinian Authority, although toward the end of his reign he seemed to be warming to Jordan. In a gesture to the Hashemite Kingdom, in January 2006, Israel granted Jordan permission to replace the main podium in the al-Aqsa Mosque from which Islamic preachers deliver their sermons.[10] The podium, partially funded by Saudi Arabia, is today considered one of the most important stands in the Muslim world. Muslims now claim it marks the "exact spot" Muhammad went up to heaven to receive revelations from Allah. The new stand bears the emblem of the Jordanian Kingdom. It replaces an eight-hundred-year-old podium believed shipped to Jerusalem by the conqueror Saladin, who recaptured the Holy City from Christian crusaders in AD 1187. The old podium was destroyed in 1969, when an Australian tourist set fire to the al-Aqsa Mosque. "This historic occasion proves that the extremist Jews will never achieve their goals of taking over the [Temple Mount.] It shows that we are much closer to liberating the al-Aqsa Mosque and Jerusalem from Israeli occupation," said Husseini of the new stand in an interview.

In recent years, Jordan has quietly purchased real estate surrounding the Temple Mount in hopes of gaining more control over areas accessing the holy site, according to Palestinian and Israeli officials who spoke with me for this book. The officials disclosed that the Jordanian Kingdom in 2006 and 2007 used shell companies to purchase several apartments and shops located at key peripheral sections of the Mount. The shell companies at times presented themselves as acting on behalf of the Waqf custodians of the Mount, according to informed sources. Jordan also set up a commission to use the shell companies to petition mostly Arab landowners adjacent to eastern sections of the Temple Mount to sell their properties, these officials said. They also described how profits from sales at any of the purchased shops would be reinvested to buy more real estate near the Mount and in eastern Jerusalem neighborhoods.

Jordan also plans to build a massive new minaret on the Temple Mount to stand at a site where Jewish groups had petitioned to build a synagogue, as I first reported.[11] A minaret is a tower usually attached to a mosque from which Muslims are called to prayer on a loudspeaker five times every day.

There are already four minarets on the Temple Mount. The new one would be the largest yet. It would be the first built on the Temple Mount in over six hundred years and would tower 130 feet over the ancient walls of Jerusalem's Old City. It would reside next to the al-Marwani Mosque, located on the site of Solomon's Stables. According to informed sources, Olmert gave permission for Jordan to construct the minaret in the future, but it was unclear if that permission would be extended during the new Israeli administration of Benjamin Netanyahu.

Jordan's King Abdullah II has issued an international tender for the minaret's design. Dr. Raief Najim, vice chairman of the committee running the project, spoke with Israeli authorities about the plan in 2006 and did not hear any objections to the minaret's proposed construction. Najim toured the al-Marwani site slated for future construction with a top Jerusalem police commander, a senior Israeli government official, and the head of the Antiquities Authority, and none of them voiced any opposition.[12]

In 2006, Knesset member Aryeh Eldad, of Israel's National Union Party, drew up controversial plans with Jewish Temple Mount activist groups to build a synagogue near the Marwani Mosque at the exact site proposed for the minaret. The synagogue was to be built in accordance with rulings from several prominent rabbis, who said that Jewish law permits Jews to ascend the Mount at certain areas. Many rabbis hold that Jews cannot go anywhere on the Mount until the building of the Third Temple, even though there are records of Jews, including some of the most prominent Jewish legal scholars, visiting the Temple ruins during the Byzantine period and beyond. Other contemporary rabbinic authorities permit entry only to the outer areas of the Mount, which can be determined from a change in the type of foundation stone.

According to Jewish law, the sanctity of the Temple Mount is structured in concentric circles. In the innermost circles, where the Holy of Holies was said to be located, the restrictions to access are the greatest. During Temple times, only the *Kohen Hagadol*, or High Priest, could enter the most restricted area, and this only once a year, on the holy fast day of Yom Kippur. The outer circles are less restricted. The rabbis who forbid Jewish entry to the Temple Mount may indirectly contribute to the Islamic consolidation of the site. The lack of a large number of Jewish visitors is likely a major factor in the Israeli government's restriction of Jewish ascent to the Mount and the belief of Muslims that few Israelis oppose their domination of the site. A top leader of the Waqf told me that Olmert's granting of permission to build the minaret in place of the synagogue "confirms 100 percent the Haram al-Sharif [Temple Mount] belongs to Muslims. This proves Jewish conspiracies for a synagogue will never succeed and solidifies our presence here. It will make Muslims worldwide more secure that the Jews will never take over the Haram al-Sharif," he said.

ARABS COMPETE FOR TEMPLE MOUNT CONTROL AS HAMAS GAINS GROUND

Jordan is not alone in seeking Temple Mount control. A number of Arab states have quietly sent agents to infiltrate the Temple Mount to determine how they can obtain more influence over Judaism's holiest site, informed security sources have told me. "It's possible that in the coming years a deal will be made that transfers the Temple Mount out from Israeli hands," said one security source. "The Arab countries are vying for influence, since they think controlling the site means big prestige in the Muslim world." The sources said the Arab agents mostly infiltrate the Jordanian-influenced Waqf by securing all sorts of positions, from Waqf garden workers to clerics, inside the Mount's many mosques. They said the agents' primary job is to collect information on how to gain more influence on the site. The agents also are to report on which Waqf officials are paid by Jordan, and on which clerics can be suspected of having good relations with Israel. "The Arab countries want to work their way in so Jordan doesn't get the most control once Israel gives up the Mount," one source said.

Saudi Arabia has sent the largest number of agents to the Mount, but other countries, including Egypt, also have sent agents. "Don't be surprised if in the near future even Somalia sends some people over to study how to have influence on the Mount," the source said.

Even Hamas has gotten in on the action. On December 19, 2007, I broke the story that Hamas featured an exclusive stream of morning prayers from the al-Aqsa Mosque on its official radio network, al-Aqsa Radio, so that Palestinians confined to the Gaza Strip and the West Bank can take part in the services.[13]

The Jewish fast day of the Tenth of Tevet, a week after Hannukah, mourns the First Temple's destruction and the siege placed on Jerusalem during the reign of the Babylonian king Nebuchadnezzar. In 2007, Jewish Temple Mount groups wanted to lead tours of the Mount on the morning of December 19, which coincided with the Tenth of Tevet that year. But the groups' plans were halted by the Israeli police, who banned Jews from ascending that day since it also marked the start of the Muslim holiday of Ein ul-Adhaa, which commemorates the Islamic belief of Abraham's willingness to sacrifice his son Ishmael for Allah. According to the Jewish and Christian traditions, Abraham nearly sacrificed his son Isaac, not Ishmael.

Asked if the police approved the Hamas broadcast, Jerusalem police spokesman Shmulik Ben Ruby told me, "As far as I know, the Israeli police is not engaged with this issue." Spokesmen for both the Jerusalem police and Israel's national police said their respective departments were not aware of Hamas's planned broadcast until I wrote an article about the issue. A senior national police source said that if, indeed, Hamas was planning programming from the Temple Mount, such a broadcast would be halted. But that day, Hamas's programming went on without a hitch. The Hamas Temple Mount morning broadcast streams continued for weeks, with Israel's police fully aware of the situation, since I had sent my articles to a number of top police officials. Eventually the broadcasts were stopped, not by Israel, remarkably, but by the PA, which realized that the broadcasts from Judaism's holiest site boosted Hamas at the expense of the rival Fatah party.

These are the woes that have befallen Judaism's holiest site. In theory, Israel controls the Temple Mount. In reality and on the ground, the Jewish state has essentially forfeited the Mount to near-complete Islamic control, including to Muslim leaders who deny any Jewish historical connection or claims to the site. Jews are barred from visiting the Temple Mount during most hours of the day, and when they are allowed to ascend, it is under heavy restriction, including a Muslim-mandated total ban on prayer. Meanwhile, gangsters can freely broadcast from the site, as Jordan and other Arab states vie for more influence on the holy Mount that has been abandoned by the Jews.

CHAPTER SIX

JOSEPH'S TOMB TRAVESTY

In Israel the dismal forfeiture of Judaism's holy sites is not limited to the Temple Mount. Nonetheless, at least Israel maintains some grasp on the Mount; Israeli police still patrol the site, although they ban Jews from ascending on most hours of the day and many times do the bidding of the Mount's Islamic authorities.

By sad contrast, Israel has completely abandoned the tomb of the biblical patriarch Joseph—considered the third holiest site in Judaism after the Temple Mount and Hebron's Tomb of the Patriarchs (*Machpelah* in biblical Hebrew). A climactic episode that took place in October 2000 is crucial because it encapsulates the Jewish state's disregard for Jewish holy sites versus its almost fawning concern for Muslim sensibilities, as well as the dire consequences of caving in to Palestinian Authority terrorism and blackmail. I personally view the episode as among the darkest in modern Israel's short history.

Joseph's Tomb is located outside the modern day city of Nablus. Historians and archeologists widely acknowledge the vicinity of the tomb as the important biblical city of Shechem. There the patriarch Abraham, upon his migration to Canaan, or biblical Israel, built an altar to God, and Jacob purchased a plot of land on which the Jews buried his son Joseph after coming up from Egypt.

Joseph's life story forms one of the most complete and instructive narratives of any personal history recounted in the Torah. The eleventh son of Jacob and the son of the matriarch Rachel, Joseph's remarkable story begins when his brothers, angry over Joseph's perceived arrogance and jealous that Joseph is Jacob's favorite son, throw him into a pit and then sell him into slavery.

Later, while living as a slave in the royal precincts of Egypt, Joseph faces false accusations of attempting to rape his master's wife and goes to prison. While in prison, Joseph makes a name for himself as a talented interpreter of dreams. Among his admirers is a fellow prisoner who had served as cupbearer for Pharaoh. The Torah relates the story of how Pharaoh has a strange dream that he needs help understanding. The cupbearer—released from prison and restored to his former position—remembers Joseph and recommends the prisoner's services to the Egyptian ruler. Pharaoh sends for Joseph who accurately interprets Pharaoh's dream about seven fat cows and seven gaunt cows as meaning that Egypt would face seven years of plenty and seven years of famine. Joseph advises Pharaoh to immediately appoint someone to oversee the storage of vast quantities of food to survive the famine. Pleased with Joseph's interpretation, Pharaoh makes him viceroy over the land of Egypt. Seven years of bounty are indeed followed by the famine Joseph predicted, and Egypt survives due to Joseph's stewardship. Joseph is eventually reunited with his brothers and father, and maintains his position of leadership in Egypt until he dies as an old man.

Shortly before his death, Joseph asks the Israelites to vow that they will resettle his bones in the land of Canaan. As detailed in the Torah, that oath is fulfilled when the Jews take Joseph's remains from Egypt and re-interr them at the plot of land Jacob had purchased earlier in Shechem, believed to be the site of the present tomb, where Joseph's sons, Ephraim and Menasheh, are also said to be buried. Exodus 13:19 describes how Moses took the bones of Joseph when he departed Egypt with the Israelites:

> And Moses took the bones of Joseph with him: for he had straightly sworn the children of Israel, saying, God will surely visit you; and ye shall carry up my bones away hence with you.

Joshua 24:32 relates the actual burial of Joseph's remains:

> And the bones of Joseph, which the children of Israel brought up out of Egypt, buried they in Shechem, in a parcel of ground which Jacob bought from sons of Hamor,

the father of Shechem, for an hundred pieces of silver: and
it became the inheritance of the children of Joseph.

The *Midrash*, the official rabbinic Torah exegesis, relates:

> There are three places regarding which the nations of the
> world cannot taunt the nation of Israel and say, "you have
> stolen them." They are: The Cave of the Patriarchs [in
> Hebron], the Temple Mount and the burial site of Joseph.

The *Midrash* explains that it is explicitly recorded in the Torah that
each of these places was purchased "for its full price" by Abraham,
David, and Jacob respectively.[1]

JOSEPH'S TOMB RETURNS TO ISRAEL

Modern Israel first regained control of Nablus and the neighboring
site of Joseph's Tomb from Jordanian occupation in the 1967 Six
Day War. The 1993 Oslo Accords signed by Yasser Arafat and
Yitzhak Rabin called for the area surrounding the tomb's site to be
placed under Palestinian jurisdiction. However, it allowed for
continued Jewish access to the tomb and the construction of an
Israeli military outpost alongside the holy site to ensure security
for *yeshiva* students and for Jewish and Christian worshippers. One
yeshiva, the Od Yosef Chai School (Hebrew for "Joseph lives on"),
was actually built at the tomb in the mid-1980s and housed
volumes of holy books and a Torah scroll. *Yeshiva* students arrived
at the tomb as early as six in the morning and studied there most
days until midnight. They continued daily learning at the school
even after the tomb area transferred to Palestinian control. The
tomb's Israeli military outpost served to protect the students and
pilgrims from surrounding Palestinians.

Data indicate that Jews of various origins worshipped at Joseph's
Tomb for more than a thousand years. The Samaritans, a local tribe
who follow an ancient religion based in part on the Torah, say they
trace their lineage back to Joseph himself and that they worshipped at
the tomb site for more than seventeen hundred years. Palestinians,
however, claim that Joseph's Tomb is not a Jewish holy site at all, but
a Muslim one. They say an important Islamic cleric who died about

250 years ago named Joseph al-Dwaik is buried there and that the tomb is actually named after him. They claim that the biblical Joseph who of course according to them was not a Jew at all but was a prophet for Islam, is buried at the Tomb of the Patriarchs in the ancient West Bank city of Hebron. Muslims also lay claim to the Tomb of the Patriarchs, Judaism's second holiest site, insisting it is a Muslim holy site that has no connection to the Jewish people. Despite these claims, it is historically documented that until Israel captured the area, Joseph's Tomb was not considered an important Islamic site.

Following the transfer of control of Nablus to the Palestinians in the early 1990s, a series of clearly orchestrated violent incidents occurred. Arab rioters and gunmen attempted to force Israel to retreat entirely by removing its lone military outpost from the tomb. This would have forced an end to Jewish worship at the site. In September 1996, in an attempt to overtake the tomb, Palestinian rioters and gunmen, reportedly with the help of Palestinian police, killed six Israeli soldiers and wounded many others, including *yeshiva* students. An eyewitness named Hillel Lieberman, who studied at the tomb's *yeshiva*, recounted:

> After a large demonstration in the central square of Nablus, Arabs began to march on Joseph's Tomb. Within minutes, the tomb was surrounded on all sides by thousands of Arabs, who began to pelt the compound with rocks and firebombs. In addition, the same Arab policemen who regularly served on the joint patrol with the Israelis now began firing at the Israeli soldiers with their Kalashnikov machine guns.

> Israeli soldiers [who were called in as reinforcements] retreated into the thick-walled building that encompasses Joseph's Tomb, and the Arabs advanced into the *yeshiva* [adjacent to the tomb], after setting fire to an army post and caravan, which housed the Israeli soldiers. At this point, the Israeli soldiers again radioed for help.

> The Arabs, upon entering the *yeshiva*, engaged in a *pogrom* reminiscent of scenes from *Kristallnacht*, when Nazis prior to the Holocaust ransacked synagogues in Germany. Sacred texts [in the *yeshiva*] were burned by Palestinians or torn to shreds, *talises* [Jewish prayer shawls] and sacred

tefillin [phylacteries] were thrown to the ground, and anything of value was pillaged. The *yeshiva's* office equipment, refrigerators and freezers, beds, tables and chairs, and all the food, were stolen.

The library was set afire, the structure of the *yeshiva* building was extensively damaged, and everything in it was in ruins. The only exception was the building of Joseph's Tomb itself, where the Israeli soldiers had taken cover, and the *yeshiva's* Torah scrolls, which the Israeli soldiers miraculously managed to save in the course of the riots.[2]

Eventually, Israeli soldiers gained control of the tomb. But the 1996 riots served as prelude for what would come next. Israel failed to arrest or take any action against the perpetrators of the deadly riots, even though the leaders of the violence, some of whom I later interviewed in Nablus, were well known to the Israeli security apparatus. In fact, according to informed security sources, a principal leader of the Joseph's Tomb riots, Jamal Tarawi, later became a legislator in the Palestinian parliament. Tarawi had been the chief of a major cell of Fatah gunmen in Nablus during the period of the riots.

Speaking to the Palestinian news media in 1996, Arafat painted the Joseph's Tomb riots as a victory for his people and a first step toward the eventual destruction of Israel. Arafat would frequently escalate tension on the Palestinian street as a way of pressuring the Israelis to retreat from more territory. Official Palestinian news media and West Bank mosques ramped up rhetoric demanding the "liberation" of Islamic holy sites, as well as of ordinary land. Sites like Joseph's Tomb, which had previously held no great value in Islam, were suddenly positioned by Palestinian leaders and sheikhs as stepping stones along the greater path toward the "liberation" of the al-Aqsa Mosque in Jerusalem and the rest of the "Muslim lands of Palestine."

Palestinians continued to attack Joseph's Tomb with regular, orchestrated shootings, and by lobbing firebombs and Molotov cocktails. Security for Jews at the site became increasingly difficult to maintain. Rumors circulated in 2000 that Prime Minister Ehud Barak would evacuate the Israeli military outpost and give the tomb to Arafat as a "peacemaking gesture." The Israeli army started denying Jewish visits to the tomb on certain days, citing the prospects of Arab violence.

Arafat returned from U.S.-mediated peace negotiations at Camp David in September 2000 and started his infamous *intifada* aimed at liberating Palestine. The Palestinians went for the kill at Joseph's Tomb during the period of one bloody week in October, and Israel's prime minister caved in. On October 1, Palestinian gunmen from Arafat's so-called military wing, the al-Aqsa Martyrs Brigades, attacked Israeli border police at Joseph's Tomb. An Israeli policeman was shot by a Brigades gunman and bled to death after Palestinian forces refused to allow his emergency medical evacuation. Heavy fighting at the Tomb continued on October 2. The next day, clashes led by Fatah's al-Aqsa Brigades injured an Israeli policeman and ten Palestinian rioters. On October 4, the Israeli Defense Forces chief of staff, Shaul Mofaz, sent troop reinforcements to the tomb, but noted he was directed to withdraw the troops if the danger to them became "too high." Barak met with Arafat and the U.S. Secretary of State, Madeleine Albright, in Paris to reach an agreement to end the Joseph's Tomb violence. They concluded a deal in which the Palestinians stated that they would stop attacks and refrain from entering the Tomb if Israel would pull back forces to pre-October positions.

Rioting again erupted at Joseph's Tomb on October 5 after Palestinian clerics used the funeral procession of a deceased rioter to incite the masses. Gun battles raged between Palestinian shooters and Israeli forces. On October 6, in the wake of rampant Palestinian attacks, Barak decided to completely evacuate the resting place of Joseph and hand over to Palestinians the sacred land promised to Joseph by the children of Israel more than three thousand years ago, and promised by the Torah as an inheritance to the Jews.

Israel's evacuation began the next day at 3:00 a.m., as soldiers clandestinely removed holy materials and a Torah scroll from the site. Palestinian gunmen led by Arafat's Brigades squad fired on an Israeli convoy as it departed the tomb, wounding one border policeman. The Israelis retreated completely while under fire. Within less than an hour, Palestinian rioters overtook Joseph's Tomb and began to ransack the site—despite Muslim claims that the tomb is the burial place of an important Muslim cleric. Palestinians hoisted a Muslim flag over the tomb. An official from Arafat's office, Amin Maqbul, visited the tomb to deliver a speech declaring, "Today was the first step to liberate al-Aqsa."[3]

Palestinian mobs continued to ransack the tomb, tearing apart books, destroying prayer stands, and grinding out stone carvings in the tomb's interior. As one BBC reporter described the scene: "The site was reduced to smoldering rubble—festooned with Palestinian and Islamic flags—by a cheering Arab crowd..."[4]

On October 8, the bullet-riddled body of *yeshiva* student Hillel Lieberman, who wrote the eyewitness account of the Palestinian attack on Joseph's Tomb in September 1996, was found in a cave near the tomb. Lieberman had disappeared a few days earlier after he went to investigate reports of violence at the tomb. The construction of a mosque was commenced on the ruins of the tomb and the *yeshiva* compound. Workers painted the dome of the compound Islamic green.

ISRAEL HALTS JEWISH PRAYER NEAR TOMB, IGNORES DESECRATION

A leader of the October 2000 attacks on Joseph's Tomb, Abu Mujaheed, told me in an interview in 2007 that Israel's retreat from the site was an important Palestinian victory. "We used to attack the tomb on an almost daily basis. Our fighters were divided into five to six cells. Each cell was composed of ten members and we used to crawl to the tomb and exchange fire with the soldiers. We led attacks in order to take away the Israeli flag. It was part of our resistance against the occupation. The goal was to chase the army of occupation from our land and the result [an Israeli retreat] proves that when we are determined we can defeat the Israeli enemy," Mujaheed explained. He went on to accuse Jews of falsifying the Torah and Jewish history to claim that the biblical Joseph was a Jew when indeed he was a Muslim, and that Joseph's Tomb houses a Jewish patriarch, when, he explained, the site actually entombs a Muslim sheikh.

I also talked with Jamil Tarawi, an al-Aqsa Brigades leader and Fatah parliament member, who called Joseph's Tomb "part of our holy sites and part of our cult and faith and not the Jews." Tarawi and Abu Mujaheed said they would never again allow Jews to establish a *yeshiva* at Joseph's Tomb as long as it is under Palestinian control. "A *yeshiva* is an institution," said Abu Mujaheed. "An institution can be the beginning of claiming rights and these claims can bring once again the Israeli army to establish a base in the place and we cannot accept this. If the Jews try to build a *yeshiva*, we will shoot at them."

Actually, Jews later did try to build a new *yeshiva* near Joseph's Tomb, but it was not Palestinians who stopped them; it was Israel. Jewish students in 2006 built a structure on the West Bank's Mount Gerizim, just outside the tomb area. The structure was used as a synagogue and was constructed on the mount so Jews could pray and study Torah as close as possible to the tomb site. Dozens of Jewish students congregated daily at the makeshift synagogue with no resistance from Palestinian gunmen. Nonetheless, the Israeli government deemed the structure—which it refused to call a synagogue—illegal, since it was built without a government permit. In line with Israeli-Palestinian talks, Prime Minister Ehud Olmert in the summer of 2007 pledged to dismantle several "illegal outposts," meaning West Bank Jewish structures constructed without a government permit. On July 31, 2007, security forces reportedly acting on direct orders from Olmert destroyed the *ad hoc* synagogue.[5] Olmert's decision to single out for demolition the synagogue near Judaism's third holiest site was challenged by national religious leaders in Israel.[6] They protested that the Israeli government regularly bulldozes Jewish West Bank construction projects deemed illegal, while the country takes little action against hundreds of thousands of Palestinians living in illegal outposts in the West Bank and Jerusalem.

The abandonment of Joseph's Tomb has had largely unreported consequences for the integrity of the site after the period in 2000 when Palestinians ransacked the structure. On February 11, 2008, Palestinians again attempted to burn the tomb. Palestinian security officials in Nablus told me they went to the tomb and found sixteen burning tires inside the sacred structure. A Palestinian police official who inspected the site told me in an interview there was some fire damage to the tomb. He said the PA immediately formed a joint committee from the organization's Force 17, Preventative Security Services and Palestinian intelligence to find out who was behind the fire. He said patrols were also stepped up around the site. A spokesman for the Israel Defense Forces later confirmed the fire reports.

An extensive search of the Israeli news media thereafter found the incident was not covered by a single news outlet in the country except by one, sole Israeli nationalist news Web site having a narrow audience.[7] Perhaps Israel's major television networks and newspapers did not deem the story of Palestinians' setting fire to one of Judaism's holiest sites newsworthy. Similarly, I could not find one U.S. Jewish group who reacted to the fire in Joseph's Tomb, perhaps because they did not know about it. Most Israelis and even American Jews probably do not understand the full consequences of Israel's retreat from Joseph's Tomb; or how this monumental decision can serve as a template for further planned Israeli evacuations from areas in the West Bank, or perhaps Jerusalem, that contain sites holy to Judaism and to Christianity. The abandonment of Joseph's Tomb is seldom mentioned in the nation's public discourse concerning handing still more territory to the Palestinians.

CHAPTER SEVEN

HOW THE U.S. FUNDS PALESTINIAN TERRORISM

It is late August 2008. A convoy of armored vehicles arrives at the Allenby border crossing between Israel and Jordan, driving from the Jordanian side. It transfers dozens of heavy crates to Israel Defense Forces trucks, which transport their cargo to the West Bank city of Ramallah, where the delivery is received in the main headquarters of the Palestinian Authority, the Muqata.

The shipment reportedly contains some nine hundred AK-47 assault rifles and ten thousand rounds of ammunition. Its origin is American.[1] That same week, after receiving a green light from Israel, America also provides Fatah with standard-issue police flak jackets to protect from oncoming fire.

This is only the latest in a series of U.S. shipments of guns, bullets, and other military-grade equipment to the militias of Mahmoud Abbas's Fatah organization, purportedly in an effort to bolster them against their rival, the violent and despotic Hamas organization. It has been well reported the U.S. also provides to Fatah militias—especially the Preventative Security Services, a kind of Palestinian police force, and Fatah's Force 17 Presidential Guard—stupendous sums of money and advanced training along with other weapons and equipment.

The American aid is sent in seemingly endless convoy loads, despite the fact that hundreds of the "moderate" Fatah security forces, including much of the group's well-known leadership, also serve openly in the barbarous al-Aqsa Martyrs Brigades. The Brigades call themselves Fatah's "military wing," and are officially classified by the U.S. State Department as a terrorist group.

In my research I obtained a list of the fifty senior Brigades leaders. I found that each of them—every last one—serves in various Fatah security forces. A few examples: Ala Senakreh, the chief of the al-Aqsa Martyrs Brigades in the northern West Bank, serves on the Preventative Security Services, as does Senakreh's number two, Nasser Abu Aziz. Kamal Ranam, chief of the Brigades in Ramallah, is an officer in Fatah's Preventative Security Services. Zacharias Zbeidi, the infamous leader of the Brigades in Jenin, serves in the Palestinian police. Serving on Fatah's general intelligence service is Ziad El-Kazaki, who was the Brigades chief of Hebron, replacing Marwan Zalum—a Brigades leader who doubled as a Fatah officer but who was assassinated by Israel for leading scores of attacks against the Jews of Hebron, including the sniper shooting of Shalhevet Pass, an infant Jewish girl. Prime Minister Ehud Olmert granted amnesty to all of these Brigades leaders were granted amnesty in 2007 and 2008, although many continue to carry out attacks.

To underscore the seamless interconnection between the terrorist infrastructure and the so-called "mainstream" Fatah militias, Abbas had, in May 2006, appointed the senior al-Aqsa Martyrs Brigades leader Mahmoud Damra as commander of the Force 17 Palestinian security unit. Damra, who later was arrested by Israel in November 2006, was on the Jewish state's most-wanted list of terrorists.

Let's take a closer look at the shipments of weapons and at the Palestinian headquarters in Ramallah to which they are delivered. The Muqata is the infamous former headquarters of late PLO Leader Yasser Arafat. It currently serves as a kind of Palestinian White House after some sections were rebuilt following Israeli bombing raids against empty wings of the building while Arafat was holed up in there in 2001. At the time, Arafat had turned down Israel's offer of a Palestinian state, instead launching the *intifada* to "liberate Palestine" primarily by terrorizing civilians. The Bush administration and the government of Prime Minister Ariel Sharon decided that Arafat was an unrepentant extremist, and worked together to isolate Arafat both physically and diplomatically. Despite this lurid history, Arafat's personal successor and his Fatah party today are called moderate.

I have visited the Muqata several times. Currently living inside are leaders of Fatah's al-Aqsa Martyrs Brigades who double as soldiers and officers in U.S.-backed Fatah security forces, meaning that known terrorists reside in living quarters inside the compound to which U.S. weapons are shipped. I found that some Brigades leaders, such as Kamal Ranam, even serve on the official Fatah team inside the Muqata that receives and inspects American weapons. One Brigades leader living in the Muqata spoke to me using his *nom de guerre* Abu Yousuf. He gets insulted if you call him anything else. Abu Yousuf is thirty-four years old, and served as a Ramallah-based chief of the al-Aqsa Martyrs Brigades. He also served as an officer of Force 17 and later moved to the Preventative Security Services, both putatively moderate Palestinian forces.

Abu Yousuf's terrorist record includes several shootings against Israeli civilians as well as some against Israeli forces operating in Ramallah. In December 2000 Abu Yousuf participated in the assassination of Benyamin Kahane, leader of the ultra-nationalist Kahane Chai organization and son of the group's founder, the well-known Rabbi Meir Kahane. Muslim radicals who later carried out the first World Trade Center bombing in 1993 assassinated the father in Brooklyn in November 1990. Abu Yousuf's specific al-Aqsa Martyrs Brigades cell has sent several suicide bombers into Israel, according to security officials. After Benyamin Kahane's murder, Arafat gave refuge to Abu Yousuf, allowing him to reside in the Muqata to avoid Israeli arrest. He still lives in the Muqata several nights a week and, as a Fatah officer, is a ranking member of the team that receives American weapons, according to informed security officials.

Also on the weapons receiving team, according to informed sources, was Khaled Shawish, an officer in Abbas's Force 17 presidential guards. Undercover Israeli police forces captured Shawish on May 29, 2007, following scores of shooting attacks he was suspected of either planning or personally carrying out. Shawish doubled as a senior Ramallah-based leader of the al-Aqsa Martyrs Brigades. He previously had boasted of involvement in the attack, along with Abu Yousuf, that killed Benyamin Kahane. Like Abu Yousuf, Shawish lived several nights a week in the Muqata, from which, according to Israeli security officials, he directed the Brigades to carry out scores of deadly shootings against Israelis driving on

West Bank roads. Israel says Shawish also directed a number of suicide bombings targeting Jewish cities, killing eight Israelis.

Notwithstanding these brutal operations, U.S. weapons shipments to Fatah are even more frequent than is reported in the news media. Before the August 2008 shipment, the last confirmed U.S. weapons transfer took place in November 2007 and reportedly consisted of one thousand assault rifles. Olmert at the time said he approved the shipment to bolster the PA's Abbas against Hamas during a crucial period when the two groups were involved in intense clashes.[2] Contradicting the mollifying explanations, sources familiar with the weapons transfer said the number of assault rifles shipped in May was closer to three thousand. Still unreported were multiple other assault rifle transfers to Fatah throughout 2007, including a cache of seven thousand rifles in January and about eight thousand more in February, according to security sources.

SHIPMENTS LINKED TO ATTACKS ON JEWS

America has been sending weapons to Fatah since the late 1990s, when Israel transferred full control of West Bank territory to Arafat in line with the 1993 Oslo Accords. Right after some previous weapons transfers, shooting attacks on Jews increased. A few days after a May 2007 American weapons shipment of a reported three hundred rifles, for instance, an unusually high number of shootings occurred against Israeli motorists in and near the West Bank; these were verified to have been carried out by al-Aqsa Brigades hitmen. Sources close to the Brigades said American assault rifles were used in three separate anti-Israeli shooting attacks carried out within weeks of the weapons shipment. One attack killed a thirty-five-year-old Israeli Arab on a major West Bank highway on the outskirts of Jerusalem. Israeli security officials say the killers likely mistook the victim for a Jew. The second attack occurred on June 13 on the same highway, lightly wounding an Israeli. The third attack, in which Abu Yousuf boasted he personally had participated, was against a busload of schoolgirls. Fortunately the bus, traveling in the northern West Bank, was armored, and three schoolgirls were only lightly injured. Security officials said that had the bus had not been armored the number and severity of girls' injuries would have been far more serious.

"It is no coincidence that as soon as these American weapons arrived, we were able to carry out these accurate shootings," Abu Yousuf said in an interview immediately following the school bus shooting. He said the U.S. sent weapons to Fatah "for its own political purposes and as part of a conspiracy to generate a civil war between us and Hamas. We are not concerned with the reasons. The first place of these U.S. weapons will be to defend the Palestinian national project, which is reflected by the foundation of the Palestinian Authority. If Hamas or any other group under the influence of Iran and Syria wants to make a *coup d'etat* against our institutions, these weapons are there to defend the PA," Abu Yousuf said.

Not surprisingly, the Fatah militant also threatened to use American weapons to target Israelis. "If we find ourselves manipulated by Israel, we cannot guarantee members of the al-Aqsa Martyrs Brigades and Force 17 will not use these weapons against Israel. Our goal is to change the occupation," Abu Yousuf said. "It's unnatural to think these American weapons won't be used against the Israelis."

Abu Yousuf told me the American weapons might be shared with other Palestinian "resistance" groups. He said that during large confrontations with Israel, such as a 2002 Israeli raid in Jenin that targeted the city's major terror apparatus, Fatah distributed weapons to their purported enemies, Hamas and Islamic Jihad. "We don't look where this piece or that piece of weapon came from when fighting the Israelis," Abu Yousuf said.

U.S. TRAINED TERRORIST GROUP

Aside from sending weapons, the U.S. has, since the late 1990s, also run training bases for Fatah militias. The American bases are located in the West Bank city of Jericho and also in the village of Giftlik, across the Jordanian border. Like many members of the al-Aqsa Martyrs Brigades, both Abu Yousuf and Shawish received U.S. training because of their status as members of Fatah forces. According to informed sources, Shawish's training took place in

Jericho in 1997. All the Brigades leaders referred to in this chapter—Senakreh, Zbeidi, Aziz, El-Kazaki, and the others—have received American training. I once met Senakreh in Nablus along with a friend of mine, U.S. radio host Rusty Humphries, and he told us he had used his U.S.-provided rifle less than twenty-four hours earlier to "shoot at the Israelis." Senakreh's cell has orchestrated at least four suicide bombings inside Israel. Senakreh's deputy, Nasser Abu Aziz, received training in Italy and Jericho. He personally has killed at least four Israelis in shooting attacks and, together with Senakreh, aided in planning several suicide bombings.

In an in-depth interview, Abu Yousuf talked about his American training: "I myself received American trainings in Jericho. Together with my Preventative comrades, I received trainings in intelligence methods and military trainings. In the intelligence part, we learned collection of information regarding suspected persons, how to follow suspected guys, how to infiltrate organizations and penetrate cells of groups that we were working on and how to prevent attacks and to steal in places. On the military level, we received trainings on the use of weapons, all kind of weapons and explosives. We received sniping trainings, work of special units especially as part of what they call the fight against terror. We learned how to put siege, how to break into places where our enemies closed themselves in, and how to oppress protest movements, demonstrations, and other activities of opposition."

Abu Yousuf related how he used his American training to kill Israelis: "We sniped at Israeli settlers and soldiers. We broke into settlements and Israeli army bases and posts. We collected information on the movements of soldiers and settlers. We collected information about the best timing to infiltrate our bombers inside Israel. We used weapons and we produced explosives, and of course the trainings we received from the Americans and the Europeans were a great help to the resistance."

Abu Yousuf claimed he shot only at soldiers and "settlers," with "settlers" meaning Jewish residents of the West Bank. In fact, he also shot at Israelis who live in central Israel, but who were driving through the West Bank, and his group also sent suicide bombers to major targets outside the West Bank, including in Jerusalem and Tel Aviv.

"All the methods and techniques that we studied in these trainings, we applied them against the Israelis," Abu Yousuf told me. "We also learned to discover agents that Israel tried to plant in our cells. I do not think that the operations of the Palestinian resistance would have been so successful and would have killed more than one thousand Israelis since 2000 and defeated the Israelis in Gaza without these [American] trainings. I am not saying this in order to irritate the Americans or the Israelis and not in order to create provocations. I'm just telling you the truth. We applied against Israel all that we learned from you Americans."

Indeed, Abu Yousuf's al-Aqsa Martyrs Brigades was one of the most active groups during the Palestinian *intifada*, in which 1,029 Israelis and more than twenty Americans have been killed as of this writing.

General Keith Dayton, who was the U.S. security coordinator assigned to the Palestinian territories, initiated a new, advanced program in 2007 for Palestinian police that trains five hundred to six hundred cadets at a time at American bases. According to informed security officials, basic training begins in Jordan and lasts for three months. It includes training in the use of weapons, conducting ambushes, fighting street crime, fighting terrorism, and dealing with hostage situations, among other courses. After the cadets successfully complete their schooling in Jordan, they continue with more advanced education at the U.S.-run base in the West Bank city of Jericho.

The U.S., Israel, and the PA supposedly screen all of the candidates for the courses. Unsurprisingly, I learned that at least two known members of the al-Aqsa Martyrs Brigades were enrolled in courses under way in both Jericho and Jordan in June 2008. To underscore the capability of Brigades terrorists to enter the U.S.-run courses, I obtained information that Muhammad Qataqi, one of the top Brigades leaders in Nablus, was officially accepted for American training in 2008. Qataqi ultimately did not enroll in the course because of a personal problem he had with Abdullah Kmeil, who was the head of the PA general intelligence office in Nablus. Kmeil is involved in the selection process for the U.S. training courses, my sources said. "Qataqi was accepted. Later on he got into a shouting match with Kmeil about politics, and he insulted Kmeil in a big way, so Qataqi wasn't allowed to enroll," a source close to Qataqi told me.

BILLIONS TO THE PA

Aside from hundreds of millions of dollars' worth of weapons and equipment, the U.S. over the years has provided vast sums of "nonmilitary aid" to the PA. The total is at least nearly $1.8 billion in direct aid to the PA and nongovernmental organizations operating in the Palestinian territories since 1994, and more than $1.1 billion to the United Nations organizations that work with Palestinians.[3]

There was a brief period when it seemed that Congress understood that the U.S. was supporting terrorism and almost blocked aid to Fatah militias. During this episode, Secretary of State Condoleezza Rice conceded she could not guarantee American money and weapons sent to Fatah won't "get into the wrong hands."[4]

The Bush administration in January 2007 pledged $86.4 million to strengthen Fatah forces, including Force 17. The funds were to be used to implement a security plan devised by Dayton calling for some $14.5 million for "basic and advanced training" for Fatah fighters, $23 million for equipment, $2.9 million to upgrade Force 17 facilities, and $3 million to provide "capacity-building and technical assistance" to the office of Mahmoud Dahlan, then Fatah's strongman in Gaza.[5] After multiple articles appeared, including several of mine, outlining how Fatah militias include terrorists, Congress blocked the aid pending a clarification from Rice. During a March 2007 Congressional hearing, Rice conceded she couldn't account for where the aid would go. She said she would request less money. "I will request less money, precisely because some of the money that I would have requested I did not think I could fully account for. I hope that is a sign for you that we take very seriously our responsibilities. I have no interest in having to come here one day and say, 'you know this funding did not end up in the right place.' I will do my very best," she told Congress.[6]

Lawmakers had caught the State Department red-handed. The U.S. was about to send money Rice admitted might get into the wrong hands. In a successful evasion, Rice simply reduced her request from $86.5 million to $59 million to fund the same terrorist-saturated Fatah militias. Congress credulously unfroze the aid, merely adding one new qualification stipulating that the money must not be used to purchase weapons. The State Department would be free to send more weapons to Fatah, which it did—just not from that particular aid package, which instead was used to train militias in which terrorists serve, but purportedly not to arm them.

During the hearings, no member of Congress expressed concern that Fatah security forces were also terrorists. Instead, they were mostly worried that Hamas might obtain weapons purchased with American aid. Hamas did, indeed, obtain a large amount of U.S. weaponry in the aftermath of a spectacular collapse of the U.S. policy of bolstering Fatah militias. In the course of less than a week in June 2007, Hamas launched a stunning coup in Gaza, taking nearly complete control of the territory and overrunning all U.S.-backed Fatah security compounds and positions there. These included Fatah's major Ansar complex in Gaza—where massive quantities of American-provided weapons were delivered and stored—and Abbas's presidential guard complex.[7] In one particularly humiliating scene broadcast around the world, masked Hamas gunmen marched soldiers from Fatah's Preventive Security Service out of their Gaza headquarters, arms raised in the air, stripped to the waist, and ducking at the sound of a gunshot.

"The Gaza Strip has fallen. It's now Hamas's land. We have lost," chief Palestinian negotiator Saeb Erekat admitted to me in an interview from Ramallah on June 15.

Years of U.S. provision of weapons, training, and funds to bolster Fatah went up in flames that June, although the Hamas coup had been in the works for years, with the group reportedly infiltrating Fatah on all levels. This incompetence reached such a pitch that at one point the U.S. was naïvely coordinating security in Gaza with agents secretly working for Hamas.

Hamas won election to power in Gaza in 2006 and for the first few months of their rule, they shared a government with Abbas's

Fatah party. However, when the U.S.-backed leader moved to dismantle the Hamas-led Palestinian national government in 2007, Hamas was furious. Fatah dismissed Hamas's elected leaders, but realizing they were stronger than Fatah in Gaza, they staged the bloody uprising and seized control. When Hamas hijacked the Fatah buildings, in the process it obtained enormous quantities of U.S. weapons. Hamas's al-Aqsa Television immediately broadcast footage of Hamas gunmen brandishing what it claimed were American assault rifles, rocket-propelled grenades, rocket launchers, and ammunition that the U.S. and other countries reportedly had provided to Fatah.

Members of Hamas's so-called military wing—all of Hamas is armed and active—released to me a list of U.S. weaponry and equipment they claimed to have seized, including dozens of mounted machine guns, approximately seventy-four hundred American M-16 assault rifles, about eight hundred thousand rounds of bullets, eighteen armored personnel carriers, seven armored military jeeps, "tens" of armored civilian cars, including pickup trucks and magnums, eight massive trucks equipped with water cannons for dispersing protests, and fourteen military-sized bulldozers. Hamas members said the long list did not even include what they said were large quantities of U.S.-provided rocket propelled grenades, grenade launchers, explosives, and non-lethal military equipment, such as boots and tents.

Abu Abdullah, a senior member of Hamas's "military wing," told me his group estimates it obtained at least $400 million worth of American weapons and equipment. While that number could not be verified, the average cost of an M-16 in Gaza during the time Hamas took over was $16,911, and the average cost of a bullet was $12.07, meaning the cost in Gaza of U.S. assault rifles and bullets alone that Hamas claims to have obtained amounts to over $137 million.

U.S. INTELLIGENCE FILES FALL INTO HAMAS HANDS

Not only did Hamas hijack American weaponry, it also claims to have obtained important CIA files, including documents that supposedly outline American intelligence networks in the Middle East. The CIA files apparently were also obtained by the Popular Resistance Committees, accused of bombing a U.S. convoy in 2003. The Committees fought alongside Hamas during the Gaza coup. Hamas and Popular Resistance Committees leaders told me they seized the purported CIA files upon taking over Gaza City's Fatah compounds, particularly the Preventative Security Services building and a U.S.-backed intelligence compound. They said that prior to Hamas's advances, Fatah officials had attempted to destroy the CIA documents, but succeeded only in eliminating some.

"The CIA files we seized, which include documents, CDs, taped conversations, and videos, are more important than all the American weapons we obtained in the last days as we took over the traitor Fatah's positions," Committees spokesman and senior official Muhammad Abdel-El told me.

According to Hamas's Abu Abdullah, "The files are crucial for our fight against the Zionists and anyone who collaborates with them, including the Americans." Abdullah said the hijacked CIA documents contained "information about the collaboration between Fatah and the Israeli and American security organizations; CIA methods on how to prevent attacks, chase and follow after cells of Hamas and the Committees; plans about Fatah assassinations of members of Hamas and other organizations; and American studies on the security situation in Gaza."

Abdullah claimed the documents also detailed CIA networks in other Arab countries and "how to help beat Islamic allies of Hamas in other Arab countries, including Egypt and Jordan."

Abdel-El boasted he found his name mentioned four times in the CIA documents on his group. "I am amazed by the material and the context of the documents," he said.

As was to be expected, Hamas says it utilized the American weapons it seized from Fatah in multiple attacks against Israel. Several times, Hamas officials said, the group used U.S.-provided shoulder-mounted heavy machine guns to shoot at Israeli helicopters operating above Gaza, including during Israel's war against Hamas that ended in January 2009.

In April 2008, Hamas attempted a major attack against Gaza's border with Israel using three explosives-filled jeeps, but the bombings were foiled by the IDF.[8] Israeli security officials called the attempted border attack the largest, most sophisticated Hamas terrorist operation since Israel had withdrawn from Gaza in 2005. Hamas's Abu Abdullah said the jeeps used in the attack were U.S. Army vehicles that his group seized from Fatah. Palestinian security officials estimated the jeeps cost American tax payers about $350,000.

While major U.S. aid to Fatah militias continues and President Obama's administration supports the continued training and arming of Fatah forces, Hamas and their allies in Gaza told me they don't mind the American policy. "We hope the Americans continue sending weapons to Fatah in the West Bank," said Abdel-El. "It will be more for the Islamic resistance organizations when we take over the territory."

CHAPTER EIGHT

THE UN "REFUGEE" CRISIS THAT KEEPS ON GIVING

Y*ou are a Jew?"* asked the stunned Palestinian boy. "You're lying."
"Yes. I am really a Jew. Why don't you believe me?" I replied,
speaking through an Arabic translator.

"Because you don't look like a pig or a monkey. Jews look
like either pigs or monkeys," the boy said with a straight face.

The boy explained to me he had learned in school that Allah
was angry with the Jews, so he turned them all into monkeys and
swine. He said his teachers told him that the Jews were guilty of
murdering Muslims and stealing Palestinian land. He said Jews
were leading a war to destroy the Palestinian people. During our
brief conversation, no matter how hard I tried I simply could not
persuade the boy that I was Jewish or that Jews were not leading a
crusade against Islam. He was convinced I was pulling his leg.

I asked what he would do if a Jew ever came to visit him.

"We'd kill him," he replied.

Our talk took place in the United Nations-run Balata refugee
camp in the northern West Bank city of Nablus. Balata is the largest
of fifty-four UN Palestinian refugee camps. Established in 1950, the
camp is said to house about eighteen thousand Palestinians,
although some estimates put the figure closer to thirty thousand.

If it weren't for local traffic, one could drive around the entire
periphery of the Balata camp in a matter of minutes. The whole
thing is less than 1.2 square miles, making it one of the most
densely populated residential zones in the world. Whole families
live in ramshackle quarters. I visited one family of six who were
living in a tiny two-room apartment that could not have been more

than 275 square feet. I had stopped to talk to the boy after an earlier interview in the camp with local leaders of the al-Aqsa Martyrs Brigades. I wanted to walk around a little bit to get a feel for the thinking of Balata's residents. Balata is home to the chiefs of the Brigades as well as to the senior leadership of multiple other major Palestinian terror organizations, including Islamic Jihad. Scores of suicide bombers have been recruited from this camp. Countless attacks against Israelis were planned or carried out from here. Balata is one of the most terrorist-dominated of Palestinian locales. In fact, just three weeks before my visit to Balata, on April 17, 2006, the carnage network there had sent a suicide bomber into Tel Aviv, where he detonated his explosives at a crowded Tel Aviv eatery and murdered eleven people, including an American teenager, plus himself, and injuring sixty others.

The Palestinian boy I spoke with, it turned out, was attending a UN-funded school in which he was apparently indoctrinated in extreme anti-Jewish propaganda. He and his family are served by UN employees who run all aspects of local life, from education through healthcare and social services, to emergency aid. The boy, in accepted parlance, is called a Palestinian refugee. The term "refugee" normally indicates a person who cannot return to his place of national origin for fear of persecution based on race, religion, nationality, membership in a particular social group, or political opinion. But as we shall see, the official UN definition of "Palestinian refugee" is drastically different from that used to classify refugees from all other regions of the world, throughout the entire history and charter of the UN.

The United Nations, which receives 25 percent of its budget from the U.S., says there are 4.25 million people registered as Palestinian refugees living in UN camps in the West Bank and the Gaza Strip, as well as in Jordan, Lebanon, and Syria.[1] Some of these people are also incorporated into population figures for the West Bank and Gaza, but Palestinian population figures differ significantly depending on whose numbers you trust. For some reason, the Israeli and U.S. governments have adopted the figures of the Palestinian Authority's Central Bureau of Statistics. This is remarkable, considering that the PA has every reason, both political and financial, to inflate those figures. The PA claims a total population in the West Bank and Gaza of 3.8 million. By contrast, a 2006 bombshell study entitled "Arab Population in the West Bank and Gaza," puts the actual Palestinian-Arab population of the West Bank at 1.4 million and Gaza 1.1 million, for a total of 2.4 million, or roughly half of the official Palestinian figure. The 2006 study was commissioned by a U.S. businessman, Bennett Zimmerman; the historian Roberta Seid, and a veteran executive, Michael Wise. The study found the PA routinely inflates its population numbers by almost 50 percent by counting some of the same populations twice, retroactively raising growth and birth rates, and even counting Palestinians who long ago emigrated abroad.

Regardless of the actual numbers, there are millions of so-called Palestinian refugees. The Palestinian leadership invariably claims its "refugees" have a "right" to "return" to their "homes" inside Israel, from which they were "expelled" during the 1948 Arab invasion of the newly-established Jewish state. Palestinian leaders generally state that the "right of return" is non-negotiable and must be granted in any comprehensive deal with Israel. The issue of Palestinian refugees is one of the most contentious, since allowing millions of Arabs to flood into Israel would definitively dilute Israel's Jewish majority and destroy its identity as a Jewish state.

The issue has long been a knife at Israel's throat, fashioned in part from lies, and sharpened collectively by the Palestinian leadership, the Arab states, the international community, and, most of all, by the UN.

THE ORIGIN OF THE PERMANENT "REFUGEES"

To understand the true genesis of this artificially maintained refugee crisis and the world's culpability therein, we must first take a trip back sixty years in time, to when and where it all began. Within one day of Israel's declaration of independence on May 14, 1948, the Arab League declared war on the nascent state of the Jews, which comprised only six hundred thousand Jewish residents at the time. Soldiers from Egypt, Jordan, Syria, Lebanon, Saudi Arabia, and Iraq converged on Israel fully intent on destroying her. At a May 15, 1948 press conference Azzam Pasha, Secretary General of the Arab League, declared it was to be a "jihad...a war of extermination and a momentous massacre."[2] When the fighting finally ended in July 1949, the Arab League had not achieved its goal. Even as Egypt, Lebanon, Jordan, and Syria were signing armistice agreements with Israel, however, the Arab League was pursuing other means to reach that same goal. Their new weapon of choice became precisely those Arabs who had fled from Israel in the course of the war.

The exact number of persons who fled is a matter of much dispute, ranging from fewer than five hundred thousand to over nine hundred thousand, depending on the source.[3] Israel officially puts the figure at about five hundred twenty thousand.[4] Similarly disputed is the specific cause of the flight. Arab narrative paints a picture of Arabs' forcibly driven from their land by Jewish troops.[5] The historical reality, however, differs substantially from the Arab narrative and is far more complex. The British historian Ephraim Karsh, who has published extensively on this subject, documents the panic that overtook the Arab population in the months before and following the advent of the war.[6] As early as the end of 1947, the British High Commissioner for (Mandatory) Palestine, Alan Cunningham, wrote, "Arabs are leaving the country with their families in considerable numbers."[7] At the same time, Jewish intelligence reported on the "evacuation frenzy that has taken hold of entire Arab villages."[8] By April 1948, at least one hundred thousand Arabs had fled, even though, according to one Arab commander, Jews "have so far not attacked a single Arab village unless provoked by it."[9]

In a historically astonishing development, at that same time various Arab leaders and military forces were driving Palestinian Arabs from their homes and villages. In the largest and best-known example, tens of thousands of Arabs were ordered or bullied into leaving the city of Haifa on the Arab Higher Committee's instructions, despite strenuous Jewish efforts to persuade them to stay.[10] Only days earlier, its own leaders, against local Jewish wishes, had similarly forced out the six thousand-strong Arab community of Tiberius.[11] Haled al-Azm, who was Syrian Prime Minister in 1948-49, wrote in his memoirs that:

[W]e have been demanding the return of the refugees to their homes. But we ourselves are the ones who encouraged them to leave...[12]

According to Karsh, the rare instances in which Jews drove out the Arabs "occurred in the heat of battle and were uniformly dictated by *ad hoc* military considerations...rather than political design."[13] The refugees fled, in the main, to Gaza—controlled by Egypt after the war—and to Judea and Samaria, which were called collectively the West Bank, and controlled primarily by Jordan and in part by Syria and Lebanon.

REFUGEE BUREAUCRACIES EMERGE

The United Nations General Assembly responded by creating what was to become a permanent bureaucracy for aiding the refugees and, as it turned out, for perpetuating the problem. UNGA Resolution 302 (IV) established UNRWA—the UN Relief and Works Agency for Palestinian Refugees in the Near East—to "carry out...direct relief and works programs" for Palestinian refugees. UNRWA began operations on May 1, 1950, superseding the emergency efforts of the International Red Cross and other relief agencies, and promptly working to register those refugees who were eligible for assistance. The initial numbers of those registered may have been inflated by at least twenty percent due to the inclusion of non-refugees, either because they had misrepresented their status or because UNRWA officials felt sympathy for them.

In 1950, the UNWRA director glaringly admitted, "...a large group of indigent people totaling over 100,000...could not be called refugees, but...have lost their means of livelihood because of the war...The Agency felt their need... even more acute than that of the refugees..."[14]

UNRWA's *Annual Report of the Director, July 1951-June 1952* contains an acknowledgment that it was difficult to separate "ordinary nomadic Bedouins and... unemployed or indigent local residents" from genuine refugees, and that "it cannot be doubted that in many cases individuals who could not qualify as being *bona fide* refugees are in fact on the relief rolls." The addition of significant numbers of needy non-refugees to the rolls likely explains why UNRWA's figure of 914,000 refugees in 1950 is almost two hundred thousand more than the 1949 estimate of the United Nations Conciliation Committee.

When UNRWA began operations, it was assumed that the refugee problem would be resolved and that the agency would function only temporarily. It was not anticipated that the Arab states, which were directly shaping the mandate of this new organization, had another idea: the refugees would be kept in camps for as long as it took, and the burden of political responsibility for them was to be placed permanently upon Israel. As one PLO document on the refugees explains: "In order to keep the refugee issue alive and prevent Israel from evading responsibility for their plight, Arab countries—with the notable exception of Jordan—have usually sought to preserve a Palestinian identity by maintaining the Palestinians' status as refugees."[15] Arlene Kushner, an Israel-based researcher on UNRWA, explains: "In other words, as a matter of deliberate policy, most Arab nations have deliberately declined to absorb the refugees or give them citizenship, and have instead focused on their right to 'return' to Israel."[16]

There was no ambiguity of intentions in the minds of Arab leaders as they planned to push Israel to take responsibility for the refugees. In 1949, the Egyptian Minister of Foreign Affairs, Muhammad Saleh Ed-Din wrote:

> Let it therefore be known and appreciated that, in demanding the restoration of the refugees to Palestine, the Arabs intend that they shall return as the masters of the homeland, and not as slaves. More explicitly, they intend to annihilate the state of Israel.[17]

Less than a year later, on April 6, 1950, the Lebanese paper *Al-Ziyyad* stated:

> The return of all of the refugees to their homes would…on the one hand eliminate the refugee problem, and on the other, create a large Arab majority that would serve as the most effective means of reviving the Arab character of

Palestine, while forming a powerful fifth column for the
day of revenge and reckoning.[18]

Even five years after the end of World War II, the range of
problems relating to the refugees of that period was still enormous
and was a major preoccupation of the international community.
Scarcely eight months after UNRWA began operation, the United
Nations General Assembly, on December 14, 1950, established
another agency to attend to other refugees worldwide: The Office of
the High Commission for Refugees (UNHCR). A July 28, 1951,
conference approved the Convention Relating to the Status of
Refugees, a cornerstone of post-war international law, which defines
the status of all refugees and outlines their rights and the obligations
of states towards them. The UNHCR, which administers all refugees
besides the Palestinians, operates according to its parameters and
stipulations. After adding a protocol in 1967, the Convention was
established as the international standard pertaining to refugees
worldwide, *with the single exception of the Palestinian Arab refugees.*
One hundred forty-one states are party to both of these instruments;
among those states that have signed neither are Bahrain, Jordan,
Lebanon, Qatar, Saudi Arabia, Syria, and the United Arab Emirates.

Once a broad-based agency was established to attend
worldwide to refugees, it was logical that UNRWA would have
been folded into it rather than being separately maintained. Due
largely to the pressure of Arab states, this never occurred.[19] The
explanation blandly, but at least honestly, offered on the UNHCR
Web site is that Arab states "feared that the non-political character of
the work envisioned for the nascent UNHCR was not compatible
with the highly politicized nature of the Palestinian question"—
which is highly pertinent to what transpired over time.[20] The UN
Secretary-General attributes refugee status to persons who suffer
from "intolerance, political breakdown, and war." By this standard,
there are few refugees to be found anywhere who are not displaced
for fundamentally political reasons. In Israel, the tiny state created
entirely to shelter refugees from one of the most horrifying crimes of
modern history, it came to pass that leaders of neighboring Arab
states—some of whom had cheerfully and overtly collaborated with
the Nazi regime—forced the resident Arab population to flee into

forty unnecessary years of increasing discomfort and sometimes misery, all under the pretense of a legitimate refugee calamity. These were the very Arabs residents whom the early Israelis had begged to stay. A situation now has evolved in which one massive agency attends apolitically to refugees worldwide according to one set of rules, while another agency stands alone, attending to only one group of refugees—the Palestinians—and making its own rules according to a tainted and opaque political agenda.

A DIFFERENT KIND OF REFUGEE

That political agenda is reflected in the significant ways in which UNRWA's definition of a Palestinian refugee differs from the definition for all other refugees drawn by the UNHCR from the Convention on Refugees. As we see after the fact, it is undeniable that UNRWA's original and continuing goal was and is twofold: to increase to the maximum the number of persons counted as Palestinian refugees and to sustain their identity as refugees so that pressure would continue to be placed on Israel. UNRWA's initial mandate did not define "refugee." The definition evolved within the agency and today UNRWA says that Palestinian Arab refugees are:

> persons whose normal place of residence was Palestine between June 1946 and May 1948, who lost both their homes and means of livelihood as a result of the 1948 Arab-Israeli conflict and their descendants...

This is a uniquely broad definition that completely ignores the UNHCR general refugee definition of a refugee as someone who:

> ...owing to well-founded fear of being persecuted...is outside his country of nationality...or former habitual residence...

The fact that UNRWA counts as Palestinian refugees persons who had been in Palestine for as little as two years means that UNHCR's stipulation about place of "habitual residence"[21] has been completely discarded. The reason UNRWA's unique definition is important is that there were many Arabs who had been in Palestine for only a relatively brief period before Israel declared independence, since Jewish economic development attracted from surrounding countries Arab workers and others desiring better living conditions. In describing this phenomenon, American foreign policy analyst Mitchell Bard writes that there was a rapid growth in the Arab population—before Israeli statehood—because "Arabs [from neighboring states] wanted to take advantage of the higher standard of living the Jews had made possible... The Arab population increased the most in cities where large Jewish populations had created new economic opportunities."[22] Karsh makes the same point.[23] The author and researcher Joan Peters argues that a significant percentage of those considered Palestinian refugees in 1948 were recent Arab immigrants—part of a hidden illegal immigration movement—who had come seeking employment.[24]

UNRWA's singular definition of "refugee" also makes no mention of UNHCR's "well-founded fear of being persecuted." Thus UNRWA defines as refugees those who fled Israel for *any* reason, including, implicitly, even orders from Arab leaders. Most significantly, UNRWA conferred the status of refugee on the patrilineal descendants of refugees, thus making it possible to sustain indefinitely and, over time, actually enlarge the original refugee population. The otherwise universal Convention on Refugees makes no mention of descendants.

Finally, the Convention on Refugees says that a person who "has acquired a new nationality, and enjoys the protection of the country of his new nationality" is exempted from the status of refugee. UNRWA alone maintains that a Palestinian Arab who has the status of refugee retains that status until returning to Israel, *no matter what new citizenship he or she may acquire.* This is pertinent in the highest degree to the hundreds of thousands of Palestinian Arabs who have acquired full citizenship in Jordan or emigrated abroad, but are still on the UNRWA rolls as refugees.

UNRWA's unique criteria for what constitutes a refugee have resulted in a Palestinian Arab refugee population that has grown enormously over the years—in fact, it is the world's only refugee population to get larger over time rather than smaller. It is also a population that has persisted in its refugee status far longer than any other group. What started fifty-eight years ago as, at most, 914,000 legitimate refugees on UNRWA's rolls has now grown to a claimed 4.25 million.[25]

The key to this situation is the ostensible Palestinian "right of return," which was placed within the UNRWA mandate. The resolution that founded UNRWA refers to UN General Assembly Resolution 194, paragraph 11, which states in its lead sentence that:

> [T]he refugees wishing to return to their homes and live at peace with their neighbors should be permitted to do so at the earliest practicable date...

The notion of the "right" of the refugees to return to Israel is predicated upon this, but it is an extremely weak basis for such an argument. This is true primarily because General Assembly resolutions are solely recommendations and have no standing in international law (although certain Security Council resolutions do). Such a resolution simply is not binding on any member state.

Then there is the fact that the true intent of the resolution has been distorted because one single phrase—not even a full sentence, but part of a sentence—has been lifted out of context. The full Resolution 194, which was passed on December 11, 1948, before the war was over, called for a Conciliation Commission that was to attempt to seek a resolution to the Arab-Israeli conflict, and it actually gives instructions to the Commission to facilitate a number of possible resolutions, including *resettlement* of refugees.[26]

Nonetheless, UNRWA has proceeded with this "right" at the heart of its policies and practices.

UN KEEPS REFUGEES IN LIMBO

In its areas of operation, UNRWA established fifty-eight camps for the so-called refugees on land provided by the administrative authority in each area. While only about one-third of the refugees actually live in the camps, most live near the camps and avail themselves of UNRWA services. The camps have remained the center of refugee life and within them UNRWA has established a large infrastructure, with schools, clinics, centers for social services, and more. This infrastructure is deemed necessary, because there has been absolutely no attempt to *solve* the problem of the Palestinian Arab refugees, as in the same way the UNHCR solves the problems of other refugees—encouraging them to get on with their lives. UNRWA simply *sustains* the refugees in a political limbo —now lasting sixty years, while at the same time delivering some very potent messages. The messages begin with the way in which the camps have been structured, with areas and streets named after villages inside Israel—serving as a constant and potent reminder of where people had supposedly come from. When registration was originally instituted, a code was utilized indicating the registrant's origins in "pre-1948 Palestine." Badil—the Resource Center for Palestinian Residency and Refugee Rights—says that, "the village structure, as it existed prior to the 1948 war, has thus been preserved by virtue of the registration system."[27]

Over the years, a variety of programs have reinforced awareness of the "[Israeli] villages left behind." For example, in 2001, a Palestinian group, the Higher Committee for the Return of Refugees, went into UNRWA schools to conduct a program with the students regarding the "predicament of refugees," in order to "bolster...their sense of belonging to the homeland." The homeland? This meant Israel within the Green Line, which is where the children's grandparents had come from, but which they had never seen. The children were given notebooks that had space for personal information on the front. One of the lines was reserved for the "hometown" of the students, which meant, of course the original village of their grandparents.[28] At the same time, UNRWA discourages any permanent resettlement of the refugees, communicating the position that this would bring them a deprivation of their "rights."

In 1985, the Catholic Relief Agency provided funds for permanent housing for refugees to be constructed by Israel near the West Bank city of Nablus. Shockingly, when Israel attempted to move refugees into the thirteen hundred homes that had been built, a General Assembly resolution was passed forbidding Israel from taking refugees out of their temporary shelters.[29] Doing this, it was said, would violate the refugees' "inalienable right of return" to the homes they left in 1948.[30] Other similar incidents were recorded.

The Arab policy of keeping the refugees discontented and sustaining their sense of impermanence and deprivation—in order to fuel their desire to "return"—can be seen vividly in a 1997 report that came out of the UNRWA refugee camp in Balata. Dr. Musallam Abu Hilu of Jerusalem Open University wrote that "it may well be that development programs have an adverse effect on the refugees' demand for return; such programs might lead to gradual and unconscious refugee integration and resettlement."[31] His first concern was the promotion of the "demand for return," not the ways in which development programs might improve the lives of the refugees. Best that the "refugees" not be too comfortable.

TERRORISTS ON UN PAYROLL?

A population trapped indefinitely in such circumstances—without citizenship or permanency, often enduring uncomfortable conditions, sensing a deprivation of their "rights"—is prone to radicalism, and this has been the case with the Palestinian Arab refugees. They have little to lose and see a change in the status quo as most desirable, which creates fertile ground for Islamic leaders to indoctrinate the ideology of jihad in the population.

Having interviewed multiple Palestinian terrorists, as well as Palestinians recruited to become suicide bombers, I have seen clearly that the poor living conditions in the refugee camps are not the main force driving Palestinian terrorism. Rather, the terrorists are very open about the fact that their main goal is to satisfy Allah by launching jihad against Israel. Of course, the desperate situation in the refugee camps does help push the population toward anger at the Jewish state; however, the refugees did not simply arrive at homicidal rage on their own. Had guidance and hope and succor been offered them, they very likely would have turned in a different, more productive direction. Lamentably, Palestinian productivity and functionality were not on the Arab agenda. Palestinian Arab refugees have been, and remain, pawns in a larger calculus to destroy Israel.

However they may deny it, UNRWA has permitted the fostering of terrorism right under its nose and communicated messages that reinforce it. Over time, hundreds of thousands of students passing through the UNRWA schools have been driven in a direction that rejects co-existence with Israel and encourages violence. UNRWA policy is to utilize in each area where it operates, the same school textbooks as are used by the administrative authority of that area: Syrian texts in Syria, and so on. In the West Bank and Gaza, the books used are those of the PA. The Committee for Monitoring the Impact of Peace (IMPACT) has conducted a thorough analysis of the PA's textbooks. Their report on the books notes that, among other things, and bizarrely by civilized standards, jihad is praised, and war against Israel is implicitly encouraged, Israel's name does not appear on any of its maps, and Israelis are represented only as occupiers and aggressors.[32]

This, however, is merely the beginning. In Gaza, UNRWA schoolchildren have been exposed directly to the ideology and incitement of Hamas. From 1990, teachers affiliated with the Islamic Bloc, which is formally associated with Hamas, have won elections as representatives of the teachers' section of the UNRWA union. By 2003, they held all seats and fully constituted the executive committee of this section of the union.[33] Saeed Siam taught in UNRWA schools from 1980 to 2003 and served as a representative to the union. The entire time he was a member of the Hamas politburo and one of the leaders of the group's so-called military wing (recall that all Hamas is a military grouping).[34] Sheikh Ahmed Yassin, the man who founded Hamas and has been immortalized by it, worked as an UNRWA teacher from 1967 to 1994.[35]

Children taught by Hamas-affiliated teachers learn only a Hamas perspective, but it gets worse: The same Islamic Bloc alluded to above—dedicated to the "Islamization" of the Palestinian issue and believing it is necessary to "liberate" all of Palestine—has been assigned by Hamas to further the goals of Hamas within the schools.[36] The Islamic Bloc works directly in UNRWA schools in order to prepare the next generation for the "liberation of Palestine."[37]

There is ample evidence of other Hamas programming. For example, on July 6, 2001, Hamas convened a conference in the

UNRWA school in the Jabalya refugee camp in Gaza, with students, teachers, and school administrators in attendance.[38] Ahmed Yassin presented his ideology, and then an official named Saheil Alhinadi, who represented the teaching sector of UNRWA, addressed the group. He praised students who had recently carried out suicide attacks against Israel, declaring that, "the road to Palestine passes through the blood of the fallen, and these fallen have written history with parts of their flesh and their bodies." The progression, then, from allowing outright terrorists to teach at UN-run schools to the major involvement of refugees in acts of terrorism was inevitable.

That involvement became starkly apparent during Israel's Operation Defensive Shield, mounted in the spring of 2002 in response to a spate of horrendous suicide bombings. In the course of a sweep of UNRWA facilities, the Israel Defense Forces discovered that the camps were riddled with small-arms factories, explosives laboratories, and suicide bomber cells.[39] Alan Baker, who was then chief counsel of the Israeli Foreign Ministry, declared that: "Bomb-making, indoctrination, recruiting, and dispatching of suicide bombers all are centered in the camps."[40] There was a particular focus on the UNRWA refugee camp of Jenin during this operation. Natan Sharansky, then serving as Israel's deputy prime minister, described in a formal government briefing on April 19, 2002, what had been discovered. The UN camp of Jenin, he declared, "had the highest concentration of explosives in the area, if not in the world."[41] Then it was discovered that the Jenin branch of Fatah had written, in a message to the terrorist leader Marwan Barghouti on September 25, 2001, that the Jenin camp is "characterized by an exceptional presence of fighters." It is no wonder, said this report, that the "Jenin [refugee camp has been called] the suiciders [*sic*] capital."[42]

Subsequent reports were also released documenting the terrorist involvement of UNRWA facilities and employees. (UNRWA employs as staff almost exclusively Palestinian Arab refugees. With a staff of over twenty thousand, fewer than one hundred are "internationals" in administrative posts.[43]) A report of the Intelligence and Terrorism Center at Israel's Center for Special Studies, released in December 2002, played a significant role in this documentation.[44] The Center, which is located at an IDF intelligence base, documented:

- A number of wanted terrorists were found hiding inside schools run by UNRWA.

- A large number of youth clubs operated by UNRWA in the refugee camps were discovered to be meeting places for terrorists.

- Ala'a Muhammad Ali Hassan, arrested in February 2002, confessed that he had carried out a sniper shooting from the school run by UNRWA in the al-Ayn refugee camp near Shechem (Nablus). He also told his interrogators that bombs intended for terrorist attacks were being manufactured inside that school's facilities.

Also documented were several instances of UNRWA employees' being implicated in terrorism, including:

- Nidal Abd al-Fattah Abdallah Nazzal, a Hamas activist from Kalkilya, arrested in August 2002, who had been employed as an ambulance driver by UNRWA. He confessed during his interrogation that he had transported weapons and explosives in an UNRWA ambulance to terrorists.

- Nahd Rashid Ahmad Atallah, a senior official of UNRWA in the Gaza Strip who was in charge of distributing financial aid to the refugees, was arrested in August 2002. He told his interrogators that during the years 1990 through 1993, in his capacity as an UNRWA official, he had granted support to families of wanted terrorists.

Additional information about arrests of UNRWA employees by Israel came in 2003 from the U.S. General Accounting Office (GAO), charged with conducting an investigation of UNRWA operations. In three instances, Israeli military courts convicted UNRWA employees of involvement with explosives. More recently, in the time leading up to and since the Hamas takeover of Gaza in the summer of 2007, there has been concern in Jerusalem about UNRWA camps being used for the manufacture, storage, and launching of rockets and mortars into Israel, as well as about residents of these camps being actively involved in launching missiles and infiltrating shooters and suicide bombers into Israel proper.[45]

The Palestinian Authority, for its part, continues to press its position that all the world's Palestinian refugees, by UNRWA's definition, must "return" to Israel. This position is obviously unacceptable for the Jewish state, although sources in Jerusalem have told me the Israeli government has recently expressed willingness to incorporate a small number of Palestinians from "refugee" camps into Israel. In the meantime, the UN-aided refugees continue to embrace terrorism and war against Israel. All the while, Palestinian leaders play the refugee card as a pressure tactic to gain extreme concessions from the Jewish state during negotiations. The refugee problem has generated a crisis of enormous proportions— an intolerable situation for Israel that will not change as long as the so-called refugees maintain their prized, but largely fabricated status accorded them by the UN.

CHAPTER NINE

HAMAS STATE IN JERUSALEM, WEST BANK?

The *radical Islamic group Hamas,* having seized control of the Gaza Strip, boldly proclaims its goal to take over the West Bank, as well. "According to our rights, we are the elected majority," Mahmoud al-Zahar, leader of the Hamas terrorist organization in Gaza, told me in an interview just prior to the writing of this book. "A majority in a democracy should control all the Palestinian areas, whether in the West Bank or in the Gaza Strip. This is not an extraordinary issue," he claimed.

Al-Zahar is the second most powerful Hamas leader following the group's overall chief, Khaled Meshaal, who lives in exile in Syria. Al-Zahar said that if Israel withdraws from the West Bank or eastern sections of Jerusalem, Hamas would have the "legitimate right" to take over the territory, just as it took control of the Gaza Strip in the summer of 2007. "You're an American," noted al-Zahar, addressing me. "Do you respect democracy? If you respect democracy, the elections in January '06 indicated Hamas is the majority and it should run the administration in Gaza and the West Bank," al-Zahar lectured.

I have interviewed Mahmoud al-Zahar several times in recent years and have followed his few other interviews with the English-language news media. Unlike some other terrorist leaders, al-Zahar is not prone to baseless boasting or empty rhetoric. While he is a dangerous terrorist, I have also found him to be an excellent political analyst who understands well the minutiae of Israeli policy and how best to advance the causes of his Islamist organization.

Hamas is perfectly explicit about its cause. The organization's nine-thousand-word charter of 1988—repeatedly reconfirmed by its leaders—rejects the possibility of negotiations with Israel and calls for the destruction of the Jewish state.

Prior to Israel's evacuation of the Gaza Strip in 2005, Hamas officials announced they would seize control of the territory after Israel retreated. They explained that they would use the land to launch rockets into neighboring Jewish population centers. Now, multiple Israeli governments and the new U.S. administration support a future Israeli withdrawal from most of the strategic West Bank and eastern sections of Jerusalem. Hamas has made clear, as al-Zahar explained to me, that if Israel retreats, Hamas will fill the void. A study was published just after Israel retreated from Gaza by a Hamas-affiliated think tank, the al-Mustaqbal Research Center. The report explained that Hamas would next focus on controlling the West Bank, from which, it stated, Hamas would then fire rockets into Israel and carry out guerrilla operations against nearby Jewish towns—precisely what Hamas began to do the moment it seized control of Gaza.[1]

Because the high grounds of the West Bank run alongside Israel's major population centers, the prospect of Qassam rockets smashing into the Jerusalem-Tel Aviv highway, not to mention Lod, Herzliya, and Netanya, may not be far-fetched, if and when Hamas gains future control of the West Bank.

Astoundingly, almost absent from public debate within Israel about the future of the West Bank is any serious discussion of the consequences of the Jewish state's recent retreat from Gaza. That it has immensely strengthened radical Islamic forces in the region, that it has created a terror sanctuary from which attacks are regularly launched on Israel proper, and that it brought about absolutely no major change in international hostility toward Israel, as then-Prime Minister Ariel Sharon had promised it would—all these failures were obvious and predictable before the withdrawal from Gaza, conspicuous to anyone who had eyes to see.

Instead, even after Israel had to go to war in Gaza in December 2008, the international community is using the Gaza Strip as a successful template to pressure Israel into even more evacuations and concessions, and it very publicly condemns desperately needed Israeli military operations occasionally carried out, simply for self-preservation, against the rocket launchers and other terrorist apparatus in Gaza.

In trying to assess the potential ramifications of an Israeli evacuation of the West Bank or perhaps even sections of Jerusalem, it is crucial to comprehend fully how Hamas, which is backed largely by Iran, was able to take over the Gaza Strip and assess if the terror group is aiming and able to repeat this scenario in the West Bank.

HAMAS INFILTRATES U.S.-BACKED FORCES

In June 2007, Hamas essentially took complete control of Gaza in less than one week, crushing the U.S.-backed Fatah organization of Mahmoud Abbas and overrunning dozens of major U.S.-supported Fatah security compounds. Scenes of humiliated Fatah officers surrendering and Fatah leaders fleeing their homes and offices were broadcast around the world. Many analysts and commentators in the West were stunned at the swift, dramatic collapse of Fatah, which barely put up a fight despite the infusion of billions of dollars in international aid since the mid-1990s, including massive direct shipments of U.S. weapons and advanced training for Fatah's various militias.

But Hamas's swift and violent takeover should not have been a surprise to anyone familiar with the situation on the ground in Gaza following Israel's retreat from the territory. As I reported in the months leading to the violence-based group's ultimate takeover, Hamas carefully sowed the seeds of an Islamist revolution.

It is well known that for many years Hamas operated a civilian infrastructure in the West Bank and Gaza Strip that openly served as a quasi-government. It tended to the local populations' needs, which Fatah, notorious for corruption and inefficiency since the decades of Yasser Arafat, often failed to do. The civil side of Hamas provided public healthcare and social and religious services; it operated schools, libraries, and charities. Hamas also endeared itself to the population by its unwavering commitment to an armed struggle against the "Zionist enemy." What is less known is how Hamas quietly and carefully infiltrated all levels of Fatah to the point that the U.S.-backed Palestinian organization was paralyzed once Hamas went for the kill.

Speaking to me in April 2007, just two months before Hamas's lightning takeover of Gaza, Israeli security officials warned that all major intelligence and security organizations associated with Fatah were in a state of "deep infiltration" by Hamas. They said Hamas had infiltrated Abbas's presidential guard unit, Force 17, which also serves as a *de facto* police force; the PA General Security Services; Fatah's general intelligence branch, and the Preventative Security Services, another major Fatah militia.

At about the same time, a Fatah intelligence official also admitted to me in an interview that Fatah had a "significant problem" of infiltration. The official, who oversaw intelligence for Fatah's police forces in the West Bank and Gaza Strip, conceded that dozens of Hamas operatives, along with members of the Iranian-backed scourge, the Islamic Jihad, were discovered serving in Fatah posts. "I can say that in some cases we diagnosed a deep infiltration to high posts in some Fatah security services," the official said. "In some cases we believe there are officers that are exposed to sensitive information."

After I published these interviews, Muhammad Abdel El, a spokesman and leader of the Hamas-allied roadside bombers, the Popular Resistance Committees, told me that Fatah's attempts to discover militants from his organization "have not even scratched the surface of our infiltration. We are very well placed within Fatah's units and their little investigations made no difference." he said. A leader of Hamas's "military wing" in the Gaza Strip, Abu Abdullah, commented that "it doesn't seem Fatah's campaign to oust Hamas from inside their organizations has made a difference for us in our penetration of Fatah." Indeed, in the months following Hamas's Gaza takeover, Fatah officials found Hamas had penetrated their security organizations at the very highest levels, perhaps explaining why there was little coordination among Fatah security agencies, including even on the local level, during Hamas's dramatic coup. There was essentially no Fatah leadership while Hamas took over. Fatah security commanders were not even present in the Gaza Strip the week of the crucial clashes in June 2007.

An official Fatah committee appointed by the Palestinian Authority president, Mahmoud Abbas, conducted an investigation into the conduct of the Fatah leaders and security officers who lost the Gaza Strip, and released a two-hundred-page report on July 27, 2007. Although it was never made public, a senior Abbas aide, Nabil Amr, who served on the committee, told reporters that Fatah security forces were in a "state of infiltration" by Hamas.[2] Another member of the inquiry committee told reporters that some six Fatah security officers would face court martial.

I learned from top Fatah sources that the state of infiltration was so deep that the U.S., which worked closely with Fatah militias in Gaza, may actually have coordinated security with a top Hamas agent. Fatah accused the director of the Preventative Security Services, Yussef Issa, of working on behalf of Hamas, the sources said. The PSS was then the largest of the U.S.-backed Fatah security forces in Gaza. The force still operates in the West Bank, where it coordinates security with the U.S., including during visits of American diplomats to the territory.

Issa was one of a handful of top Palestinian militia leaders to hold regular security meetings with the American security coordinator in the region, Lieutenant General Keith Dayton, and with Dayton's U.S. team. These meetings aimed at implementing the Dayton Plan, which called for the U.S. to strengthen Abbas's security forces against their rival Hamas. Perversely, Issa is suspected of being "one of the most important Hamas infiltrators in Fatah," a top Preventative Security Services source in Ramallah told me. The source said Issa's wife is the sister of the wife of Siad Siam, who served as Hamas's Interior Minister and is a founder of Hamas's so-called Executive Force militia in Gaza. The source speculated that the family relationship had facilitated Issa's initial recruitment to work on behalf of Hamas. Notably, he said Issa is also suspected of accepting significant sums of money from the expansionist jihadists. "Hamas has been buying off agents at all levels both in Gaza and in the West Bank," said the PSS source. "The buying is still going on." Asked on the record if Issa was listed as a suspected Hamas agent, a member of the Fatah team that released the two-hundred-page report told me he could not release any names, but pointed out that Abbas had downgraded Issa from colonel to the rank of soldier. "So there's your answer. You can infer from that what you will," said the Fatah team member. Abbas's aide Nabil Amr admitted that Fatah security forces were in a "state of infiltration" by Hamas.

Some assert that the model of the Gaza Strip is not relevant to an Israeli withdrawal from the West Bank or eastern Jerusalem. Israel's disengagement from Gaza was unilateral, this argument goes, leaving behind a security vacuum that was ultimately filled by Hamas. In the case of a likely future Israeli West Bank withdrawal, they contend, the Jewish state plans to hand the strategic territory to its Fatah "peace partner," with which it will coordinate an evacuation instead of beating a unilateral retreat, and then coordinate security with a strong Fatah in the aftermath. To that end, Israel and the U.S. have been strengthening Fatah forces in the West Bank to withstand a possible Hamas takeover. American security coordinators recently launched the most advanced training courses ever provided to Fatah.

A quick review of this argument suggests an almost irrational naiveté in the notion that Fatah is or could be a partner in peace, even within itself, and certainly not with Israel. Fatah is structurally unstable, internally divided, and avidly disliked by many Palestinians who recall too vividly the depredations of Yassir Arafat's goons. It was and is permeated at all levels by a better-run, more effective outfit that bases itself on theological imperialism. Fatah barely stands a chance.

FATAH FORCES RUN SCARED

Large quantities of U.S.-provided weapons have been shipped to Fatah in the West Bank. In the new, advanced six-month U.S. training course being conducted for Fatah security officers, the first three months take place at U.S.-controlled bases in the Jordanian village of Giftlik. The six hundred elite PA soldiers train in weaponry, ambushes, fighting street crime and terrorism, and dealing with hostage situations. The second, more advanced training is at a U.S.-run base in the West Bank city of Jericho.

The Fatah graduates of this new program are billed as the most professional Palestinian police force ever assembled. According to General Dayton, while he was the U.S. security coordinator, U.S. security officials rented an apartment in Jericho and personally oversaw "every aspect of the new units' trainings."

An important trial balloon was launched in February 2008. Five hundred members of the new elite Palestinian force were deployed to assume security control in the northern West Bank city of Nablus, a major stronghold of Fatah's al-Aqsa Martyrs Brigades's carnage faction. Israel allowed the deployment and coordinated with the PA. These Nablus police were to be responsible for public security, and for fighting crime and terrorism. Careful observers were not surprised in April 2008 when Israeli security officials closely monitoring the unit's progress resigned themselves to the fact that the units were largely failing. "They cannot fight terrorism," one security official privately told me. "The Israel Defense Forces must do most of the work for them in that regard. When it comes to public security, they can block off streets and create a perimeter and carry out other basic duties, but beyond that, fighting crime isn't going well."

A major episode evidencing the new unit's failure to fight terrorism played out in early April 2008 after thirteen senior leaders of the al-Aqsa Martyrs Brigades—pardoned in an amnesty deal by Prime Minister Ehud Olmert—publicly took up arms and vowed savage attacks on Israel. The proud terrorists had received amnesty on the conditions that they disarm, refrain from attacks, spend three months in PA detention facilities, and another three months confined to the city in which they reside. In a challenge to the new Nablus police force, the thirteen senior Brigades leaders publicly reneged on their amnesty agreement, departed their PA detention facilities, openly took up arms, and created a stronghold in the Old City of Nablus. These cutthroats also challenged a few pragmatic leaders of the al-Aqsa Martyrs Brigades itself, who held back on publicly attacking Israel while the amnesty agreement was being implemented. Calling themselves the Night Warriors of al-Aqsa, the maverick cell members vowed imminent attacks in central Israel.

According to informed security sources, among those rejecting the agreement were Hanni Caabe, Mahdi Abu Jazaleh, and brothers Omar and Amer Haqube—all high-ranking Brigades executioners.

The U.S.-trained Fatah police unit, under Dayton's direct watch, was called on to eject the al-Aqsa terrorist rebels from Nablus's Old City. The operation was seen as a major test of the capabilities of the West Bank's future protectors. A large Fatah force did attempt to raid the terrorists' stronghold several times, but according to security officials the force repeatedly failed. "We are talking about six attempts so far, where five of the attempts utilized more than three hundred policemen against the thirteen terrorists and all attempts failed miserably," a security official told me while the fiasco was going on. "They couldn't even get near the stronghold without being heavily fired on and then retreating."

Finally, the IDF raided the Brigades's stronghold on April 20, killing Brigades leader Caabe during a shootout and sending at least five other rebel Brigades terrorists into hiding. "Israel had to come in and do the work for the Palestinian force," said an Israeli security official. "I don't know how they can handle security without Israel backing them up."

With the first trial balloon of Fatah forces having miserably failed, the U.S.-backed unit saw another chance in the first week of May in 2007. This time consisting of 480 members of the elite U.S.-trained force, the second unit deployed in the northern West Bank city of Jenin. The Jenin force's commander, Suleiman Amran, duly announced to the news media that the deployment was an important day for the town and that "there's no chance for troublemakers to return to Jenin."[3] Less than thirty minutes into their second major mission, the Fatah forces retreated. According to eyewitnesses I spoke to, the Fatah force simply scrammed, panicked by the armed hooligans they were charged with combating.

The episode began on Tuesday, May 7. The Fatah team embarked on its first mission—to clear out a section of Cabatiya, a Palestinian camp just south of Jenin considered a major base of the Teheran-funded, Hezbollah-commanded Islamic Jihad. About two hundred policemen attempted to engage in fire clashes in Cabatiya with members of Islamic Jihad, Hamas, and even some renegade members of Fatah's al-Aqsa Martyrs Brigades. In less than thirty minutes from the start of the clashes, according to witnesses, including al-Aqsa members, the best-ever Palestinian police force bolted, cut and ran, retreated from the scene. Israeli security officials monitoring the fight confirmed this. "The security men ran away scared. They didn't arrest anyone," said one al-Aqsa witness.

Both Israeli and U.S. security coordinators are well aware of Fatah's failures during these crucial tests of their capabilities. Soothingly, Fatah's inability to arrest Hamas members without the IDF standing over its shoulder doesn't seem to be a deal breaker for Israel or the U.S. when it comes to a West Bank withdrawal. Instead, the myth that Fatah will be able to stabilize the West Bank or eastern Jerusalem is an accepted part of withdrawal plans and logic. There has been some talk about deploying international forces in the Palestinian territories, particularly an Egyptian contingent in Gaza and a Jordanian one in the West Bank. A key policy maker in Prime Minister Benjamin Netanyahu's office told me the recently elected Israeli leader favors working with Jordan on assuming security control of the West Bank. But neither Egyptian nor Jordanian troops will fight to protect Israel; and besides, Hamas has made clear they will not go along with any internationalization plan. "Hamas's position is resisting this idea strongly, because there is no need for such things," Ahmed Yousef, the chief Hamas political advisor in Gaza, told me. "We can handle security and don't need to bring forces and internationalized solutions," Yousef explained. Following Israel's twenty-two-day war against Hamas in Gaza that ended in January 2009, the Islamist group agreed to allow international monitors to deploy along the Gaza-Egypt border—although the border agreement is unlikely to change the situation on the ground, as we will detail in the final chapter.

HAMAS SET FOR WEST BANK TAKEOVER

Meanwhile, Hamas already seems to be setting the stage for an eventual West Bank takeover. An amazing scenario unfolded just hours before the start of the November 27, 2007, U.S.-sponsored Annapolis summit, in which Israel intended to hand over most of the West Bank to Fatah. The night before the summit, Israel cracked down on a cell of leading Palestinians suspected of setting up a Hamas military arm in order to take over the strategic territory.

According to Israeli security sources, the IDF arrested seven top members of Fatah suspected of working on behalf of Hamas to establish a special forces unit in the West Bank. One of the arrested Fatah officials was the assistant to the secretary-general of Fatah in Gaza and a member of the PA parliament, Maged Abu Shamaleh. Shamaleh, along with his assistant and another six arrested militants, moved to the West Bank immediately following Hamas's takeover of Gaza.

Just one month after Annapolis, a senior Palestinian security official told me, an internal Fatah investigation revealed that Hamas had, with some success, tried to establish a military operation in the northern West Bank city of Jenin, the longtime Fatah stronghold (although Islamic Jihad also has a major presence there). The official explained that Hamas gunmen in Jenin were originally thought to have numbered in the dozens, but Fatah later found out that Hamas purchased over six hundred high-powered assault rifles and distributed them to its fighters in the city. Fatah raids confiscated about one hundred rifles, but they believed five hundred more were handed out by Hamas in Jenin alone. The Fatah investigation also found that many of the Fatah Brigades gunmen —who had been granted amnesty by Olmert—had sold their weapons to Hamas, which stockpiled and then distributed the rifles in Jenin. The amnesty was supposed to have been conditioned on Brigades terrorists' handing in their weapons to the PA for a fee.

A noticeable spike in the price of assault rifles in the West Bank sparked the Fatah investigation. The Palestinian security official said Fatah also confiscated $350,000 in cash from a Hamas official in the West Bank city of Ramallah in early December 2007. He said the cash had been meant to purchase more weapons for Hamas gunmen in the West Bank. The Fatah investigation also found that members of the al-Aqsa Martyrs Brigades in Jenin were turncoats recruited by Hamas with the offer of larger paychecks.

In response to the Fatah investigation, the Hamas-allied Committees spokesman, Abdel-El, declared in an interview with me,

"We thank [Israel] for this gift to the American tool [Abbas], because it is only a matter of time before the Islamic resistance [Hamas] will come to the West Bank just as we took Gaza."

The chief of Hamas's so-called special forces in Gaza, Abu Oubaida al-Jara, called on all Fatah members "not to resist because the Islamic project [Hamas] is coming very soon to the West Bank."

WHO SUPPORTS A WEST BANK WITHDRAWAL?

Both U.S. and Israeli leaders have repeatedly claimed that the majority of the Israeli public supports a West Bank withdrawal.

"I speak for the entire country, who are with me," Olmert said in a November 2007 address regarding an evacuation from the West Bank.[4] That same month, U.S. Secretary of State Condoleezza Rice told American Jewish leaders at the General Assembly of the United Jewish Communities meeting in Nashville: "I believe that most Israelis are ready to leave most of the—nearly all of the West Bank—just as they were ready to leave Gaza, for the sake of peace."[5]

But several days before Rice's sweeping statement a survey released in Israel found 61 percent of Israelis opposed to withdrawing from the West Bank, citing their fears that the Palestinians would use the strategic territory to fire rockets into central Israel. Some 77 percent of Israelis said they believed Fatah lacked the power to prevent attacks from the West Bank.[6]

Israel's security apparatus is also leery of any West Bank retreat. In one notable interview, a liberal activist and former IDF Gaza commander called an Israeli withdrawal from the West Bank a "mistake" that if implemented would result in rockets fired at major population centers. "Olmert's [withdrawal] plan is a mistake," said Colonel Shaul Arieli, an activist for Israel's left-wing Meretz party, which supports final status negotiations leading to a Palestinian state.[7] "This is not the way to solve the Israeli-Palestinian conflict," the former Israel Defense Forces commander in northern Gaza said. "The West Bank withdrawal plan will lead to the same result [as the Gaza withdrawal]—firing of Qassams and Grads at Israel. But then the front won't only be here in the south, it will also encircle the state of Israel's eastern border."

Former Israeli Defense Minister Moshe Arens, a conservative politician, in an interview with me slammed the "failed" policy of withdrawal, calling it a "victory for Palestinian terror." Arens is a seasoned Israeli diplomat who has served several times as defense minister, including during Israel's foray into Lebanon in the early 1980s.

Not only most Israelis, but also some Arab countries, especially Egypt and Jordan, seem to oppose more Israeli evacuations. Jordan borders the West Bank, mostly along the eastern littoral of the Jordan River, while Egypt lies immediately to Gaza's south. In a June 2006 interview with Israel's leading daily, *Yediot Aharonot*, Jordan's King Abdullah stated, "Such a unilateral step [as evacuating the West Bank] would foster insecurity and doubts, not only in the Palestinian Authority, but among the rest of the peace partners in the region."[8] Israel's retreat from Gaza has already had an enormous impact on Egypt. The Cairo government has repeatedly clashed with Gaza's Hamas rulers, who are ideologically allied with the Muslim Brotherhood, the outlawed Islamist opposition in Egypt. In fact, Hamas was founded as a violent offshoot of the Egyptian Muslim Brotherhood, which, in turn, had been established to promote Islamic *sharia* law. The Egyptian group soon joined international politics as its founder, Hassan al-Banna, became an admirer and friend of Hitler. Hamas has already, on numerous occasions, organized the storming of the Egypt-Gaza border, threatening Egyptian security. In May 2006 Egyptian authorities announced that bombers who had attacked the Egyptian Sinai resort town of Dahab that month had trained for the operation in the Gaza Strip with local Palestinians.

Still, the agenda of further Israeli evacuation from the West Bank and perhaps Jerusalem, pushed by Israeli, American, and European leaders and welcomed by Israel's radical Muslim enemies, rolls on. It is difficult to see what will prevent the rapid transformation of the West Bank and perhaps eastern Jerusalem into a Taliban-style mini-state.

CHAPTER TEN

LOSING LEBANON

T*hings are looking up*. Our country will continue to move toward independence," former Lebanese Prime Minister Michel Aoun told me in an interview.

Lebanon's Druze leader Walid Jumblatt concurred. "There have been major developments for the future freedom of Lebanon," he said to me from his Shouf Mountain headquarters by phone.

Both leaders spoke in the aftermath of the "Cedar Revolution," a series of massive demonstrations in central Beirut they helped lead against Syria's nearly thirty-year military occupation of their country. The Cedar protests erupted after the assassination in Beirut one month earlier of former Prime Minister Rafik Hariri, who was killed in a car bomb blast widely blamed on Syria. Crowds from across Lebanon, at times estimated at over a million people, gathered in Martyrs' Square in central Beirut to demand the immediate withdrawal of Syrian troops, the firing of Syrian backed Lebanese intelligence forces, and an international inquiry into Hariri's killing. Soon the Iranian- and Syrian-backed Hezbollah political and military organization led counter-protests in Beirut. These also drew large crowds, who demanded the opposite—that Damascus maintain its military presence in Lebanon. These counter-demonstrations foreshadowed a renewal of sectarian violence that would again plague Israel's neighbor to the north.

For a time, the Cedar Revolution succeeded. In April 2005 Syria withdrew its nearly twenty thousand troops from Lebanon. Syrian officers held a public farewell ceremony in the Bekaa Valley for the heads of Syrian intelligence, and claimed that all Syrian agents and troops were departing the country. Then, in the months that followed, a string of bombings and political assassinations began to target pro-democracy leaders and media personalities in Lebanon. Syria, which maintained a grip on much of Lebanon's security apparatus, was charged with carrying out the assassinations and large-scale bombings in a bid to destabilize the country. Despite the onslaught of horrifying political assassinations, Lebanon seemed to be on the road to independence. As part of an international investigation into the Hariri murder, major military leaders with ties to Syria were arrested. Progress was made toward establishing an independent Lebanese parliament and replacing the country's president, Emile Lahoud, long considered a Syrian puppet. Lebanese pro-democracy leaders also pressed political and public relations campaigns for Hezbollah to disarm.

OLMERT DECLARES WAR

All that changed on July 12, 2006, when Hezbollah raided the Israeli border, firing rockets at Israeli towns while launching an anti-tank missile at two armored trucks patrolling Israel's side of the border fence. Three IDF soldiers were killed in the raids, and two more—Master Sergeant Ehud Goldwasser and First Sergeant Eldad Regev—were dragged off (probably dead or near death) by Hezbollah to Lebanon.

Prime Minister Ehud Olmert promptly declared Hezbollah's border attack an "act of war." He warned that Lebanon would "bear the consequences of its actions" while promising a "very painful and far-reaching response."[1] With an inexperienced defense minister, Amir Peretz, at his side, Olmert led his country to war.

Well, sort of. The Israel Defense Forces attacked numerous targets in Lebanon with artillery and air strikes while Israel's Security Cabinet, consisting of top ministers, met to discuss a larger response. In the opening hours of what would later be officially termed a war, the Israeli leadership was already conflicted about the goals of its actions. Olmert repeatedly blamed the Lebanese government for Hezbollah's provocative raid, explaining the attack was launched from Lebanon while Hezbollah had two ministers serving in the Lebanese parliament.[2] The IDF chief of staff, Dan Halutz (who was later infamously found to have sold off his investment portfolio three hours after the Hezbollah raid was launched), endorsed Olmert's plan to hold the government of Lebanon accountable, stating, "If the soldiers are not returned, we will turn Lebanon's clock back twenty years."[3]

But four days into the conflict, on July 16, the Knesset's Security Cabinet released a statement explaining that, although Israel had engaged in substantial bombing operations across Lebanon, its war was not against the Lebanese government. The *communiqué* stated: "Israel is not fighting Lebanon but the terrorist element there [Hezbollah], led by [Hassan] Nasrallah and his cohorts, who have made Lebanon a hostage and created Syrian- and Iranian-sponsored terrorist enclaves of murder."[4]

Amidst uncertainty over just what or who was the target in Lebanon, Olmert eventually set forth the major goals of Israel's Second Lebanon War—to ensure the return of Regev and Goldwasser and to "decimate" Hezbollah strongholds in South Lebanon. Those goals would change repeatedly during the military confrontations to come. In the war's opening days, according to security sources who spoke to me, the IDF presented Olmert with alternative battle plans to devastate Hezbollah within three to five weeks. The plans had been drawn up by Israel's leading military strategic experts and refined and improved over several years. They called for an immediate air campaign against Hezbollah strongholds in South Beirut. Then key sections of the Lebanese-Syria border were to be bombed to halt Syrian resupply of arms to Hezbollah and to ensure that the kidnapped soldiers were not transported out of the country. The centerpiece of the military's battle plans called for the immediate deployment of up to forty thousand IDF infantry troops to South Lebanon's Litani River. The troops would then work their way south back to the Israeli border, while surrounding and then cleaning out Hezbollah strongholds under heavy aerial cover. From the Litani south to the border would cover the entire swath of territory from which most Hezbollah rockets were being fired.

To the great dismay of Israeli military officials—and of Lebanese democrats and perhaps of the American Pentagon—Olmert drastically curtailed their plans, primarily the mass deployment of Israeli ground troops. Instead, he initially allowed only a limited Israeli air campaign focused on some high-profile Hezbollah targets, such as the group's stronghold in the capital's Dahiyeh neighborhood, the Beirut International Airport, and roads that led from Beirut into Syria. The main smuggling routes between Syria and Lebanon, sites very well known to Israeli intelligence, were essentially off limits to the Air Force because Olmert feared bringing Damascus into the conflict, according to senior IDF sources.

Then Hezbollah met Israel's air campaign with massive, devastating rocket attacks against Israel's northern cities, placing nearly one-third of its population centers under direct rocket attack. The IDF again presented Olmert with a plan for a large ground deployment to the Litani River. The Israeli prime minister—under heavy public pressure to commit ground forces and step up operations in response to Hezbollah missile fire—approved only a limited ground offensive of up to eight thousand soldiers who were not permitted to advance to the Litani. The IDF was directed merely to clean out Hezbollah's bases within about three miles of the border. Small forces did manage to advance further while isolated special operations were carried out deep inside Lebanon. Many IDF commanders operating in Lebanon later complained that they did not receive proper direction or proper definition of the goals of their ground campaign.

Hezbollah's missile attacks inside Israel prompted Olmert to announce yet another goal of the Second Lebanon War: to stop the rocket attacks. To that effect, the IAF apparently succeeded in taking out Hezbollah's longer-range rockets, such as Iranian-supplied Zelzal missiles capable of reaching Tel Aviv, although some security officials believe Hezbollah was not interested in escalating the conflict by crossing an unspoken but understood red line.

Olmert was already accused by various critics of using excessive force and he feared charges of firing indiscriminately into population centers. He limited the IAF to strategic bombings of large-scale targets only. In many important instances, the air force was not allowed to clear access routes for ground troops to enter. Thus the IDF—with a force one-fourth the size it had requested—

engaged in heated, often face-to-face combat over the course of weeks with a well-armed, Iranian-trained Hezbollah militia who had planned up to six years for this battle. Hezbollah had made good use of the time following Israel's withdrawal from the Lebanese border in 2000, a retreat, as we will discuss shortly, understood as a victory both by Hezbollah and by the larger Middle East terrorist community.

Israeli soldiers found themselves up against Hezbollah gunmen who fought in civilian clothing and hid behind local civilian populations. Well-orchestrated Hezbollah ambushes took tolls on Israeli troops. Iranian-supplied advanced anti-tank missiles proved quite effective against Israeli combat vehicles. Due to the lack of sufficient ground troops, the IDF suffered in very specific ways on the battlefield.

One example is a battle I watched closely that began July 25. The Israeli army attempted to besiege Bint Jbail, a town of about thirty thousand, commonly referred to as the "Hezbollah capital" of South Lebanon. Because there were not enough troops to surround the strategic village completely, Bint Jbail's northern entrance was not sealed off and, according to army sources, hundreds of Hezbollah fighters joined the 150 or so Hezbollah gunmen already inside. As a result, the IDF had to contend with a much larger Hezbollah contingent. Nine IDF soldiers were lost in heavy fighting the next day. Another fourteen soldiers were killed at Bint Jbail over the next two weeks. There was also a public setback for the Israeli navy. On July 14 Hezbollah fired two Iranian-provided Chinese C-802 Silkworm missiles that struck the INS Hanit warship, causing significant damage and four fatalities. The Israeli ship possessed several sophisticated multi-layered missile defense capabilities, but reportedly they had intentionally been disabled.

DIPLOMACY KILLS ISRAELI SOLDIERS?

In perhaps the most tragic aspect of the war, a large number of Israeli casualties resulted. from diplomatic demands in Olmert's office, according to angry senior IDF sources I spoke to. On several occasions, the pace of the fighting was interrupted while heavy diplomacy looked to be gaining momentum. Most notably, during a visit to the region by Secretary of State Condoleezza Rice, the IAF was conducting a campaign in which some civilians died in the Southern Lebanese village of Qana. Olmert's office told the IDF to halt most operations and troop advances for up to thirty-six hours while U.S.-backed negotiations ran their course. Military leaders later charged that some troop battalions, instructed to hold positions outside villages but not to advance, actually became sitting ducks for Hezbollah anti-tank fire, which killed at least thirty-five young soldiers. After that burst of diplomacy failed, including during Rice's visit, soldiers carried on.

During my reports from Jerusalem, Tel Aviv, and the rocket-battered north, I learned from military officials of several meetings in which IDF officers petitioned Olmert and Defense Minister Peretz during the war for a larger ground force and for heavier aerial cover; or at least for authorization for ground troops already in Lebanon to reach the Litani River in hopes of cleaning out Hezbollah-dominated villages and towns, such as nearby Tyre, from which many missiles were being launched into Israel. These petitions became more frequent as Hezbollah rockets continued to rain down, eventually killing forty-three Israeli civilians and wounding some 4,262 more.

Finally, toward the beginning of August, tens of thousands of troops went on standby in northern Israel, but could not enter Lebanon. The smaller IDF numbers already on the ground inside Lebanon carried on, eventually with instructions to create a buffer zone of about three miles within which the Hezbollah infrastructure would be entirely eliminated. That zone would do little to stop rocket fire into northern Israel, since most rockets were fired from positions deeper inside South Lebanon. Officials told me that toward the middle of the war the IAF was still held in check from targeting key positions close to the Syrian border in the Bekaa Valley; it was from these that Hezbollah received regular shipments of rockets and other heavy weaponry originating in Iran, after having been transported via Syria. Israel did eventually bomb roads in an area a few kilometers from Syria, but many weapons-smuggling routes at the border remained intact.

While Syria placed its military on high alert, Olmert told reporters several times that Israel had no intention of bringing Damascus into the war, a clear, although likely unintended, signal to Syria it could and can continue to arm Hezbollah with little consequence.

Finally, on August 6, three and a half weeks into the war, after Hezbollah rockets killed a record fifteen Israelis in one day, including twelve army reservists resting near the Lebanese border, Olmert's cabinet finally gave the green light for an enormous IDF ground invasion and for an advance to the Litani River.[5] Israeli military officials were elated that the IDF would finally hold the authority to do what it had wanted to do nearly one month before. The cabinet, though, left the timing of the new operation to Olmert, who held the advance back until the weekend of August 12. The IDF then charged ahead on four main fronts, reaching the Litani River and even beyond in full force and prepared for an intense battle to overtake the areas used by Hezbollah as its rocket-launching base. The IDF estimated it would need another four to six weeks to successfully wipe out the Hezbollah infrastructure. A day later, on August 13, Israel approved a UN ceasefire resolution. On the morning of August 14, the truce officially took effect. The IDF and IAF made many important gains, clearing out some villages and bombing strategic Hezbollah sites that would clearly set back the eager guerillas. Since Hezbollah answers to Iran and not to the Lebanese population, we may never know how many Hezbollah fighters were killed or the extent of damage inflicted by the Jewish state during the war. By most criteria, Israel lost the war. It did not achieve a single one of Olmert's shifting goals: Regev and Goldwasser were nowhere to be found. In a clear victory for Hezbollah, the UN ceasefire heavily negotiated by Foreign Minister Tzipi Livni postponed to a later date negotiations to secure the freedom of the two kidnapped soldiers. Olmert had repeatedly vowed the war would stop only after Hezbollah returned the abducted Israeli troops, but the prime minister ended the conflict without even vague promises of the soldiers' assured safety or any indication that they were alive.

Although it was far from a knockout, Israel dealt a major blow to Hezbollah, another of Olmert's publicly declared aims. The terror group retained a good deal of its infrastructure in South Lebanon and proved it had the ability to fire hundreds of rockets per day into Israel during the last days of the war. On August 13, on the final day of the war, Hezbollah fired over 240 rockets—its largest one-day volley—into northern Israel, killing one civilian and wounding at least twenty-six others. Clearly Israel had not depleted Hezbollah's arsenal of medium-range missiles, despite Olmert's pledge to the Israeli public of removing the rocket threat.

CEASEFIRE LETS HEZBOLLAH RE-ARM

The ceasefire that ended the war called for the deployment of up to fifteen thousand international troops to police South Lebanon, including the Lebanon-Israel border—an increase from the two thousand that had ineffectually patrolled the border area until then. The UN troops in Lebanon were to be joined by fifteen thousand Lebanese soldiers. For Israel, the main effect of an international force on its border was to provide little deterrence to Hezbollah operations while impeding the ability of the IDF to respond to any future conflict. Previous international forces or observers, including in Lebanon, Gaza and Hebron, had done little to stop terrorists from arming or attacking Israel. Nor was Hezbollah dismayed by the deployment of the international force, as it later blithely ignored them while openly replenishing its rocket arsenal and rebuilding its strongholds in South Lebanon, including along the Israeli border. Hezbollah was probably ecstatic about the deployment of fifteen thousand "soldiers" from the Lebanese Army to replace Israeli troops in the south. The Lebanese Army was short on troops and ill-equipped, and had to recall Lebanese soldiers who had served during the previous five years—all of which meant that many unprepared ex-soldiers were charged with protecting the Israeli border. Taking into account the Shi'ite-Sunni sectarian divisions in Lebanon's army—with many soldiers sympathetic to Hezbollah's cause—what was left was a force that, at best, did little to contend with Hezbollah and at worst might prompt an internal civil war or openly assist Hezbollah.

The ceasefire further called for "all Lebanese militias" to disarm. Hassan Nasrallah, chief of Hezbollah, soon repudiated this clause. Instead, he declared victory in the war and quickly undertook the complete rearmament of his movement. Israeli security officials say Hezbollah now has more rockets pointed at Israel than before the 2006 conflict. They also say Hezbollah may have secured anti-aircraft missiles that would pose a major threat to the IAF in any future conflict, although this information was not confirmed. More than two years on, Hezbollah has not only completely rearmed, but has taken control of the Lebanese parliament. Israel's poor showing in the war also eased Syria's diplomatic isolation after a long period of Damascus taking the blame for the Hariri assassination.

To realize the full consequences of Israel's failure during the Lebanese war, and how that failure is directly tied to potentially dangerous future Israeli policies towards the Palestinians and Syria, we must take a step back to look at Israel's historic retreat from a South Lebanese "security zone" in 2000.

Starting in the late 1960s, Yasser Arafat's Palestine Liberation Organization, then mainly based in Jordan, carried out scores of cross-border raids against Israel from South Lebanon. After Jordan expelled the PLO in 1971, Arafat set up guerrilla headquarters in Lebanon and repeatedly used the territory to direct and launch terrorism at the Jewish state. In 1978, following a large-scale PLO terror attack, planned and launched from Lebanon, Israel invaded its neighbor and successfully pushed back the PLO. Heavy international pressure forced the Jewish state to withdraw, however, leaving South Lebanon to an interim UN force and to the South Lebanese Army, or SLA. The PLO soon retook its bases in South Lebanon and resumed its campaign. Eventually, the IDF re-invaded Lebanon in 1982 to expel the PLO, forcing Arafat's group from most of South Lebanon and eventually forcing Arafat and his cronies to decamp to Tunis. Israel withdrew to a small buffer zone it created at the border with the help of the SLA. Together they kept terrorists away from the Israeli border. The IDF maintained bases at the border from which it could attack deeper into Lebanon when necessary.

Using this Israeli security zone as a pretext, Hezbollah in 1985 announced its armed struggle against the Jewish state, with its goal being an Israeli retreat out of Lebanon. Over the years Hezbollah launched scores of attacks, including border raids or attempts to infiltrate Golan Jewish communities, but most of these were halted before they reached Israel, due to the IDF's strong position in South Lebanon.

Then in May 2000, Israeli Prime Minister Ehud Barak hastily pulled the IDF out of South Lebanon. Barak, with Bill Clinton in the White House, was engaged at the time in intense negotiations to offer Arafat a Palestinian state. Under Barak, Israel's retreat from Lebanon was disorderly, and left most of Israel's Christian allies in the south to their fate under Hezbollah. The Lebanese jihadis immediately declared the withdrawal a victory and quickly worked to solidify near-complete control over South Lebanon. They went about building bunkers and erecting rocket launchers, in some cases just meters from the border with Israel. The IDF's evacuation greatly boosted Hezbollah's image in Lebanon and garnered the Syrian-paid group broad support in many regions in the country.

Thus did Israel's retreat from South Lebanon in 2000 set the stage for Hezbollah's successful provocation of the Second Lebanon War six years later. One would imagine that the consequences of the 2000 withdrawal, coupled with the obvious failure of Israel's retreat under fire from the Gaza Strip five years later, would have constituted a giant wake-up call for Israel's government and its people, but that was not to be. Both of the Israeli prime ministers involved—Barak in 2000 and Ariel Sharon in 2005—had promised and predicted that once Israel disengaged from the territories in question, the international community would more than understand if Israel ever needed to reenter those territories to carry out anti-terror operations. These pledges proved illusory. Instead, the international community repeatedly condemned Israel's 2006 war in Lebanon just as it now urges an immediate end to any Israeli military incursions into Gaza to suppress rocket and missile attacks from there. In making their cases for both withdrawals, Barak and Sharon pledged that Israel's security would be enhanced. The reverse occurred: the retreats set the stage for armed gangs, mercenaries of different stripes, Iranian- and Syrian-sponsored paramilitary groupings, and cohorts of youthful looters to fill the void, with Hezbollah now in control of most of Lebanon and

Hamas ruling Gaza and threatening a takeover of the West Bank. Incomprehensibly, the consequences of Israel's retreats from Lebanon and Gaza rarely enter into Israeli public debate regarding whether or not the Jewish state should withdraw from still more territory, including eastern Jerusalem, the strategic West Bank, or the vital Golan Heights. It is as if no one wants to face what Israel's concessions have already led to.

ISRAEL SEALS HEZBOLLAH'S VICTORY

Olmert was apparently not content with failing to achieve his declared objectives during the 2006 Second Lebanon War. He soon handed Hezbollah another victory on a silver platter. In an emotional day for the Jewish state, on July 16, 2008, Israel traded live Lebanese terrorists, including Samir Kuntar, the man responsible for one of the most gruesome of anti-Israel attacks, in exchange for two coffins containing the remains of Goldwasser and Regev. Kuntar is considered a hero in the greater terrorist community. He had been serving four life sentences in an Israeli prison for murdering four Israelis—including a father and his young daughter—in a bloody 1979 kidnapping and multiple-murder attack in northern Israel. Kuntar reportedly sent Hezbollah a letter from his Israeli prison cell saying he would like to join the Lebanese massacre group once he was released by Israel. For Hezbollah, Kuntar's freedom was the sheer vindication of terrorism. Securing Kuntar's release had been the very excuse Hezbollah used for carrying out its 2006 cross-border attacks that provoked the war in the first place. Since the 1980s, securing Kuntar's freedom had been maintained by Hezbollah as one of the main goals of its war against Israel. When Olmert traded Kuntar for the bodies of Regev and Galdwasser, the Israeli leader handed Hezbollah their prize.

In what, if provable, would be a scandal in Israel of major proportions, security officials told me that Israel has had information since 2006 that Eldad Regev and Ehud Goldwasser were almost certainly dead. Yet it was not until late June 2008, just minutes before the Security Cabinet agreed to the prisoner exchange, that Olmert finally told the Knesset that Israeli intelligence strongly believed the abducted army reservists were not alive. The gladdening prospects for the return of the two live Israeli solders, as well as Olmert's claim that the soldiers' fates were unknown, had been used in part by Olmert's government and the Israeli news media to sell to the public the idea of a significant prisoner exchange with Hezbollah.

In Lebanon, Hezbollah used the prestige of having secured Kuntar's pending release, and the intense street violence it had started two months earlier, effectively to seize control of the Lebanese parliament. On July 11, only days after Kuntar's release was agreed to by Israel, Lebanese Prime Minister Fuad Siniora formed a national unity cabinet allowing Hezbollah and its allies veto power over all government decisions. This means that any attempt by the Lebanese parliament to disarm Hezbollah will immediately be squashed. Even though the veto deal was marketed by Siniora as a sign of national unity and conciliation, any elementary analyst knows it leaves Lebanon hostage to the whims of Iran and Syria, meaning that Israel's enemies now exert control over the Jewish state's northern borders.

Lest there be any ambiguity about who the true enemies are, in November 2008 the president of Syria, Bashar Assad, presented the infant-killer Kuntar with Syria's highest medal.

Following the war, Israel lost major deterrent power everywhere. I argue that Israel's loss in 2006 was its most devastating defeat in recent memory and has resulted in the escalation of some of the greatest threats the Jewish state has ever faced. Israel's military loss to a small, hired army run by Iran via Syria officially reversed the trend of 1967, in which Israel defeated Egypt, Jordan, and Syria and established itself as the Middle East's preeminent military power. Although that position had been eroded in the 1990s by Israel's surrender of strategic territory to Arafat and the Jewish state's 2000 withdrawal from Lebanon, Hezbollah's 2006 victory on the battlefield has changed the game. Enemy states and guerrilla organizations took note of how contemporary Israel can be defeated if the proper military tactics are deployed. For example, Hezbollah's victory completely redefined the Palestinian terrorist strategy for defeating Israel. Both Hamas and Fatah witnessed the importance of rockets and of building Hezbollah-like guerrilla armies capable of storming the Israeli border and engaging Israeli troops. Israeli security officials say Hamas has sent hundreds of Gaza-based militants to Iran for prolonged periods of advanced training. The militants then return to Gaza where they retrain more gunmen in Hezbollah-like tactics. Since 2006, Palestinian terrorists in Gaza have repeatedly attempted to storm Israel's border in operations similar to Hezbollah's border raids.

"We are turning Gaza into South Lebanon," a northern Gaza leader for the al-Aqsa Martyrs Brigades, Abu Ahmed, told me in an interview. "We learned from Hezbollah's victory that Israel can be defeated if we know how to hit them and if we are well prepared. We are importing rockets and the knowledge to launch them, and we are also making many plans for battle."

Palestinian security sources confirmed the development of war bunkers inside Gaza similar to the underground Hezbollah lairs Israel faced during the war in Lebanon. During its confrontation with Hezbollah, Israel destroyed scores of complex bunkers that snaked along the Lebanese side of the Israel-Lebanon border. (By contrast, during Israel's recent twenty-two-day war against Hamas in Gaza the IDF did not destroy many of the Islamist group's bunkers) Military officials said they were surprised by the scale of the Hezbollah bunkers, in which Israeli troops reportedly found war rooms stocked with advanced eavesdropping and surveillance equipment, much of it labeled, "Made in Iran." Abu Ahmed said the most important tools in the Palestinian resistance arsenal were rockets. He said his group learned from Hezbollah that Israel can be defeated with missiles. "We saw that with the capacity to bombard the Israeli population with hundreds of rockets every day we can change the strategic balance with Israel," he said.

Israel's loss to Hezbollah has consequences far beyond the Jewish state. The Second Lebanon War was viewed by Israel's enemies as a proxy military campaign in which Israel represented the West, particularly the U.S.; while Hezbollah represented its master Iran and Tehran's client state Syria, as well as their proxies, including the various Palestinian terrorist gangs in the Gaza Strip and West Bank. During the war, the paramount Druze leader, Walid Jumblatt, told me that Iran was using Hezbollah's confrontation with the Jewish state to test the capabilities of Iranian weapons and to observe Israeli military performance ahead of a possible future conflict between Tehran and either Israel or the U.S. "Iran is bringing in [to Lebanon] sophisticated weaponry," said Jumblatt. "The Iranians are actually experimenting with different kinds of missiles in Lebanon by shooting them at the Israelis. Iran is using this violence to test certain abilities." Iran is thought to supply Hezbollah with most of its rockets, weapons, and munitions. If Jumblatt's accusations are correct, Iran has gained important lessons from Hezbollah's victory; and, as the world press has reported, not only in its proxy war against Israel but in its direct military involvement in fueling the insurgency against U.S. troops in Iraq.

Israel's loss to Hezbollah greatly damaged U.S. influence in the region and cleared the way for a major reorientation in the Middle East: Iran's hegemony grew while Russia was reintroduced as a major player in the region, announcing the reopening of naval bases in Syria and taking a more outward role in supporting America's foes. Following the war, polls in multiple Arab countries, including in U.S. "allies" such as Egypt, consistently found Hezbollah's chief, Nasrallah, to be the most popular figure. That, combined with Israel's loss, no doubt gave pause to Arab countries oriented toward the West, including Egypt and Jordan, about the wisdom and value of an alliance with America and its Israeli ally.

CHAPTER ELEVEN

ROMANCING SYRIA

Just after midnight, Israeli Air Force warplanes crossed into Syrian air space and delivered their bombs targeting a mysterious building compound in the remote Deir ez-Zor region of eastern Syria, along the upper Euphrates River. The daring air raid culminated months of intense intelligence work, some of it in coordination with the United States.

Only six months after the September 6, 2007, bombing did the CIA and other intelligence officials brief select congressional committees on details of the strike. Bush administration spokesmen confirmed U.S. and British news media reports that the target had been an early-stage Syrian nuclear reactor, constructed with assistance from North Korea. CIA Director Michael Hayden said the site would have had the capacity to produce enough nuclear material to fuel one to two weapons a year. It was of a "similar size and technology" to North Korea's Yongbyon reactor, Hayden said.[1] White House press secretary Dana Perino explained that the "Syrian regime was building a covert nuclear reactor in its eastern desert capable of producing plutonium.[2] "We are convinced, based on a variety of information, that North Korea assisted Syria's covert nuclear activities. We have good reason to believe that reactor, which was damaged beyond repair on September 6 of last year, was not intended for peaceful purposes." The U.S. accused Syria of hiding its partially constructed reactor from the International Atomic Energy Agency (IAEA). Tellingly, Syria released not a word about the raid; rather, immediately after the Israeli air strike, Damascus sent in bulldozers to remove nearly every square meter of earth around the building—the radioactivity would easily have been identified by the IAEA—and created a sort of small park, thus burying evidence of the reactor's existence. "This cover-up only served to reinforce our confidence that this reactor was not intended for peaceful activities," the White House statement read.

Syrian officials, including President Bashar al-Assad, immediately denied any involvement in illicit nuclear activity and dismissed Washington's accusations as part of a campaign to discredit their government. In response, the U.S. demolished Syria's denials when it released detailed satellite images of the reactor, including one clearly showing the fuel cell rods and another showing the reactor's exterior, which turned out to be a duplicate of other known North Korean reactors. Syria was left humiliated and defeated. It had been caught red-handed violating international nuclear protocols. It had nearly succeeded in altering the balance of power in the Middle East in favor of its partner pariah state, Iran. Suddenly, Israel and the U.S. were strategically positioned to enforce an effective international isolation of Syria. At last it was payback time to the Assad regime for supporting the insurgency against U.S. troops in Iraq; for assassinating former Lebanese Prime Minister Rafiq Hariri and destabilizing Lebanon; for arming, training and funding the Hezbollah terror group; and for openly providing sanctuary to the leaders of Hamas and Islamic Jihad.

MYSTERIOUS REVERSAL OF COURSE

Versus Syria, Israel was presented with a winning set of cards on a silver platter. Its next move? To throw in those cards and bring the Syrians back into international respectability by abruptly announcing "peace talks" with Damascus.

Immediately following the air strike, Israel's military censor inexplicably imposed a total media blackout on the Israeli press regarding the Deir ez-Zor bombing, restricting Israeli reporters to parroting foreign press reports of the attack, and forbidding reports with any new information or quotes of sources discussing the raid. With the government mum and the Israeli public in the dark about just what the Israeli Air Force had bombed, Prime Minister Ehud

Olmert on September 17, 2007, announced he was ready to make peace with Syria "without preset conditions and without ultimatums."[3] This just eleven days after Israel bombed an early-stage Syrian nuclear facility that could have terminated the Jewish state's very existence.

Two months later, Israel agreed to allow Syria to attend the U.S.-backed Annapolis Summit, which sought to create a Palestinian state before 2009. At the summit, Syria was allowed to place on the agenda its recovery of the Golan Heights at a panel discussion about the Israeli-Palestinian conflict. Why was Syria allowed to introduce this issue at all, let alone in an unrelated session? The Olmert government was vague about its reasons. "Israel sees in a positive way the high-ranking participation of Syria in a conference which is clearly about the Israeli-Palestinian track, but could open additional avenues to peace in the Middle East," said Miri Eisin, an Olmert spokeswoman.[4]

The Golan Heights is strategic mountainous territory above the northeasternmost corner of Israel, overlooking Israeli population centers. Twice Syria used it to launch ground invasions into the Jewish state. Israel recaptured the Heights after Syria launched a massive tank assault from the territory in 1973.

While Damascus attended high-level summits and placed its recovery of the Golan on the Annapolis agenda, inside Syria the country furiously armed itself. According to informed Egyptian and Jordanian security officials, Syria—with aid from Iran—in late 2007 and early 2008 acquired a large number of Russian surface-to-surface missiles, including advanced, laser-guided missiles capable of striking the entire Jewish state. The officials told me that Syria had acquired the latest Russian Iskander rockets, having a range of 173 miles, and also upgraded Russian Scud-D missiles, whose range covers all of Israel. The security officials said both the Iskanders and the new Scuds are "smart missiles," fitted with laser guidance systems capable of striking specific targets. They said the projectiles, some of which can be fitted with non-conventional warheads, were purchased from Russia in part with financing from Iran.

One of the main reasons Damascus did not retaliate after Israel carried out its September 6 air strike, one official said, was that

Syria's rocket infrastructure was not yet complete. After the Israeli strike, Syria picked up the pace of acquiring rockets and missiles, largely from Russia with Iranian backing. He said Syria is aiming to possess enough projectiles to fire over one hundred rockets per hour into Israel for a sustained period of time. A Jordanian official said that as of 2008 Syria had achieved its goal: "They have enough rockets to fire five thousand in the opening hours of a war and then sustain a prolonged missile and rocket campaign against Israel," the official told me.

Meanwhile, Olmert was not content with simply allowing Syria to attend prestigious conferences. In February 2008 he quietly launched indirect talks with Syria, through Turkish mediation, regarding renewed negotiations over an Israeli retreat from the Golan Heights. At the time, Olmert faced multiple criminal investigations for corruption and countrywide pressure to resign following his glaring failures of leadership during the Lebanon war. His government was becoming increasingly rudderless. He needed some reason to justify remaining in office. In a coalition largely with leftist parties favoring Israeli withdrawals, Olmert decided to launch intense negotiations with the Palestinians as well as talks with Syria. (The current Israeli administration under Benjamin Netanyahu has sent messages to Damascus that it would be willing eventually to continue peace talks with Syria, according to top sources working for Netanyahu.)

Syria's Bashar Assad was more than happy to oblige Olmert, even if the talks were otherwise useless. Already isolated by U.S. congressional sanctions, Assad was still facing down an international probe into the assassination of Hariri, murdered in a 2005 car bomb blast widely blamed on Syria. Further, Assad was coming under increasing fire for his open military alliance with Iran and for destabilizing Lebanon. Syria was fully implicated in a string of bombings and political assassinations in Lebanon that had targeted anti-Syrian politicians and leaders. Assad saw the negotiations with Israel as a way to ease international opposition to his regime and find his way back into the world community, preferably making as few concessions as possible.

That is exactly what happened. On May 21, 2008, Olmert's office and Assad's headquarters both publicly announced they were negotiating. Syrian Foreign Minister Walid Moallem then claimed that Olmert agreed to withdraw from the entire Golan. Olmert's office neither confirmed nor denied Moallem's claim. A Syrian source familiar with the negotiations told me at the time that Israel had not yet brought up Syria's relationships with Iran, Hezbollah, and Palestinian terrorist organizations. He said he assumed those relationships would be discussed in the future, while calling it "unlikely" that Syria would agree to cut ties with Iran. In other words, according to Syria, at least, Israel initiated the talks without setting as a precondition that Syria's relationships with Iran, Hezbollah, or Palestinian terrorists would end.

As soon as the talks were announced, Assad started fielding phone calls from European countries offering renewed diplomatic contact with his no-longer-untouchable regime. Just weeks later, Assad attended a French-initiated regional conference at which financial deals between Syria and the European Union were discussed. French President Nicolas Sarkozy promised Assad to make a state visit to Damascus, which he later did, and he immediately sent a delegation of high-level French businessmen and legislators to Syria in a major repudiation of U.S. sanctions imposed on Syria.

A furious Walid Jumblatt, the leader of Lebanon's Druze minority and a prominent anti-Syrian politician, in a personal interview accused Israel of "opening the doors of Europe to Assad. They have opened the door to Europe freely to Assad without mentioning his wrecking of Lebanon and the Hariri tribunal," he fumed at the time. "I am afraid Assad is now at ease, waiting for a new administration in the United States. President Bush will leave and then the isolation that was around Bashar will be over." Indeed, President Barack Obama has not disguised his willingness to directly engage with Syria and bring Damascus into the international fold.

John Bolton, former U.S. Ambassador to the United Nations, told me he "cannot understand" why Israel was negotiating with Syria while that country continued supporting terrorism. "Israel should be isolating the Syrian regime and working toward its replacement. The talks won't break the Iranian-Syrian connection," said Bolton. "I don't see the upside to talks that will grant the Ba'ath Party [led by Assad] longevity and legitimacy."

Not only did Israel summon Europe to Assad's doorstep, but apparently even the U.S. discussed with Syria a deal to bring Damascus back into the diplomatic arena. A senior Syrian official told me that offers were discussed wherein if the U.S. helped facilitate billions of dollars in business for Syria and built up Damascus as the primary American ally in the Arab world in place of Saudi Arabia, the Syrians would be willing to scale back alliances with Iran and make peace with Israel. The official said Syria recently conveyed this message to numerous visiting foreign dignitaries, including U.S. congressmen and Turkish mediators. He said Syria also demanded as a key condition for considering altering its alliances that the U.S. cease opposing Syrian influence in Lebanon. "Syria is the key to the Arab world," said the official, who spoke by phone from Damascus on condition his name be withheld. "We have influence with Hezbollah and Lebanon and hold many cards in the Palestinian and Iraqi arenas. The U.S. needs to rethink the value of the investment it places in Saudi Arabia." Security officials in Jerusalem confirmed their knowledge of the Syrian offers to the U.S., which they said prompted a major blowup between Syria and Saudi Arabia. The rift was highlighted at the March 2008 Arab Summit, a major annual meeting of Arab leaders held that year in Damascus. Saudi Arabia sent only a low-level representative—a major snub to Syria—and used the platform to blast Damascus. The Syrian official also told me he had received numerous messages from then-Senator Barack Obama's team that the U.S. would be ready to engage Syria in the near future, although the U.S. may not accept all Syrian demands.

ASSAD PLAYS THE RUSSIAN CARD

Syria, meanwhile, has essentially thumbed its nose at Western entreaties; instead, it has publicly enhanced its strategic relationship with Russia while doing nothing to diminish ties with Tehran. Sparking widespread fears of a major military buildup with its erstwhile Cold War partner in the region, the Syrian regime began receiving warships and advanced weaponry from Russia. In August 2008, Assad paid a two-day visit to Moscow, where he reportedly discussed with President Dmitry Medvedev ways to expand mutual military ties. Topping the Russian wish list was a revival of its Cold War-era naval bases on the Mediterranean at the Syrian ports of Tartus and Latakia. Moscow also maintained naval bases in Damascus during the Cold War but Russia's influence in the region weakened after the collapse of the Soviet Union. According to informed security sources, Syria struck a deal with Russia that allows Moscow to station submarines and warships off Tartus and Latakia. In exchange, Russia agreed to supply Syria with weaponry at bargain prices, including an advanced missile defense system as well as aircraft and anti-tank and anti-aircraft missiles. In Russia's *Kommersant* newspaper Assad rationalized that Russia's 2008 conflict with Georgia, in which Moscow says Georgian forces were trained by Israelis and utilized Israeli weapons and technology, gave ample reason for Russia and Syria to tighten their defense cooperation.[5] Israel denies that it trains or supplies arms to other countries, but says that private Israeli firms conduct equipment sales and training with the Israeli Defense Ministry's approval. Stated Assad: "I think that in Russia and in the world everyone is now aware of Israel's role and its military consultants in the Georgian crisis. And if before in Russia there were people who thought these forces can be friendly then now I think no one thinks that way. Of course military and technical cooperation is the main issue," said Assad. "Weapons purchases are very important. I think we should speed it up. Moreover, the West and Israel continue to put pressure on Russia."

While Israel has replaced the Olmert government, its extended romance with Syria has far-reaching consequences that continue today with the doors to the world opened to Damascus. A mainstay of Obama's presidential campaign was advocating dialogue with America's foes; and, beyond campaign rhetoric, he has put in prominent positions senior policy officials such as his envoy to the Mideast Dennis Ross, who has long petitioned for economic and diplomatic coordination with Syria.

THE JEWISH GOLAN HEIGHTS

While Syria has been partners with Russia and Iran, and has been embraced by Europe and the U.S., it has not lost sight of regaining the Golan Heights. Indeed, since 2006 in particular, Syria has been moving swiftly to reestablish its control of the territory, regarded by many as crucial to Israel's security.

The Golan Heights is a plateau and mountainous region of about 690 square miles, bordering Syria and Lebanon. Israel conquered it during the 1967 Six Day War, in which Syria joined other invading Arab armies in attacking the Jewish state, with Syria's line of attack running down the Golan. In 1981, Israel unilaterally annexed the Golan—meaning that the full regime of Israeli domestic law would henceforth apply there—although that move was not recognized by most of the international community. In forty years of the Golan being under Israel's control, there has been only one outbreak of major hostilities between the two countries—the 1973 Yom Kippur War—and that war would not have been much of an engagement had Syria not begun by first taking the Golan as a staging ground to attack Israel.

News media accounts routinely bill the Golan as having been "undisputed Syrian territory" until Israel "captured the region" in 1967. In actuality, the Golan has been out of Damascus's control for far longer than the nineteen years it was within its rule from 1948 to 1967. Even while Syria did briefly hold the Golan, some of it had been stolen from Jews. Jews purchased tens of thousands of acres of farmland on the Golan as far back as the late 1800s. The Turks of the Ottoman Empire kicked out some Jews around the turn of the century, but Jews still farmed some of the Golan until 1947, when Syria first became an independent state. Just before that, the territory transferred back and forth among France, Great Britain, and Turkey before it became a part of the French Mandate of Syria. When the French Mandate ended in 1944, the Golan Heights became part of the newly independent state of Syria, which quickly seized land worked by the Palestine Colonization Association (Jewish) and the Jewish Colonization Association. A year later, in 1948, Syria, along with other Arab countries, used the Golan to attack Israel in a war to destroy the newly formed Jewish state.

Despite this undisputed history, most people in the world today—even in Israel itself—think that the Golan Heights has always been a Syrian territory, that it is inarguably Syrian real estate.

The Golan is steeped in Jewish history and is connected to the Torah and to the periods of the First and Second Temples. The Torah referred to the Golan Heights as "Bashan"; the word "Golan" apparently derived from the biblical city of "Golan in Bashan." The book of Joshua relates how the Golan was assigned to the tribe of Menasheh. Later, during the time of the First Temple, King Solomon appointed three ministers in the region and the area became contested between the northern Jewish kingdom of Israel and the Aramean kingdom based in Damascus. The book of Kings relates how King Ahab of Israel defeated Ben-Hadad I of Damascus near the present-day site of Kibbutz Afik in the southern Golan, and the prophet Elisha foretold that King Jehoash of Israel would defeat Ben-Hadad III of Damascus, also near Kibbutz Afik. The online Jewish Virtual Library has an excellent account of how in the late sixth and fifth centuries BC the Golan was settled by Jewish exiles returning from Babylonia, modern day Iraq. In the mid-second century BC, Judah Maccabee's grandnephew, the Hasmonean King Alexander Jannai, added the Golan Heights to his kingdom.[6]

Gamla (now the namesake of a fine Israeli wine) became the Golan's "capital city" and was the area's last Jewish stronghold to resist the Romans during the Great Revolt in which the Second Temple was destroyed. The revolt at first succeeded, until Rome dispatched its top general, Vespasian, who conquered the Golan city by Jewish city. Despite the ultimate failure of their revolt, Jewish communities on the Heights survived, and even flourished. The Golan hosted some of the most important houses of Torah study in the years following the Second Temple's destruction and subsequent Jewish exile; some of Judaism's most revered ancient rabbis are buried in the territory. The remains of some twenty-five synagogues from the period between the Jewish revolt and the Islamic conquest in AD 636 have been excavated. The Golan is dotted with ancient Jewish villages.

Today the Heights has a population of about thirty-five thousand—roughly eighteen thousand Jewish residents and seventeen thousand Arabs, mostly Druze. The Arab residents retain their Syrian citizenship, but under Israeli law can also sue for Israeli citizenship. Based on many reports I filed from the Golan, I would say that more than half the territory's Arab residents are happy to live under Israeli rule, while the others are Syrian nationalists who would prefer Assad as their president.

On September 27, 2006, Assad issued a decree urging his citizens to move to the Golan Heights, claiming the International Committee of the Red Cross, or ICRC, would help flood the Golan with Syrians. The text of the decree, which I obtained, urged Syrian officials, humanitarian workers, public service providers, and their families to move to the Golan with the help of the ICRC. Assad's signed statement said Syrians who wished to move to the Golan would be granted approval by "all the relevant authorities." A United Nations contingent monitors Golan border zones. The ICRC has authority to operate in the area purportedly in humanitarian cases to facilitate civilian crossings into and out of Syria. Israel must approve any cases of Syrian residents moving to the Golan. The Red Cross can also petition for entry for Syrian aid workers assisting its programs.

Dorothia Krimitsas, a spokeswoman for the ICRC, told me her organization is "neutral" and seeks to help Syrians only in "humanitarian cases." "We are aware of Assad's decree [for Syrians to move to the Golan via the Red Cross] but we are a nonpolitical organization. We help facilitate movement between Syria and the Golan in humanitarian cases, like weddings and important unions," said Krimitsas, speaking from Geneva. To the contrary, Jerusalem officials have long accused the ICRC of anti-Israel bias. For nearly sixty years the organization refused membership to Israel purportedly because the Jewish state wanted to use its own emblem—a Star of David—instead of the traditional cross or Muslim crescent. Only after years of intensive lobbying efforts by the American Red Cross and millions of dollars allocated toward cooperation was Israel finally admitted in 2006. The ICRC also, anomalously, treated Hezbollah fighters on the battlefield during the 2006 Second Lebanon War. Some Israeli military officials accused Red Cross ambulances of helping transport Hezbollah fighters. "The moment a Hezbollah fighter is injured, he is considered a noncombatant, so we must take care of him," said an ICRC spokeswoman, Carla Haddad.[7] During a major Israeli anti-terror raid in the northern West Bank city of Jenin in 2002, the ICRC along with the Palestinian Authority and the UN accused the Jewish state of attacking civilians and denying medical treatment to injured Palestinians for six days. The charges later were comprehensively disproved.

Assad in recent years has significantly escalated his government's involvement in the Golan Heights. Israeli officials have told me that in 2006 Assad started paying official state salaries to some Golan public workers, principally public teachers. Until then, most Golan public workers, including teachers and local officers, drew salaries from Israel, although a few public officials have been collecting salaries from Syria since the 1970s. This story was reported only by me and was not picked up by the Israeli news media. Then, a Syrian official informed me that top members of Assad's Ba'ath Party were advised in a private briefing to purchase real estate in the Golan Heights because, they were told, the strategic territory will "very soon" be returned to Syria. "This is not a political recommendation. It was made in private to top officials because it is absolutely estimated that Syria will very soon get the Golan Heights back," the official said. "We've been instructed to purchase what will become prime real estate for us."

And so, due to almost farcical Israeli missteps and myopia, Syria finds itself a team player in the world community, all the while fully in partnership with Iran, Hezbollah, and Palestinian terrorists. At present, it is consistently arming itself to the hilt with rockets and missiles capable of devastating Israel. It moves to reassert its role on the Golan Heights—territory vital for Israel's security, but that Damascus expects to regain in the near future, including under the new Benjamin Netanyahu regime.

CHAPTER TWELVE

IRAN PURSUES ARMAGEDDON

Of all the grave security threats facing Israel today, Iran is by far the single greatest. Controlled by a fanatical regime of Shi'ite Muslim revolutionaries, Iran today is a semi-fascistic country of more than 65 million whose leaders routinely threaten to annihilate the Jewish state. Its nuclear program, on the brink of weaponization, is clearly intended for hostile purposes. Among global political analysts, no one doubts that a nuclear Iran would be a game changer. It would irrevocably alter the balance of power in the Middle East, placing Tehran and all of its proxies (Syria, Hezbollah, Hamas) under the protection of a nuclear umbrella, and would give Iran the technical option of wiping Israel off the map.

Iran's nuclear program is not a threat to Israel alone. Tehran could easily strike U.S. military installations in the Middle East with its existing missile arsenal, including Shehab-3 medium-range ballistic missiles, which experts deem fully capable of reaching all U.S. bases in the Gulf. Iran is further said to be developing missiles capable of reaching Western Europe and eventually even the U.S. mainland, according to many experts. Of grave concern is the fact that Iran would always have the option of transferring nuclear material to any organization to carry out an attack anywhere in the world. Prudent consideration points to Salafist groups in North Africa, Lashkar-e-Toiba in India, Jemaa Islamiya or Abu Sayyaf groups throughout Southeast Asia, al-Qaida in Central Asia and throughout Western Europe, Shining Path in Peru or narcoterrorists in Colombia, and, of course, Hezbollah and Hamas. Despite its repeated calls for Israel's destruction, Iran has so successfully marketed its brand of Shi'ite belligerence as being a threat only to the Jewish state that many in Europe and the U.S. seem either to have resigned themselves to a nuclear Iran or to hope that feisty little Israel will somehow take care of the problem.

In December 2007, the U.S. intelligence establishment hoisted what could only be viewed by Tehran as an American white flag. Faced with an Iranian regime on the verge of obtaining nuclear weapons, the U.S. government released one of its occasional National Intelligence Estimates, this one said to represent the consensus view of all sixteen American spy agencies. In an opening salvo that left astute readers thunderstruck, the 2007 NIE judged with "high confidence" that Iran had halted its nuclear weapons program in 2003. The synopsis of the report judged with "moderate confidence" that Iran had not restarted its nuclear weapons program as of mid-2007. "But we do not know whether [Iran] currently intends to develop nuclear weapons," stated the NIE report.[1]

This document of vital importance totaled nine pages. The first page was a colored cover with no information. Four more pages provided the background history of the NIE, with just one page focusing on the scope of the report on Iran and another page, including a coded chart, on how to read the report. One page compared the report to a previous estimate. Only two pages of the NIE focused on the report's key judgments on Iran, which were worded as blanket statements and were not supported in the report by any specific information. The NIE also related that some intelligence agencies judged Iran could produce enough enriched fissile material to make a nuclear weapon by 2010—in line with some Israeli estimates—while other agencies, including the State Department's Intelligence and Research Office, believed that the earliest time Iran could likely have enough enriched uranium to produce a bomb would be 2013.

The release of the 2007 NIE was a bombshell that effectively ended any chance the U.S. would force a showdown with Tehran over its nuclear program. The report's publication was followed by a series of largely ineffectual international trade sanctions lobbed against Iran. Half a year later, in July 2008, the U.S. sent William Burns, then third in line at the State Department and a proponent of engagement with Tehran, to meet Iran's main nuclear negotiator, Saeed Jalili, in the highest-level American diplomatic contact with Iran since the humiliating U.S. embassy hostage crisis of 1979.[2] Iran duly noted the change in U.S. attitudes toward its regime and made clear that under no circumstances would it halt its nuclear ambitions or fully cooperate with international inspectors.

The window is swiftly closing for a successful military strike to set back Tehran's nuclear program. Israel has warned that Iran may receive Russia's advanced S-300 anti-aircraft missile system by mid-2009. The presidential victory of Barack Obama, who campaigned on a platform of dialogue and direct negotiations with Iran, sent the Tehran regime a signal that the American people have resigned themselves to Iran's nuclear ambitions or at least plan to present the carrot without the stick. While the election in Israel of Benjamin Netanyahu, who made curbing the Iranian nuclear threat the major platform of his campaign, likely sent shivers done the spines of the Ayatollahs, Netanyahu must contend with a U.S. president who wants to engage Iran and may not support Israeli action against Tehran.

THE IRANIAN NOOSE

Meanwhile, Iran has tied a noose around Israel's neck that U.S.-Israeli policy has actually been strengthening in recent years. I am referring to concessions to Iran's proxy war, which is killing Jews and strangling Israel at the country's borders. The Islamic Republic is the principal military sponsor of the Ba'athist regime in Syria. Iran also directs, funds, arms, and trains the Lebanese Hezbollah south-facing combat group on Israel's northern border. Iran is the main financial and military backer of the Palestinian terrorist organizations that border the Jewish state's major population centers.

In March 2008 the head of Israel's Shin Bet Security Services, Yuval Diskin, told the Knesset that Hamas, committed to the obliteration of Israel, had "started to dispatch people to Iran, tens and a promise of hundreds" to receive advanced military training.[3] The testimony prompted a skeptical reaction from a reporter for London's *Sunday Times*. She took the trouble to pull an Aaron Klein and query a senior "commander" of Hamas's Izzedine al-Qassam Brigades, the killer assemblage so-called military wing proud to be responsible for hundreds of suicide bombings, shootings, rocket attacks, and cross-borders raids. The unnamed Hamas official not only confirmed to the *Sunday Times* that Iran was indeed providing training for his group—which he said had been taking place since Israel's 2005 disengagement from Gaza—but suggested that Diskin had actually understated the nature of Iran's relationship with Hamas.

The "commander," who withheld his name since he said he was a target of Israeli forces, told the *Sunday Times* that Hamas had been sending fighters to Iran for training in field tactics and weapons technology. He said some Hamas members travel to Syria for more basic training.[4] "We have sent seven 'courses' of our fighters to Iran," he said. "During each course, the group receives training that he will use to increase our capacity to fight." The most promising members of each group stay longer for an advanced course and return to the Gaza Strip as trainers themselves, the Hamas representative claimed.

The goal in Gaza is to build Hezbollah-like guerrilla armies capable of waging a serious proxy war for Iran against Israel. Israeli security officials note with increasing concern that Hamas in recent years has groomed a well-organized militia resembling an army—complete with battalions, companies, platoons, special forces for surveillance, snipers, and explosive experts. According to *bona fide* terrorist sources in Gaza with whom I spoke, a major part of Hamas's success is due to aid from Iran. One senior terrorist told me his group is receiving help from the Iranian proxy Hezbollah to import long-range rockets and train in guerrilla warfare tactics. "We have warm relations with Hezbollah, which helps with some of the training programs," the informant said. "We don't have anything to be ashamed of—that we are dealing with Hezbollah and that we are receiving training and information from them." He said Hezbollah maintains cells in the Egyptian Sinai desert, which adjoins Gaza. "The Sinai is an excellent ground for training, the exchange of information and weapons, and for meetings on how to turn every piece of land into usable territory for a confrontation with Israel."

Iran apparently trains Palestinian terrorists not only in its own country, in Syria, and in the Sinai, but also within Gaza itself. Before Hamas humiliated the Palestinian Authority and President Mahmoud Abbas's U.S.-backed Fatah organization by kicking them out of Gaza in June 2007, PA forces claimed to have captured seven Iranian military trainers—including a general of the Iranian Revolutionary Guards—at a purported Hamas training facility in the Gaza Strip. Fatah officials told me that a raid of the Hamas-dominated Islamic University in Gaza (to be later targeted by Israel) yielded the Iranian agents one thousand Qassam rockets and equipment to manufacture the Qassams. According to the Fatah officials, one of the Iranian agents attempted suicide prior to his capture.

Nor is Iran's backing of Palestinian terrorism within Israel limited to Hamas. Israel's "peace partner," Fatah, is in bed with Tehran, too. I personally know of numerous al-Aqsa Martyrs Brigades members who work as paid links between Fatah and the Iranian-backed Hezbollah. Some of those Brigades men moonlight from Fatah's official security forces, which receive hundreds of millions of dollars per year in U.S. and international aid.

In March 2006, the al-Aqsa Martyrs Brigades in Gaza announced the importation of new, longer-range Qassam rockets aimed at the Jewish state. Abu Ahmed, a Gaza-based leader of the Brigades who had been involved in coordinating the group's missile network, told me the new rockets were named after the Iranian Shehab missile and dedicated to Iranian President Mahmoud Ahmadinejad "because of his courageous position toward the enemy."

Several times, Palestinians in Gaza have fired Grad rockets at the strategic port city of Ashkelon, home to some 125,000 Israelis. (Ashkelon also houses a major electrical plant that powers most of the Gaza Strip.) Grad rockets are longer-range projectiles similar to the Katyusha rocket, which Hezbollah successfully deployed during the 2006 Second Lebanon War to barrage northern Israel. Israel has said the Grad rockets were transferred into Gaza by Iran.

Israeli security officials also say Iran directly pays for Palestinian attacks on Israelis. Security officials in 2006 intercepted a series of communications, including phone calls and e-mails, between Hezbollah and West Bank Fatah terrorists revealing that

Hezbollah had been trying to recruit Fatah suicide bombers to carry out attacks. One security official told me at the time that previously intercepted bank transactions suggested that Hezbollah had raised its cash offers to Palestinian terrorists and was willing to pay $100,000 for a suicide bombing operation. In the past, information indicated that Hezbollah paid only $20,000 for such attacks. Major General Yaacov Amidror, former head of Israel's military intelligence research, told me, "The money comes straight from Iran. At one point, we had information Iran once told Islamic Jihad if they didn't carry out a suicide attack within sixty days, they would cut back their funding. That just illustrates the kind of relationship Tehran has with them. Also with Hezbollah."

At other times, Palestinian carnage groups act as wholly-owned subsidiaries of Iran. Iran is accused of directly ordering multiple Palestinian attacks, including border raids and rocket firings, which at times have visibly supported strategic objectives for Tehran. One example is the daring June 2006 cross-border raid from Gaza, in which Hamas and two allied mercenary groups kidnapped Israeli infantryman Gilad Shalit. Israeli security officials said that Iranian Revolutionary Guard units and Hezbollah guerrillas trained the terrorists who carried out the raid and Shalit's ensuing abduction. The kidnapping prompted a major Israeli troop call-up in which Prime Minister Ehud Olmert allowed some ground troops to enter the Gaza Strip in the first significant Israeli incursion into Gaza since Israel's withdrawal one year earlier. That Israeli retaliation drew a firestorm of international media attention and furious condemnations from world leaders. The focus on Israel was a welcomed distraction for Iran, which itself was facing mounting international pressure against its regime and from a world summit that had been set to focus on Iran's suspected illicit nuclear program but instead also dealt with the Gaza violence.

COMMON ENEMY

There are, of course, major ideological differences between the Palestinian organized terrorist groups, who are Sunni Muslims, and their sponsor and handler Iran, which is dominated by the Shi'ite

Islamic denomination. Shia Muslims believe that Muhammad's progeny—the Twelve Imams—were the best sources of knowledge about the Koran and Islam, and were the most trustworthy carriers and protectors of Islamic tradition. They believe in a dynasty of Islamic authorities and promote a hereditary class of spiritual leaders who, they believe, have divine powers.

Sunni Muslims in part follow the teachings of Muslim *caliphs* who proclaimed their leadership after Muhammad's passing, but were not his blood relatives. The *caliphs* interpreted important parts of Muhammad's *hadith*—or oral tradition—that Shias reject. Sunni Muslims make up about 85 percent of Muslims worldwide.

The largest sect of the Shias, called the Twelvers, believe that of the Twelve Imams after Muhammad, the twelfth and last one, born in 868 AD, is the Imam Mahdi who still lives, but cannot be seen until Allah determines it is time to prepare the faithful for Judgment Day. The Twelvers count current Iranian president Mahmoud Ahmadinejad among their faithful. They believe Imam Mahdi will return to lead the forces of righteousness against the forces of evil in a final, apocalyptic world battle. Some Middle East analysts attribute Ahmadinejad's pursuit of nuclear weapons in large part to a desire to precipitate the final, Mahdi-led battle. In a speech in Tehran in November 2006, Ahmadinejad said his main mission is to "pave the path for the glorious reappearance of Imam Mahdi, may Allah hasten his reappearance." His cabinet has reportedly given $17 million to the Jamkaran Mosque, site of a well, at which Shia Muslims believe the Mahdi disappeared over a thousand years ago.[5]

Palestinian terrorist groups do not share Ahmadinejad's Shia beliefs. I once talked to a senior Hamas leader who said that he quietly fears the spread of Shia values under the Iranian umbrella. Nonetheless, Palestinian organizations willingly and openly cooperate with Iran since they share a common hatred for Israel.

INDOCTRINATING CHILDREN

The Palestinians are just one arm of the Iranian proxy war against the Jewish state. Hezbollah, which like Iran practices a fundamentalist form of Shia Islam, is another. A look at just a small section of Hezbollah—the group's youth militia, called the Mahdi Scouts—illustrates the symbiotic relationship between Iran and the Lebanese militia. Hezbollah's Mahdi Scouts was established in 1982 and operates under the jurisdiction of the Lebanese Ministry of Education. According to Israel's Center for Special Studies, a think tank specializing in terrorism information and analysis, the Scouts has about forty-two thousand Lebanese males and females between the ages of eight and sixteen, organized into 499 groups.[6] Hezbollah's forty-two thousand Mahdi Scouts reportedly undergo military training at summer camps in Shi'ite communities in Beirut, the Bekaa Valley, and South Lebanon. At these youth camps, Scouts learn the basic use of arms along with physical training and marching exercises while dressed in Scout uniforms or camouflage suits. An investigative report published in August 2006 by the Egyptian daily *Ruz al-Yusuf* claimed the first lesson Hezbollah teaches its Scouts is the destruction of Israel. "[This lesson] is always an important part of the curriculum and is always aimed at children and adolescents who are new to the program. [The objective is to train a] high-caliber Islamic generation of children who would be willing to sacrifice themselves for the sake of Allah in the campaign against Israel," *Ruz al-Yusuf* reported.[7]

The Center for Special Studies analyzed scores of documents and material captured by the Israeli Defense Forces during the 2006 Second Lebanon War and found that the major activities at Mahdi Scouts summer camps, including sports and social programs, aim to inculcate Iranian Islamic revolutionary principles into Scout members—some as young as eight years old. The material revealed that Iranian Revolutionary Guard units played a central role in establishing the Mahdi Scouts and their regular programs and summer camps. The Center said a large volume of materials collected in Lebanon by the IDF "illustrates how members of Hezbollah's youth movement had been indoctrinated with the principles of the Iranian Islamic revolution and the personality cult of [the Supreme Iranian leader] Ali Khomeini."[8] Among the scouting literature discovered were books and magazines glorifying Khomeini as a hero worthy of emulation. That emulation is evident at all levels of Hezbollah, whose leaders regularly travel to Iran and whose militia is reportedly trained, armed, and funded by Tehran, with managerial help from Syria.

According to Israeli security officials with whom I spoke, Iran completely controls and directs all branches of Hezbollah. The self-congratulatory Lebanese paramilitary group cannot make a single major decision—political, military, or social—without first securing Iranian approval. The working relationship between Tehran and Hezbollah is so close that during the Second Lebanon War there were reports, some of which originated with this reporter, that Iranian Revolutionary Guards were fighting Israeli soldiers alongside Hezbollah. In late July 2006, various trusted sources told me that Revolutionary Guard units stationed in Lebanon had fired some of Hezbollah's missiles and rockets. In a well-circulated report, on July 23, Lebanese sources told me that between six and nine Iranian Revolutionary Guards, killed in clashes with Israel, were taken by truck into Syria for flight back to Iran.[9] They said the bodies were transported along with tens of thousands of Lebanese civilians fleeing Lebanon into Syria.

SYRIA REPORTS TO IRANIAN MASTERS

The Ba'athist regime of Syria, which evinces many qualities of Soviet tyranny and manages to integrate plainly fascist principles, is also a client state of Iran. As discussed in the previous chapter, Iran has for years shipped large quantities of rockets and missiles to Damascus. The Syrian president, Bashar al-Assad, has been known to maintain a regular Iranian liaison (read: handler) by his side. According to Israeli military sources, Iran has been working since 2006 to overhaul Syria's military to the point where many top Syrian military commanders now report directly to Tehran. The sources said that even if Assad wanted to make peace with Israel he could not do so since Iran could use its control to stage a military coup.

Iran's sponsorship of Israel's encircling enemies provides Tehran the ability to mount a massive, coordinated response to any Israeli strike against its nuclear program, without Iran visibly attacking the Jewish state directly. Indeed, Palestinian terrorists interviewed for this book claimed that Iran is anticipating an Israeli military strike on its nuclear facilities, and has been providing Palestinian terrorists and other regional allies with contingency plans for attacks against Israel and American regional interests in the event of war. One Islamic Jihad terrorist in the West Bank claimed that during any Israeli strike on Iran his organization has been directed to "wreak havoc" on Israel with suicide bombings, rocket attacks, and "special surprises." He said rocket attacks would be launched from both the Gaza Strip and from the West Bank, which borders Jerusalem. He also threatened that his column would target American interests in the Middle East whether a strike against Tehran were carried out by Israel or by the U.S. "The Zionists and the Americans are coordinated 100 percent. It doesn't matter who attacks Iran, we are planning to hit them both," said the Islamic Jihad leader, who spoke on condition of anonymity, because he said the topic was "very sensitive."

Muhammad Abdel-Al, spokesman for the very active, Hamas-allied Popular Resistance Committees in Gaza, told me that during any U.S. or Israeli military strike against Tehran, a response would be directed against Israel and American interests by Iran, Syria, Hezbollah, and Palestinian terrorists combined. "The war will be a war on more than one front. It will be everybody against everybody. Iran, Syria, Hezbollah, and the Palestinian organizations will work together. War with Iran is coming and it means the Middle East will not remain the same after it," the Committees leader said.

These claims should not be chalked up merely to boastful rhetoric. Were it launched, a combined onslaught by Syria, Hezbollah, and the multiple Palestinian gangs and trained terrorists could place the entire Jewish state under sustained rocket onslaught. The Israeli Air Force would need to work quickly to preempt as many rocket and missile attacks as possible by taking out any known locations of missile and rocket storage and launch sites, but a large number of rockets would no doubt get through, as they did during the Second Lebanon War and when Israel went to war in Gaza two years later.

Israeli security officials said the greatest threat that Syria poses to the Jewish state is now from its missiles. They noted that Syria recently test fired two Scud-D surface-to-surface missiles, which have a range of about 250 miles, covering most Israeli territory. The officials said that the Syrian missile test was coordinated with Iran and is believed to have been successful. It is not known with what type of warhead the missiles were armed. In addition to longer-range Scuds, Syria is in possession of shorter-range missiles such as 220mm and 305mm rockets, although some of these have been passed on to Hezbollah.

Since the 2006 war, Hezbollah has completely replenished its rocket arsenal. Hezbollah chief Hassan Nasrallah has several times warned that Israel faces a "colossal surprise" in any future war with his organization. Any Israeli attempt to attack Lebanon "will be faced with a colossal surprise likely to change the fate of the war and the region," Nasrallah said in August 2007.[10] Nasrallah has repeated that threat on numerous other occasions, as have other Hezbollah figures. According to informed sources with whom I spoke, the "surprise" Nasrallah is referring to is his group's new ability to fire missiles that can target Israel's international airport.

This information about Iran's proxies readying for combat comes as Ahmadinejad has made clear that his country's nuclear program will not be halted. "Iran has obtained the technology to produce nuclear fuel and Iran's move is like a train…which has no brake and no reverse gear," Ahmadinejad said in February 2007, according to Iranian state media.[11] Manouchehr Mohammadi, a deputy at Iran's foreign ministry, commented, "We have prepared ourselves for any situation, even for war."[12] Iranian military commanders have said recent military displays demonstrate Iran's readiness to counter any attack.

I am not arguing here against a military strike targeting Iran's nuclear sites. Such strikes were necessary against Iraq (in 1981) and Syria (in 2007), and would seem to be the only hope of halting or seriously delaying Tehran's nuclear program. I am only pointing to Tehran's consolidation of proxies targeting Israel which, if not neutralized, can lead to disaster. With Syria, Hezbollah, and the Palestinian combat corps in place, and with negotiations afoot to create what in all likelihood would eventually become a Hamas-led state in most of the West Bank and perhaps even eastern Jerusalem, Iran's ability to wreak havoc on Israel while it pursues sufficient means utterly to destroy the Jewish state grows stronger by the day.

CHAPTER THIRTEEN

HAMAS HANDSHAKE ON WHITE HOUSE LAWN?

The embrace of Hamas is unfolding at a feverish pace, even while it has made clear its goal is the destruction of Israel. This has far-reaching, dangerous ramifications for the Jewish state. It means a growing segment of the international community is willing to cede power and legitimacy to Israel's mortal enemy without demanding it first renounce its lethal goals. Several factors have coalesced to create a perfect storm to provide the terrorism *cadre* with international legitimacy.

In December 2006, I interviewed the chief political advisor to Hamas Prime Minister Ismail Haniyeh. The advisor, Ahmed Yousef, told me that Hamas officials had already met in Europe with high-ranking American figures, "especially members of the Democratic party." He then also claimed that Hamas had met with European leaders, including members of the British Parliament. Yousef did not specify exactly when the meetings took place, nor with which members of the Democratic Party the State Department-sanctioned terrorist group had supposedly met, but he claimed the meetings were "fruitful" in introducing the Hamas "political vision" to the international community.

Fast forward fifteen months to April 2008, when former U.S. President Jimmy Carter toured the Middle East and held court with Hamas's most senior leadership in the West Bank, the Gaza Strip, and Syria. Hamas sources told me the meetings with the Democrats in 2006 had been feelers, initiated by Carter's people, that led to the ex-president's solidarity visit with Hamas less than a year and a half later. In his visit to the West Bank, Carter attended a reception with the Hamas leader Nasser Shaer. Shaer is a former deputy prime minister and education minister in the Hamas-led Palestinian government (later unilaterally disbanded by the rival Fatah faction in 2007). Shaer also served a sentence in Israeli prison for terrorist activities. Hamas's reception for Carter was closed to the news media, but according to participants, and to Shaer himself, Carter hugged Shaer and kissed him on each cheek, the customary Islamic greeting for friends, although many U.S. diplomats refrain from kissing Palestinian officials. "He gave me a hug. We hugged each other, and it was a warm reception," Shaer told the Associated Press.[1] "Carter asked what he can do to achieve peace between the Palestinians and Israel...and I told him the possibility for peace is high." One day after embracing Shaer, Carter traveled to Egypt (since Israel denied him direct access to Gaza), where he met with the Gaza Strip's senior Hamas leaders Mahmoud al-Zahar and Saeed Seyam. The two men are identified by both Israeli and Palestinian security officials as the most important leaders of Hamas's so-called military wing—in reality its anti-civilian terrorism wing—which carries out suicide bombings, border raids, kidnappings, shooting attacks, and rocket launchings aimed from Gaza at Jewish population centers.

Al-Zahar is both chief of Hamas in Gaza and leader of its most radical faction, besides being commander of its paramilitary trained primarily to fire at or blow up unarmed civilians or Israeli soldiers. He served as foreign minister in the Hamas-led Palestinian government. Israeli officials say al-Zahar is more radical than Khaled Meshaal, Hamas's overall chief, who resides in exile in Syria. At a rally in March 2007, al-Zahar told a crowd of thousands that Hamas's short-term goal is "to liberate Palestine. Our final goal, which will be achieved, is that Islam will enter every house and will spread all over the world."[2]

Saeed Seyam oversees Hamas's so-called Executive Force, the group's main militia. He served as Hamas's interior minister, and then was one of the main architects of Hamas's takeover of the Gaza Strip in June 2007, when it expelled the U.S.-backed Fatah organization, overtaking all Fatah security compounds and reportedly seizing American weapons. Seyam would later be eliminated by Israel during its twenty-two-day war in Gaza ending January 2009.

CARTER'S ELUSIVE BREAKTHROUGH

Carter initiated the meeting with al-Zahar and Seyam, Hamas's spokesman Fawzi Barhoum told me. Carter glowingly announced that al-Zahar and Seyam would accept a "peace agreement" if the Palestinians approved it in a referendum. Al-Zahar, however, later qualified in an article published by the *Washington Post* that even to begin peace talks with Israel, the Jewish state would have first to withdraw from "all the land" it occupied in the 1967 war— meaning the Golan Heights, the Gaza Strip, the West Bank, and eastern Jerusalem, including the Old City, and the Temple Mount; release all Palestinian prisoners held in Israeli jails, and end its "air, sea, and land blockade of Palestinian land."[3] These concessions, al-Zahar stressed, would not result in a "peace agreement"; instead, the retreats are necessary preconditions to start negotiations.

Carter went on to Syria to meet with Hamas's overall chief, Khaled Meshaal. Afterward, Carter triumphantly announced his mediation efforts had been successful—Hamas agreed to a ten-year truce in exchange for Israel withdrawing to the pre-1967 borders. "There's no doubt that both the Arab world and the Palestinians, including Hamas, will accept Israel's right to live in peace within the 1967 borders," Carter told reporters effusively at a press conference.[4]

But Hamas chieftain Khaled Meshaal was more reserved: "We agree to a [Palestinian] state on pre-'67 borders, with Jerusalem as its capital, with genuine sovereignty, without settlements, but without recognizing Israel."[5]

"We have offered a truce if Israel withdraws to the 1967 borders, a truce of ten years," Meshaal said. Meshaal did not repeat Carter's assertion about accepting Israel's right to live in peace. Rather, he agreed to accept a Hamas state along pre-1967 borders, "without recognizing Israel."

Hamas spokesman Barhoum clarified to me that in order for any truce to take effect, Israel would need to evacuate "every centimeter of the West Bank and every centimeter of east Jerusalem." Those pre-1967 borders would leave Israel with a truncated state, difficult or impossible to defend. A well-known 1967 report by the U.S. Joint Chiefs of Staff argued in a memorandum to the Defense Department that to ensure its security, Israel must retain control of much of the Golan and "the prominent high ground [of the West Bank] running north-south." The report has since been upheld by over one hundred retired U.S. generals and admirals. No Israeli-Palestinian peace plans, even those drafted by extreme leftist Israeli parties such as Meretz, call for the Jewish state to evacuate the entire West Bank, citing security concerns for retaining at least a small portion of the territory.

In an interview, another Hamas spokesman in Gaza further upped the ante. The Jewish state must allow "all Palestinian refugees" to "return" to Israel as a precondition for any Israeli-Hamas truce, Sami Abu Zuhri told me. The "right of return" for millions of "Palestinian refugees" is a formula that Israeli officials across the political spectrum recognize as a code for Israel's destruction by flooding the Jewish state with millions of generationally-expatriated Arabs, thereby eliminating its Jewish majority.

In the end, Carter's truce boiled down to Israel withdrawing to indefensible borders and accepting millions of Arabs who would destroy Israel from within, all in exchange for a promise by Hamas to refrain from terrorist attacks for a period of ten years. Carter actually achieved nothing new: Hamas has been floating that exact truce proposal for years. In January 2007, for example, the prime minister of the Hamas-led Palestinian government, Ismail Haniyeh, announced that Hamas was willing to accept a temporary Palestinian state in the West Bank, the Gaza Strip, and eastern sections of Jerusalem in exchange for a ten-year truce with Israel.[6] He stressed that Hamas would not give up "liberating" all of Palestine. "We are for liberating any inch of Palestine, but we will not close the door for the next generation, because the weak don't always stay weak, and the strong won't stay strong," Haniyeh said in a televised address. At the same time Haniyeh was outlining his truce position, a Hamas spokesman told me that Hamas was still working to destroy the entire state of Israel. "Hamas will be able to free most of the territories of the historical Palestine occupied in 1948 [the state of Israel] and bring back the Palestinian refugees to their lands and houses," said Hamad al-Ruqb. "This step will be followed by a struggle to release the rest of the lands that will remain under occupation." He added that Hamas has a ten-year plan to defeat Israel that includes setting up a massive army composed of all Palestinian factions that would train for a period of ten years.

Haniyeh accurately used the term *hudna* to describe a truce with Israel, as had Meshaal during Carter's mediation efforts. The word was used by Muhammad in the Koran when he declared a ten-year "truce" with the Quraysh tribe that controlled Mecca. Two years later, Muhammad acquired enough troops and arms to conquer Mecca, so he abrogated the *hudna* eight years early, waging war and defeating the Quraysh tribe. Muslims thus understand that a *hudna* is truce of convenience, to be abrogated whenever advantageous to a righteous Muslim cause. The word does not carry the Western-language connotation of preparation for peaceful coexistence.

Carter's meetings with Meshaal, al-Zahar, and other Hamas figures marked the highest-profile encounter between that terrorist group and a Western figure until that point. It opened the floodgates for other countries to initiate relations with Hamas, in direct defiance of official U.S. and Israeli efforts to isolate them. On March 19, 2008, the French Foreign Minister, Bernard Kouchner, confirmed that Paris had held talks with Hamas. "These are not relations, they are contacts," Kouchner told Europe 1 radio.[7] "We are not the only ones to have them." Hamas spokesman Ashraf Barhoum announced Hamas had "met a delegation from the European Parliament, and they are supporting the Palestinian legitimate rights and Palestinian democracy; and they emphasized their full support for Hamas, because Hamas is the democratic choice for the Palestinians."[8]

"There was a delegation from France, the government," Barhoum said, speaking from Gaza, "and from Italy and Norway and from the EU parliament and from Carter. All of these are supporting Hamas, and they have a plan to support Palestinian rights and interests." The Hamas spokesman claimed there were "several meetings between Hamas and Europe, and they want finally to support Hamas." Barhoum would not name any of the EU officials he claimed had met with Hamas.[9]

The EU, for its part, denied any talks with the proscribed terrorist group. The Italian government also denied that its officials had met with Hamas. In August 2007, however, the Italian Prime Minister, Romano Prodi, broke with EU official policy by stating, "Hamas exists. It's a complex structure that we should help to evolve—but this should be done with transparency. One must push for dialogue so that it happens, and not shut anyone out."[10] Norway's deputy foreign minister, Raymond Johansan, admitted meeting with Hamas's chief leader Haniyeh.[11]

Hamas explicitly credited Carter's visit for breaking its international isolation. Hamas's chief political advisor told me, "His visit is a good step and a positive step in the right direction. It would engage with the world community. To what degree he succeeds depends on the people in Europe and the U.S," said Ahmed Yousef, just prior to Carter's visit.

OBAMA: HAMAS HAS "LEGITIMATE CLAIMS"

Hamas was formed in 1987 as a violent offshoot of the Egyptian Muslim Brotherhood, which seeks to establish an Islamic state first in Egypt and then around the world. The U.S. State Department classifies Hamas as a terrorist group, because it is responsible for scores of deadly suicide bombings and thousands of shooting attacks and rocket firings aimed at Israeli civilians. Hamas's official charter states that Israel "will exist and will continue to exist until Islam will obliterate it, just as it obliterated others before it." It defines the entire land of Palestine as "an Islamic *Waqf* [trust] consecrated for future Muslim generations until Judgment Day. It, or any part of it, should not be squandered; it, or any part of it, should not be given up." Rejecting any possibility of negotiations leading to peace with the Jewish state, the charter declares, "There is no solution for the Palestinian question except through jihad. Initiatives, proposals, and international conferences are all a waste of time and vain endeavors." The charter further claims that Zionists created the French Revolution, the Russian Revolution, European colonialism, and both world wars. It also claims that the Freemason and Rotary clubs are Zionist fronts. It warns that Israel is an expansionist regime that "aspire[s] to expand from the Nile to the Euphrates. When they will have digested the region they overtook, they will aspire to further expansion, and so on. Their plan is embodied in the *Protocols of the Elders of Zion,* and their present conduct is the best proof of what we are saying."

Jimmy Carter may be the most radical example to date, but he is by far not the only important American to imply that Hamas is legitimate. During numerous unscripted interviews with reporters, Secretary of State Condoleezza Rice referred to Hamas as a "resistance" movement. Meeting in November 2007 with the *Dallas Morning News* editorial board, Rice was asked by a reporter if supporting democracy in the Middle East was really in U.S. interests, citing the Palestinian elections that Hamas had dominated. Rice replied: "And what you've at least got now in Palestine and what you've at least got in Iraq now is contestation between healthy political forces and more radical forces. Hamas loved it when it could run the streets, faces covered, toting a few guns, and [having] no responsibility for what happened to the Palestinian people. They were the great resistance force, and their only purpose in life was to threaten Israel."[12]

During a June 2007 interview with the *New York Daily News* editorial board, Rice also was asked about the recent history of democratic elections in the Middle East resulting in the rise to power of terrorist groups such as Hamas.[13] Rice told the paper it was "very interesting to see Hamas trying to come to terms with no longer being really a resistance movement, but having to deal with politics." During the same interview she referred a second time to Hamas as a resistance movement: "A moderate Palestinian friend of mine said, 'You know, they [Hamas] used to be the great resistance." These were clearly not momentary slips of the tongue. I found six other instances in 2007 and 2008—all transcribed on the State Department Web site— where Rice called Hamas a "resistance" movement.

In diplomacy, as in law, semantics are crucial, for it is in the phraseology of policy that true attitudes can be divined. That is why I try to read as carefully as possible any interviews from top U.S. policymakers regarding Hamas and other terrorist groups. Over lunch in Tel Aviv in May 2008, I was browsing the *New York Times* opinion section and was startled by an interview then-presidential candidate Barack Obama had given to *Times* columnist David Brooks. Obama stated that the Hamas and the Lebanese Hezbollah terrorist organizations have "legitimate claims...weakened" by the violence the terrorist groups carry out.[14] Obama compared Hezbollah to Hamas, asserting that they both need to be compelled to understand that "they're going down a blind alley with violence that weakens their legitimate claims."

Brooks did not press Obama as to what exactly were Hamas's and Hezbollah's "legitimate" claims. He was speaking to Obama for clarification on an earlier statement the politician had made implying that Lebanese militias should be tempered with enticements.

THE OBAMA "ENDORSEMENT"

For their part, Hamas officials made positive statements about Obama from the very beginning of the 2008 presidential campaign. Ahmed Yousef, Hamas's chief political advisor in Gaza, told the U.S. radio host John Batchelor and me during a broadcast interview in mid-campaign that he "hopes" Obama becomes president. "We like Mr. Obama, and we hope that he will win the elections," said Yousuf in the interview, which made world headlines. "I hope Mr. Obama and the Democrats will change the political discourse.... I do believe [Obama] is like John Kennedy, a great man with a great principle. And he has a vision to change America to make it in a position to lead the world community, but not with humiliation and arrogance," Yousuf said, speaking from Gaza. Asked specifically if he believed Democrats would engage Hamas if the party took the White House, Yousuf replied, "I do believe Democrats will make a drastic change in American foreign policy. I hope they are able to fix the damage done by [President] Bush and the Republicans and engage again in a very positive way with the Arab and Muslim world, where most of their vital interests lie."

Yousef's unsolicited praise of Obama became a prominent theme of the presidential debates. Obama's opponent, Senator John McCain, used the Hamas quotes to claim that the Iran-funded group had endorsed Obama, even though Obama had repeatedly condemned Hamas as a terrorist group that should be isolated until it renounced violence and recognized Israel. While I wouldn't describe Yousef's statements to me as an endorsement *per se*, it was clear the Hamas figure at the very least was excited about Obama's announced policy of engaging America's foes, most notably the Islamic Republic of Iran, Hamas's main sponsor.

Following Obama's victory in November 2008, Yousef claimed to *Al-Hayat*, the leading Arabic-language newspaper, that Hamas maintained regular communication with Obama's aides. "We were in contact with a number of Obama's aides through the Internet, and later met with some of them in Gaza, but they advised us not to come out with any statements, as those may have a negative effect on his election campaign and be used by Republican candidate John McCain [to attack Obama]," Yousuf told *Al-Hayat*.[15] Yousuf claimed that Hamas's contact with Obama's advisors was continuing, adding that relations were maintained after Obama's electoral victory. Obama's senior foreign policy advisor, Denis McDonough, rejected Yousef's claims. "This assertion is just plain false," McDonough told the *Jerusalem Post*.[16]

While Obama has condemned Hamas, there remain doubts about what his policy will be regarding the Egyptian-born, Iranian-funded mob. His administration has called for reconciliation talks between the U.S.-funded Palestinian Authority and Hamas. Some Obama policy advisors favor engagement with Hamas. Charles Freeman, appointed by Obama to head the U.S. National Intelligence Council, has called for dialogue with Hamas. The NIC is a crucial component of the U.S. intelligence apparatus, serving as the center for midterm and long-term strategic thinking within the American intelligence community. It provides intelligence briefs for Obama and key U.S. agencies and produces reports that help determine American policy on crucial issues, such as Iran's nuclear program. Also, a former ancillary advisor, Robert Malley, argued in numerous opinion pieces in top U.S. newspapers that Hamas should not only be talked to, but provided with aid. Malley resigned after it became public that he had held talks with Hamas. And then there are Obama's little-noticed remarks to the *New York Times* about Hamas's (and Hezbollah's) "legitimate" claims. In February 2009, Secretary of State Hillary

Clinton outlined preconditions for Hamas to join the so-called peace process. "Hamas knows the conditions…. They must renounce violence, they must recognize Israel, they must agree to abide by prior agreements," she said. Most of those conditions call for Hamas to simply pay lip service by "renouncing"—but not ceasing—violence; "recognizing;" and "agree[ing] to abide"—leaving open the possibility of Hamas not actually abiding to "prior agreements." Sound familiar? These were almost the exact same conditions set out for arch-terrorist Yasser Arafat to join the international arena.

In mid-February 2009, Senator John Kerry, who heads the Senate Foreign Relations Committee, paid a visit to United Nations installations in the Gaza Strip, becoming the most senior U.S. government official to enter Gaza since 2000. The Massachusetts lawmaker announced his trip was aimed at surveying the humanitarian situation in Gaza following a large-scale Israeli operation there (to be discussed in the next chapter); he stated his trip did not signal any change in U.S. policy toward Hamas.[17]

While in Gaza, Kerry accepted a letter from UN workers. The communication was determined to have been a plea from Hamas to be passed to Obama. FoxNews.com quoted Kerry spokesman Frederick Jones as claiming the Democratic senator was not aware the letter was from Hamas and only heard of its true origin from news media reports, prompting Kerry to forward it to the U.S. consulate in Jerusalem.[18] Hamas's Yousef confirmed to me the communication, a two-page appeal which he himself wrote, congratulated Obama on his election victory and petitioned the U.S. president to open dialogue with his Islamist group.

Mushir al-Massri, a Hamas spokesman and parliament member, told me Kerry's visit to the Hamas-controlled Gaza Strip was a "big sign" of a "change" in the U.S. position toward the Islamist group. Speaking from Gaza, al-Massri said, "This is part of a new era regarding Hamas in the international community. Kerry can say there is no change," al-Massri continued, "but Hamas controls Gaza. It's very important that he came here. I hope next time the U.S. can more openly support Hamas."

On March 2, 2009, the Obama administration formally pledged a $900 million U.S. aid package for the Palestinians, pending

Congressional approval. Clinton told reporters the funding, which included $300 million for reconstruction efforts in Gaza, was meant to foster regional peace and would not fall into the hands of the Hamas terrorist organization.[19] But the aid is slated to be received by both the PA and the UN Relief and Work Agency, or UNRWA, which administers aid to millions of Palestinian "refugees" in the Gaza Strip and the West Bank. As documented in chapter eight, the UNRWA openly employs Hamas members. The PA, meanwhile, had been in talks with Hamas about establishing a unity government at the time the aid was announced.

Israeli security officials warned that since Hamas controls the Gaza Strip, any reconstruction efforts in the territory are likely to bolster Hamas, whether the Islamist group directly receives the funds or not. They also said the PA has previously used donor funds to pay salaries for Hamas officials and the terrorist group's police force in Gaza, which include scores of terrorists among its ranks.

U.S. JEWS EMBRACE HAMAS

Even some left-wing Jewish groups push for U.S. engagement with Hamas. In February 2006, the U.S. Congress attempted to push tough legislation aimed at financially and diplomatically isolating the newly Hamas-led Palestinian government. Some liberal American Jewish groups worked to block the anti-Hamas efforts, with some of the organizations asserting that Hamas may be willing to make peace with the Jewish state. "We oppose the legislation. The U.S. should be extending carrots to Hamas, and not just slapping them with sticks. We should be trying to encourage Hamas to recognize Israel, not shutting them out completely," M. J. Rosenberg, the policy director of a prominent leftist think tank, the Israel Policy Forum, told me.

Rosenberg was one of several liberal Jewish leaders opposing a bill initiated in the House of Representatives by Ileana Ros-Lehtinen (R-FL), and Tom Lantos (D-CA), that called for a strict termination of aid to the new Hamas-dominated government. Americans for Peace Now, an offshoot of its Israeli namesake, supports final status negotiations to create a Palestinian state. APN's assistant director, Lewis Roth, told me his organization "has a problem" with the bill demanding that Hamas must recognize Israel. "This new call for the [Hamas-led] PA to recognize the existence of Israel as a Jewish state is not agreeable," Roth said. "It's something the U.S. has never applied before in negotiations with the Palestinians or with regard to Jordanian treaties. The clause is clearly drafted with Hamas in mind. It makes no sense." Another far leftist group, the Brit Tzedek v'Shalom Jewish Alliance for Justice and Peace, actually initiated an online petition calling for Americans to oppose the anti-Hamas legislation.

These are just a few of the cracks in the front to isolate Hamas, a few of the facets of the inability of some to distinguish evil from good. It starts with language, continues with talks and public meetings, moves into diplomatic commitments and then into formal policy that engages and recognizes a terrorist group sworn to destroy Israel.

In the 1970s, when Arafat's PLO was hijacking international airliners and murdering foreign diplomats, many observers probably would have considered it unimaginable that one day Arafat would become a top dignitary, address the United Nations, take over strategic territory handed to him by Israel, shake the hand of Israel's leader at a ceremony on the White House lawn, and receive a Nobel Peace Prize plus billions in aid and direct U.S. and European weapons shipments, all while maintaining his campaign of death and horror against the Jewish state.

The embrace of Hamas by Jimmy Carter and others in the international community cannot be viewed as simple pragmatism, the pure belief that since Hamas is a central player in the Palestinian arena, the Islamist organization must therefore be accorded recognition. An appropriate and perfectly acceptable policy toward Hamas—one that is universal domestic practice by all "moderate" Muslim countries against their Islamist foes—would be not to deal with them at all, to isolate them and impose heavy sanctions on the gang of thugs, until at the very least it renounces violence and accepts Israel's right to exist.

I believe that the acceptance and legitimization of Hamas by the international community that we are witnessing largely reflects growing anti-Semitism: either its direct embrace or at least acquiescence to it. I agree with the general premise that since public, overt Jew-hatred went out of fashion in the West following the Holocaust, age-old anti-Semitism has been replaced *en bloc* by anti-Zionism, by attempting to de-legitimize and defeat the Jewish state instead of aiming directly at Jews as individuals. Radiating from the Muslim world, and backed up by both oil billions and jihadists, anti-Semitism is at the core of the growing Western embrace of Israel's enemies, from Hamas to Fatah to Hezbollah—the drive to force Israel to accept extreme concessions and forfeit strategic territory on its way to complete termination.

INCOHERENT ISRAELI POLICY

Sadly, the international community's willingness to treat with Hamas is fueled by Israel's own failure to follow a coherent policy toward this multinational, politico-theological murder cohort. On one hand, Israeli leaders claim that Hamas must be isolated, and they routinely chide any Western country that seems on the verge of developing relations with Hamas. Simultaneously, Israel negotiates with it and carries out policies that directly aid Hamas's consolidation of power on the Palestinian street.

From the beginning, in the late 1980s, Israel aided in the establishment of Islamist charities in the West Bank and the Gaza Strip, from which Hamas emerged. The hope was that those charities and their attendant civilian infrastructures would serve as rivals to the Palestine Liberation Organization. When Hamas in the 1990s began to distinguish itself as one of the deadliest Palestinian murder groups, largely focused on attacking the Jewish state while currying favor with the Palestinian population, Israel began to adopt a mostly unified public front against Hamas. By the time of the Oslo Accords of September 1993, Israel was justifying its decision to bring Arafat back to power by asserting that Arafat's "secular" Fatah would disarm and suppress Islamist groups like Hamas. At least this was the template in other secularist Middle East regimes, such as those in Egypt and Jordan, where fighting the Muslim Brotherhood, from which Hamas descended, was standard public policy.

That all changed in January 2006 after Hamas trounced its Fatah rivals in PA parliamentary elections, taking seventy-six of the 132 seats in the Palestinian legislative chamber. In response, Israel simply upheld all normal contacts with the Hamas-led PA, negotiating with the malefactors toward creating a Palestinian state while claiming it was only holding talks with the Fatah section of the Palestinian government, as if Hamas did not dominate the parliament.

In June 2007, Abbas unilaterally dismantled the Hamas-led government, leading Hamas to a violent takeover of the Gaza Strip. At once, Israel was provided the perfect scenario to isolate Gaza and its Hamas rulers. How could any Western nation argue against isolating a terrorist group sworn to Israel's destruction, which took control of a territory from a rival organization perceived as moderate, and then used the land it gained to build ravaging armies and militant training camps while firing rockets toward Jewish homes and launching scores of massive cross-border raids? Instead, while Israel has called on other states to boycott Hamas, it has all the while subsidized the Hamas regime in Gaza and conducted sporadic negotiations with it.

With the exception of occasional, temporary cutbacks in response to rocket fire, the Israeli Electric Company supplies nearly 70 percent of Gaza's electricity while the Israeli army oversees the transport of tons of humanitarian aid into Gaza. Israel routinely allows diplomatic delegations, mostly European, into and out of Gaza while knowing full well that many of these delegations meet with Hamas leaders. Israeli banks send convoys of new Israeli shekels once per month to infuse the cash-strapped Gaza Strip with the Jewish state's currency, meaning that Israel is partially fueling the Hamas-controlled Gazan economy. An *exposé* by Reuters—of all news agencies—found that once the Israeli cash shipments are delivered to Gaza, the shekel convoys are protected by Hamas's Executive Force.[20]

Israel also conducts indirect, and at times direct, talks with Hamas. Egyptian officials served as middlemen in Israeli-Hamas talks on border issues, ceasefire negotiations, and parleys aimed at freeing kidnapped Israeli soldier Gilad Shalit, according to security officials. According to Hamas sources with whom I spoke, Prime Minister Ehud Olmert's special representative regarding the return of kidnapped Israeli soldiers, Ofer Dekel, even met Hamas leaders incarcerated in Israeli prisons in an effort to broker a deal to free Shalit.

Moreover, yet unsurprisingly, there is a growing campaign within Israel's liberal intellectual elite pushing for dialogue with Hamas. Israel's major newspapers frequently feature opinion pieces, often penned by prominent academicians, outlining the pros of an engagement policy.

Perhaps Israel's greatest gift to Hamas was agreeing to a ceasefire after Hamas seized power in June of 2008. The truce—an Israeli-generated *hudna*—provided Hamas with crucial downtime, not only to smuggle weapons into Gaza and construct longer-ranger range rockets, but also to consolidate its power in Gaza and work toward extending its reach deep in to the West Bank. The ceasefire conferred enormous legitimacy upon Hamas, since it was able successfully to maintain the truce for a long period of time—much longer than any previous truce has held with Fatah militants. The ceasefire also sent mixed messages to an international community that watched in confusion as Israel forged agreements with a crowd of Egyptian-led, Persian-sponsored criminals that was supposed to be isolated. It remains to be seen if the new Israeli administration led by Nenjamin Netanyahu will follow suit and continue to empower Hamas, but the cracks in the wall of international isolation may already be too wide to cement over.

CHAPTER FOURTEEN

THE GAZA WAR: AGAIN ISRAEL FAILS TO WIN

B *efore taking his country to war* against Hamas, Israel's prime minister issued a warning: "I am telling them now that this may be the last minute. I'm telling them: Stop [the missile attacks]. We are stronger," Prime Minister Ehud Olmert exclaimed in comments directed at the leadership of the radical Islamic government of Hamas in the Gaza Strip.[1]

Olmert delivered his plea on December 25, 2008. Two days later, the Israel Defense Forces would embark on a twenty-two-day military campaign aimed at seriously damaging Hamas's governmental and missile-launching terrorist infrastructure. The war was incited by Hamas's earlier announcement that it would not renew a six-month ceasefire that expired on December 19. To drive home its point, within one week it had fired a scourge of dozens of rocket and mortars from Gaza into nearby Jewish civilian centers.

The primary war chief of Hamas, who lives under state protection in Syria, on December 14 told a Hamas television station in Damascus, "There will be no renewal of the 'calm' after it expires."[2] Khaled Mashaal made that statement only hours after a personal meeting with former U.S. President Jimmy Carter.[3]

According to sources in Hamas with whom I spoke, Hamas was actually willing to extend the ceasefire, but was bluffing by making bold declarations and launching rocket attacks; by this mechanism, it was holding out for better terms than a mere freeze on Israeli military operations in Gaza as embodied in the terms of the previous lull. Hamas wanted an agreement with Israel whereby the Gaza-Israel borders would be more open, including for commerce. With the exception of humanitarian aid, Israel had tightly closed its borders with Gaza after Hamas seized control of the territory in the summer of 2007 from the U.S.-backed Fatah organization. An agreement to reopen the borders would have marked a major victory for Hamas, and much endeared the group to the local population.

This time, Hamas overplayed its hand. Israel launched the aerial portion of its military campaign, dubbed Operation Cast Lead, at 11:35 a.m. Jerusalem time on Saturday, December 27. In the opening minutes, more than fifty fighter jets and attack helicopters entered Gazan airspace, dropping more than one hundred bombs on at least fifty targets, including Hamas military bases, training camps, underground Qassam rocket launchers, a police station and largely empty Hamas government buildings and institutions.[4]

At the war's outset, Olmert announced two main goals for his campaign against Hamas. The first was decisively to smash the group's terrorist infrastructure, especially the rocket-manufacturing locations and the materiel resupply network. Olmert's second goal was to put a stop to three years of regular Hamas rocket attacks from Gaza aimed at nearby Jewish communities. As it turned out, neither goal was accomplished, while Hamas's drive to open the Gaza borders succeeded. During the campaign, Olmert announced a third goal: to alter the situation on the ground so that Hamas would not be able to continue smuggling weapons into Gaza from neighboring Egypt. That goal is in failure.

MEDIA ACCEPT HAMAS PROPAGANDA

A few hours after Israel's first-day air strikes, I checked on television and was astounded by the misinformation on Palestinian casualties delivered by the cable news outlets, especially CNN and the BBC. I conducted scores of searches of print media sources, most of which immediately reported as fact that at least 205 people, mostly civilians, had been killed during the first few hours of the Israeli strikes. Each news outlet failed to mention that the casualty numbers were provided by Hamas, and at first claimed that only three of the casualties were actual Hamas "military" leaders.

With somber music playing in the background, both CNN and the BBC aired continuous loops of what the networks claimed were Palestinian civilian casualties being rushed into a local hospital. Both networks aired the same footage, provided to them by al-Jazeera, the Arab satellite channel sponsored by the government of Qatar—which is openly pro-Hamas. CNN interviewed a man identified as a Gaza-based physician who claimed that two-thirds of the "over two hundred casualties" were women and children. The network also featured—without challenge—a man identified as a Gaza-based human rights activist, who accused Israel of deliberately targeting civilians and perpetrating a "massacre" in Gaza. A Hamas spokesman told the BBC the casualties were "mostly women and children."

"Does hitting so-called Hamas institutions mean over two hundred civilians killed?" a BBC anchor twice asked the Israeli government spokesman, Mark Regev. In an interview with me a few minutes later, Regev cautioned, "The Hamas government in Gaza instituted a Taliban-like regime and has systematically destroyed independent civil society, which makes it pretty difficult for there to be independent verification of these numbers." He continued, "One must keep in mind Hamas has a major propaganda interest in highlighting civilian casualties while at the same time minimizing the number of Hamas combatants killed."

It would later be determined that 140 members of Hamas's so-called police forces were killed that first day, including police chief Tawfiq Jabber. In other words, even if Hamas's initial claim of 205 killed (later changed to 225) had been true, the overwhelming majority of casualties were from Hamas's armed forces. The Western media trend of parroting Hamas's claims as fact, and without attribution, would repeat itself throughout the conflict, as the news outlets constantly berated Israel for purportedly killing more than 1,250 Palestinians. IDF clarifications, with additional data, that the majority of those were armed militants were seldom, if ever, reported.

Of much historical significance was, and is, Hamas's established practice of using civilians as human shields. The international news media rarely reported this lurid fact during the war. "Entire families in Gaza lived on top of a barrel of explosives for months without knowing," stated IDF Brigadier General Eyal Eisenberg. He charged that Hamas sent civilians, including women and children, to transfer weapons to gunmen engaged in battles with Israeli forces, and he accused Hamas of booby-trapping many of the civilians' homes. He labeled Hamas's alleged use of civilians as "monstrous" and "inhumane."

Similar reports were provided to me while the battles with Hamas were going on. In one fight focusing largely on the Hamas infrastructure in the city of Jabaliya, an Israeli commander described how Hamas drew Israeli forces into populated civilian areas, shooting at Jewish fighters from occupied homes while women and children were inside. In another case, Israel's *Haaretz* daily quoted an Israeli commander describing how Hamas sent a boy who seemed to be about ten years old into the battlefield in full view of the Israeli military, to remove a gun from a felled terrorist and then pass the weapon to another terrorist. The commander at the scene said he ordered his troops to halt their fire as the Israeli soldiers watched.

This appalling event defines the profound, perhaps unbridgeable, differences between the Israeli and the fundamentalist Muslim cultures. The contemporary nation of Israel derives its values substantially from a Biblically-generated Western ethos that places immeasurable value on each human life, whereas jihadism proclaims a disposition to die or to kill in order to follow the somewhat ambiguous demands of a seventh-century warrior prophet.

A commander told me how Hamas snipers used the windows of a Jabaliya house that was clearly occupied by women and children to shoot at his unit. "The aim is to draw us into killing civilians to bring about international pressure to end our operation," the commander said. Clearly, this tactic for the most part succeeded.

During the conflict, I interviewed scores of Hamas members wanted by Israeli security. In two instances, I could hear children playing or screaming in the background while I spoke with the Hamas figures, who almost certainly topped Israel's most-wanted list.

Another unreported datum is a nearly unique practice of the IDF: to telephone civilians to warn them of an imminent attack. The IDF maintains a database of telephone numbers in Gaza. While it cannot possibly call each home before danger occurs, it maintains an automated system with which it regularly warns civilians of incoming attacks via phone calls or text messages. The IDF routinely employed what it terms "roof knocking"—just prior to a targeted bombing, the building in question received a telephone call in Arabic warning the occupants that the structure was going to be bombed.

At one point, the U.S. and international news media falsely portrayed an Israeli air strike against a Hamas-run university in the Gaza Strip, claiming that a "women's wing" had been targeted, when, according to the Israeli military, the target was a weapons lab at the school's chemistry department. In a series of air aids on December 28, one precision strike hit a building of Gaza's Islamic University. A widely circulated Associated Press report claimed, "One strike destroyed a five-story building in the women's wing at Islamic University, one of the most prominent Hamas symbols in Gaza."[5] The report did not—could not—cite the source of the information.

CNN also reported that a "women's wing" had been targeted, as did London's *Independent* newspaper and China's Xinhua news agency. BBC Online described the building as a "science center" and painted the university as "a center of support for the Islamist militant group that controls the narrow coastal strip." Reuters claimed the university was a "significant Hamas cultural symbol."

Avital Lebovich, a spokeswoman for the Israel Defense Forces, told me that Israel had targeted only one chemical laboratory at Islamic University, which she said was specifically used for the manufacture of Hamas explosives. "This is the first university in [the] world that gives out bachelor's degrees in rocket manufacture," she said. Lebovich asserted that the targeted building did not house any women's wing.

Islamic University was founded by the Hamas spiritual leader, Ahmed Yassin, assassinated by Israel in 2004. Previous Israeli raids of the main university campus in Gaza yielded mass quantities of weaponry and Hamas incitement material. As I previously documented, officials from Palestinian Authority President Mahmoud Abbas's Fatah party claimed to me in February 2007 that they had captured seven Iranian military trainers–including a general of the Iranian Revolutionary Guards–inside Gaza City's Islamic University. They said the facility was being utilized as a

Hamas military training ground. The Fatah officials said at the time they had also found about one thousand Qassam rockets, with equipment to manufacture the rockets, inside the university. They previously had suspected that kidnapped Israeli soldier Gilad Shalit was held for a time on the university grounds.

In a 2007 interview for my previous book, *Schmoozing with Terrorists*, Muhammad Abel-Al, a leader and spokesman of the Popular Resistance Committees (a Hamas-affiliated terrorist group) acknowledged that Islamic University is "extremely important" for recruitment of militants. Abdel-Al, who also goes by the name Abu Abir, said several members of his group studied chemistry at the university to aid in the manufacture of explosives and suicide belts.

Abu Abdullah, considered one of the most important operational members of Hamas's so-called military wing, Izzedine al-Qassam Martyrs Brigades, also spoke with me during an interview for the book. He willingly explained that Islamic University was regularly used by Hamas to support "resistance activities." "It is no secret that we utilize all tools at our disposal, including our fighters at Islamic University, in preparations to fight the Zionists," he expounded.

Meanwhile, Israeli air strikes continued targeting both symbolic Hamas institutions, such as government buildings, and the group's military infrastructure, including rocket caches, police stations, explosives factories, and smuggling tunnels between Gaza and neighboring Egypt.

On the evening of January 3, 2009, the IDF campaign moved on to its second phase, when the military launched a ground operation aimed at dividing the Gaza Strip into three zones, and initially securing the areas in northern Gaza from which rockets were being launched into Israel. Throughout the campaign, Hamas fired an average of thirty-three rockets per day into Jewish population centers, killing three Israelis and gradually increasing the distance of its rocket attacks, eventually reaching about twenty-five miles into the Jewish state and placing civilians as far as Beersheva and Gadera on rocket alert. Even the Tel Aviv municipality was reportedly put on alert.

ABBAS ASKS FOR THE ATTACK

Significantly, the Israeli assault was strongly condemned in public by Mahmoud Abbas and his Fatah party, who termed the IDF campaign "barbaric" and "unnecessary." According to informed diplomatic sources in Jerusalem, however, Abbas for months had been petitioning Israel to launch a massive military raid against his Hamas rivals in Gaza. The sources, speaking on condition of anonymity, said Abbas and his top representatives waged a quiet campaign asking the Israeli government to target Hamas in Gaza just before his term in office was scheduled to expire on January 9, 2009.

For their part, Hamas leaders had repeatedly warned they would not recognize Abbas as PA president after the ninth, and that they would launch a major campaign to de-legitimize the PA president and install their own figures to lead the Palestinian government. Abbas hoped that a large-scale Israeli military campaign in Gaza would distract Hamas from undermining his rule, the diplomatic sources said. Abbas's bet was spot on. Hamas put up little resistance as he stayed in office past his term without even having the PA pass a decree that would keep him in power legally. In early 2009, speculation is that once Hamas stabilizes, Abbas may declare "emergency rule" and attempt to remain in office, then face a Hamas campaign to oust him.

GOALS NEVER ACHIEVED

Israel began the third stage of its assault on the morning of January 11 with the deployment of some reservists to Gaza. IDF ground attacks focused on suburbs of Gaza City and also advanced toward a major Hamas headquarters in the northern Gaza neighborhood of al-Karramah. According to IDF sources, the proposed third phase of the operation was to be an extensive, large-scale ground operation that would have cleaned out central and northern Gaza of Hamas's intact "military wing." The sources stressed the completion of the third stage was crucial were Israel to deal a decisive blow to Hamas.

It was not to be. On January 17, following a security cabinet meeting and just two days before the inauguration of U.S. president

Barack Obama, Olmert announced a unilateral ceasefire without any agreement or coordination with Hamas. Defense Minister Ehud Barak explained, "First a ceasefire is declared. If Hamas stops firing rockets then Israel pulls its forces out of the Gaza Strip. If rocket fire resumes then the IDF goes back in, this time with the international backing gained by having tried a truce."[6]

Olmert declared that his military objectives had been met.[7] Was the prime minister correct? Wars are won or lost based on which side achieves its goals. In Israel's three-week offensive against Hamas, the Jewish state made many impressive gains, but largely failed to achieve its declared objectives.

As noted at the outset, Olmert's announced goals were decisively to smash Hamas's capabilities and stop the terrorist group from rearming. Israeli air strikes did deal a strong blow against Hamas's governmental institutions and some of its weapons caches. While the IDF will not publicly confirm the percentage of Hamas military infrastructure it wiped out, other defense sources have said privately that Hamas lost about 38 percent of its rockets and a sizable portion of its explosives development program. Nevertheless, the sources said Hamas's estimated six thousand-man force, trained in Iranian-style guerrilla tactics, was left largely in place along with the majority of the group's underground bunkers and large numbers of explosives factories. In addition, a significant percentage of Hamas's rocket arsenal and most of its weapons caches were stored well and so remained safely tucked away.

Israel destroyed so many Hamas buildings (the Israel Air Force almost ran out of targets) that the group's ability to govern on the ground should have been severely damaged, since it was not left with many government compounds from which to rule. Hamas's government infrastructure, including office buildings, police headquarters and even financial institutions, was badly damaged. Israel also temporarily scared into hiding some Hamas leaders with its successful elimination of many top Hamas members, including Jimmy Carter's friend Siad Siam, the chief of Hamas's Executive Force, a Hezbollah-like militia heavily involved in carnage and despoliation. All the same, Hamas leaders are quite used to living under assassination threat; thus, about three weeks after the IDF withdrew, Hamas's military chiefs emerged from their shells.

Olmert's stated goal of destroying Hamas's ability to rocket Israel fell short, as Hamas continued to fire undiminished numbers of rockets every single day during the entire conflict. The group even shot at least twenty rockets and eight mortars in the twenty-four hours following Israel's un-negotiated, unilateral truce declaration.

Olmert also made some farcical claims, telling the Israeli media that Hamas would find it difficult to continue smuggling weapons into Gaza and that at the time he spoke (on January 19) the IDF controlled the northern Gaza Strip—the area from which most rockets are launched into the Jewish state. On the ground, the IDF on January 19 absolutely did not control the entire northern Gaza Strip, as was clearly evidenced by Hamas's ability to keep firing rockets from that zone on that day.

Crucial to bleeding Hamas dry was for Israel to find a way to halt the rampant weapons smuggling from Egypt into Gaza. Indeed, this was one of Olmert's declared goals, and this, too, would not be achieved. As this book went to press, Israel was negotiating an international monitoring mechanism it hoped would stop the enormous Egypt-Gaza weapons transfers, even though previous international monitors stationed along that border had fled their duty and repeatedly failed to stem Hamas in its determined and incessant munitions smuggling. The absent monitors had been stationed at the border, on the Philadelphi Route, following Israel's 2005 evacuation of the Gaza Strip.

Even if a beefed-up international force is eventually established inside Gaza—and this is not currently in the works—it is unlikely that any such force would, in fact, accomplish its assignment. An example of failure is the thirteen thousand-strong UNIFIL force in southern Lebanon that was established following the 2006 war there. The Iranian-backed Hezbollah militia has rebuilt its extensive and complex system of tunnels and completely rearmed its warehouses and personnel, often in full view of the international "peacekeepers," according to Israeli defense officials.

RELYING ON FAILED POLICIES

If the flow of weaponry to Hamas is ever to be choked off, the burden of accomplishing that will rest heavily upon Egypt. To that end, according to Egyptian security sources, the U.S. Army Corps of Engineers, this past January, arrived in the Egyptian Sinai desert, which borders Gaza, to train Egyptian troops in the use of advanced American machinery to detect Hamas smuggling tunnels. Egypt also has pledged to clamp down on local Sinai tribes involved in the weapons trade. While there have been some signs that Egypt has taken its charge seriously, in the long run it is doubtful that the Mubarak government, which has done little to stem rampant weapons smuggling in the past and whose poorly paid soldiers are said to be bribed by Hamas, could or would truly follow through.

A new agreement being negotiated also calls for the participation of Fatah forces in border patrols. This is the same Fatah that received hundreds of millions of dollars in U.S. and international aid, and advanced military training, but which was humiliatingly expelled from the Gaza Strip in less than one week by Hamas gunmen.

The final agreement also seems likely to open Gaza's borders more than they were before Israel's operation began—meaning that Hamas's primary goal before the war, a better truce deal, was achieved.

The timing of the Gaza offensive, of course, was instructive. Abbas needed a distraction. Olmert, slammed for his leadership failure during the Lebanon war, was on his way out of office and thought he could certainly gain some stature for his legacy from a successful military campaign. Foreign Minister Tzipi Livni and Defense Minister Ehud Barak were facing national elections in Israel, both running for the top slot against the opposition leader, Benjamin Netanyahu, who had positioned himself as the hardline defense candidate. Barak personally oversaw Operation Cast Lead's military strategy while Livni ran the diplomatic and public relations aspects of the war. They calculated that a publicly perceived win against Hamas might reposition both of them as credible defense alternatives to Netanyahu. Throughout the campaign, the Israeli news media largely trumpeted Israel's "victory" over Hamas.

Another probable consideration was the expected change in U.S. politics. The military operation was launched just weeks before Barack Obama took office. The war was tacitly supported by President Bush, who did not ask Israel to halt its offensive. While a trusted IDF source told me that he had heard Obama's team had informed Israel they would like to see the offensive against Hamas scaled back before January's inauguration, a representative from Olmert's office denied to me that there had been any contact between the Israeli government and Obama or his team regarding the Hamas offensive.

Hamas for its part proved in the days following Operation Cast Lead that it was still on top of its game. Exactly one week after the operation formally ended, Hamas resumed governance activities and was acting at about 85 percent capacity in administering Gaza—this according to Hamas officials and activists from the independent al-Mizan human rights organization in Gaza with whom I spoke. Fully functioning within the week, they asserted, were Hamas' interior ministry, court system, and ministries of transportation, education, police, and health services, as well as scores of other official institutions. Additional sources in Gaza confirmed that the Hamas government was soon close to fully functioning.

Forced to improvise following the Israeli air raids that targeted its institutions, Hamas took over dozens of apartments within civilian complexes from which it based its new government infrastructure. That move obviously could complicate Israeli efforts to target Hamas in the future. Speaking in a joint interview with a representative of the Israeli Ynetnews.com Web site and me, one Hamas official said his group had made back-up copies of government files for storage within apartment buildings.

As expected, Hamas declared victory over Israel, although that may be overstating things. Hamas's "victory" came by default since its only goal was to survive the IDF beating. It did achieve that, not due to its might, but because the IDF did not finish the third stage of its attack, which could have devastated the organization and perhaps have annihilated it.

One real Hamas victory did occur in the form of the international legitimacy accorded the group during and after the offensive. The Obama administration called for Hamas to join a unity government with their Fatah rivals. Senator John Kerry visited the territory. Hamas sources claimed that their group was in direct contact with Italy, France, the EU and U.N. representatives, many of whom, the sources said, expressed willingness to bring Hamas into the international fold and out of its diplomatic isolation. Immediately following the war, Tony Blair, the former British prime minister and Mideast envoy representing the international quartet of the UN, EU, Russia and the USA, advocated that Hamas be brought into the "peace process."[8] In an arresting version of the fox guarding the chicken coop, the new border agreement in Gaza looks to grant Hamas a role in patrolling the territory, meaning that Hamas would be a central participant in a process purportedly meant to ensure that Hamas cannot rearm.

A clear winner or loser of this war cannot easily be determined. Both sides gained and lost. If we judge which side best achieved its objectives, Israel clearly failed. Soon after the war, observers speculated that Hamas would probably continue reducing, but not halting, its rocket attacks against Israel, since it is in the group's best interests not to provoke any further IDF operations, for fear that Hamas' military infrastructure would be targeted anew. When the time is right and when its arsenal has been replenished by Iran, Hamas will again resume its war to destroy the Jewish state.

It was with a heavy heart that I decided to name this book *The Late Great State of Israel.* Just thinking about the possibility of the destruction of the Jewish state—after all it has achieved and after all the odds it has overcome—fills me with urgent concern. That is precisely the reason for this title: to provoke an immediate reaction; to wake up Israel's friends and its own citizens from a dangerous slumber; to prod the world into pondering the unthinkable; and to shed light on the scope of the calamitous threats facing the Jewish state and the substantial changes in policy that are required to deal with those perils.

I write these concluding words from the heart of Jerusalem just after it became clear that the Jewish nation's next leader is Likud chairman Benjamin Netanyahu, who ran on a platform stressing Israel's security needs. Netanyahu has made clear that his primary goal as prime minister will be to halt Iran's drive to obtain nuclear weapons. He has also made strong statements about defeating Hamas and retaining vital territories, such as the Golan Heights and some of the West Bank.

Yet Netanyahu is known to be a pragmatic politician. From top sources both in his administration and in the Palestinian Authority, I have direct information about his plans to initiate eventual negotiations with Syria and to try to coax Jordan into working more with the PA to take over key West Bank territories. Netanyahu's team had no immediate comment on this report.

Careful observers recall that as the ninth prime minister of Israel, from 1996 to 1999, Netanyahu established intensive, secret negotiations with Syria in which he offered to evacuate much of the Golan Heights. He also infamously signed the Wye River

Accords, which transferred vital West Bank territory, including a portion of the holy city of Hebron, to the control of Yasser Arafat and his Fatah killers. In partial exoneration, Netanyahu signed the Accords under heavy pressure from President Bill Clinton, whose policies built up Arafat as a statesman willing to make peace with Israel even while the Palestinian leader orchestrated continuous waves of terrorism against Jews.

From the first, the Wye River Accords were a strategic disaster that gave the Palestinians a physical platform from which to launch attacks, helping to pave the way to the Second *Intifada*. The word on the Israeli political street was that Netanyahu had "caved" to Clinton and to the everything-is-negotiable politics of the State Department.

Now, Israel's returning leader must again contend with a White House intent on pushing the same failed formulas—of building up Fatah and of brokering negotiations in which the Jewish state would be compelled to relinquish most of the West Bank—this time, while Hamas quietly prepares to take over the strategic land just as it did in Gaza. Indeed, President Barack Obama has brought back many of the same personalities, including Middle East envoys Dennis Ross and George Mitchell, whose strategies and influence during the Clinton years helped bring the Middle East to its current destabilized, powder-keg state of crisis.

Obama seems at least as determined as Clinton to travel the "land-for-peace" path, where Israel gives substantial land to its lethal enemies in exchange for a promise of no more armed hostilities. This is a vow forsworn in the very scripture of their holy book, which specifically advocates that Muslims offer to infidels short-term peace agreements that must, obligatorily, be abrogated within ten years.

According to a top PA official, the Obama administration has promised that understandings reached with Israel during negotiations while President Bush was in office would be utilized as starting points for current and future talks. Bush launched the Annapolis summit of 2007, which initiated negotiations meant to create a Palestinian state in the Gaza Strip, West Bank and perhaps eastern Jerusalem. "With Obama, the number of settlers to be removed from the West Bank will much be more important than sixty thousand," the PA official told me, referring to last year's bargaining in which Israel expressed a willingness to withdraw from up to 94 percent of the West Bank and move about sixty thousand homesteaders into central settlement blocks closer to Jerusalem.

There has also been some concern in Jerusalem that Obama will categorically not support another large-scale Israeli operation against Hamas in Gaza. Indeed, the U.S. is slated to provide hundreds of millions to reconstruct the Gaza Strip, meaning any future Israeli raid in that territory could target infrastructure funded by America and the international community. The Islamist movement, for its part, claims openly that Obama's administration favors bringing Hamas into the so-called peace process, while Obama's team has so far flatly denied having any talks with the terrorist organization.

On Syria, Obama has made clear he favors dialogue and bringing Damascus out from isolation into the international arena. As Iran's military partner in the region, Syria provides crucial support for Hamas's and Hezbollah's war against Israel. During the 2008 presidential campaign, some of Obama's advisors asserted that they would like to see Israel open negotiations with Syria.

More than on any other issue, the stated views of the new Israeli and American leaders clash most pointedly regarding Iran and its drive to obtain nuclear weapons, which would threaten Israel's existence and provide Tehran and its terrorist proxies with a nuclear umbrella. Obama's team claims it can convince Iran to refrain from going nuclear with direct talks and incentives, such as financial aid and international legitimacy.

If Netanyahu decides to oppose Iran or promote a hard-line policy, he will have to contend with an unfriendly White House and State Department. This would be likely to generate a crisis in U.S.-Israeli relations, especially if Netanyahu acts while Obama is in the midst of diplomatic engagement with Iran. I believe that Netanyahu understands that regarding the threat from Tehran, Israel must move to protect its interests. Regrettably, due in part to U.S. and Israeli mismanagement, Iran, as I have documented here, has been allowed to lay the foundations for yet another costly future war that could wreak havoc on the Israeli home front.

The view from where I sit in Jerusalem is beautiful and dramatic. The often-rubbled and rebuilt walls of the Old City serve as testament to the dangers Israel currently faces. While those ancient walls are today only a symbol of the threat, a look just to the east, where the so-called security fence threads its way along the border of Jerusalem, reveals the living resurgence of the age-old danger, stirring the disturbing feeling that history is repeating itself. I trust and believe that Israel will ultimately survive—against all odds and in spite of the threats from within and without—only through the grace of God. But for now, things don't look good.

Abdel-Al, Muhammad. Spokesperson and senior leader, Popular Resistance Committees, Fatah-allied terrorist group. Interviewed by phone and at times on live national radio (ABC Radio, John Batchelor Show), December 28, 2006; January 8, 2007; April 6, 2007; May 3, 2007; May 14, 2007; May 30, 2007; June 14, 2007; June 15, 2007; June 18, 2007; June 19, 2007; July 26, 2007; September 3, 2007; November 8, 2007; December 19, 2007; January 31, 2008; February 19, 2008; April 20, 2008; May 25, 2008; June 20, 2008; July 1, 2008; November 24, 2008; December 12, 2008; December 15, 2008.

Abu Abdullah. Senior leader, Hamas's so-called military wing. Interviewed by phone April 23, 2006; June 1, 2006; June 6, 2006; July 5, 2006; October 2, 2006; October 19, 2006; November 27, 2006; November 30, 2006; December 6, 2006; December 18, 2006; December 22, 2006; January 2, 2007; January 30, 2007; March 8, 2007; March 20, 2007; April 4, 2007; April 24, 2007; May 14, 2007; May 31, 2007; June 7, 2007; June 12, 2007; June 13, 2007; June 14, 2007; June 18 2007; June 19 2007; June 20, 2007; July 26, 2007; September 3, 2007; November 1, 2007; November 21, 2007; January 31, 2008; March 16, 2008; April 20, 2008; June 20, 2008; July 6, 2008; September 1 , 2008; December 15, 2008.

Abu Ahmed. Northern Gaza Strip commander, al-Aqsa Martyrs Brigades, Fatah-allied terrorist organization. Interviewed by phone June 7, 2006; October 2, 2006; October 17, 2006; October 24, 2006; November 12, 2006; November 27, 2006; November 30, 2006; December 27, 2006; January 4, 2007; January 29, 2007; February 26, 2007; March 14, 2007; March 28, 2007; April 23, 2007; April 26, 2007.

Aoun, Michel. Former Lebanese prime minister. Interviewed by phone May 5, 2005; May 10, 2005; August 23, 2005; November 13, 2006.

Abu Aziz, Nasser. Deputy commander, al-Aqsa Martyrs Brigades, Fatah-allied terrorist organization. Interviewed in person in Brigades's stronghold inside the Balata refugee camp in Nablus, November 11, 2005. Subsequent interviews on April 27, 2007; May 31, 2007; June 27, 2007; August 7, 2007; August 19, 2007; November 8, 2007; July 27, 2008.

Barhoum, Fawzi. Hamas spokesman in Gaza. Interviewed by phone April 16, 2008; May 19, 2008.

Erekat, Saeb. Senior negotiator, Palestinian Authority. Interviewed by phone and at times on live national radio (ABC Radio, John Batchelor Show), on September 14, 2004; November 5, 2004; December 17, 2004; June 9, 2005; April 15, 2005; September 8, 2005; March 2, 2006; May 8, 2007; June 15, 2007.

Jumblatt, Walid. Leader, Progressive Socialist Party, leader of Lebanon's Druze minority. Interviewed by phone February 19, 2005; February 24, 2005; March 18, 2005; April 25, 2005; May 10, 2005; August 23, 2005; September 22, 2005; December 1, 2005; December 12, 2005; December 29, 2005; February 6, 2006; May 12, 2006; May 29, 2006; July 14, 2006; July 27, 2006; November 13, 2006; November 22, 2006; July 9, 2007; May 8, 2008; July 16, 2008.

Masri, Mushir, al-. Hamas parliament member and spokesman. Interviewed by phone February 20, 2009.

Abu Muhammad. Chief of Islamic Jihad terrorist organization in Jenin. Interviewed in person in Jenin, November 16, 2006.

Ruqb, Hamad. Hamas spokesman in Gaza. Interviewed by phone January 21, 2007.

Senakreh, Ala. Northern West Bank chief, al-Aqsa Martyrs Brigades, Fatah-allied terrorist organization. Interviewed in person in Brigades's stronghold inside the Balata refugee camp in Nablus, November 11, 2005. Subsequent interviews July 21, 2006;

November 10, 2006; March 15, 2007; May 3, 2007; August 7, 2007; October 11; 2007.

Tarawi, Jamal. Member of Palestinian parliament, former Nablus-based leader of Fatah's Tanzim militia. Interviewed on December 12, 2006.

Yousef, Ahmed. Chief political advisor to deposed Hamas prime minister Ismail Haniyeh. Interviewed by phone and at times live on national radio (ABC Radio, John Batchelor Show), April 13, 2008; April 17, 008; May 8, 2008; June 5, 2008; July 6, 2008; November 11, 2008.

Yousuf, Abu. Senior leader in Ramallah, al-Aqsa Martyrs Brigades, Fatah-allied terrorist organization. Doubles as member of Fatah security forces. Interviewed in person in Ramallah January 8, 2005.

Zahar, Mahmoud al-. Chief of Hamas in Gaza. Interviewed by phone and at times live on national radio (ABC Radio, John Batchelor Show), April 13, 2005; October 10, 2005; January 4, 2006; February 15, 2006; December 20, 2006; October 22, 2007; November 11, 2007; September 17, 2008.

Ziliani, Dmitri. Spokesman for the Jerusalem section of Palestinian Authority President Mahmoud Abbas's Fatah Party. Interviewed by phone June 12, 2008.

Zuhri, Sami Abu. Hamas spokesman in Gaza. Interviewed by phone April 17, 2006; April 23, 2006; April 20, 2008; April 21, 2008.

CHAPTER ONE: MEET ISRAEL'S "PEACE PARTNER"

1. *WorldNetDaily*, "U.S. peace partner's group shoots at Jew," WorldNetDaily.com, January 17, 2008, http://www.wnd.com/index.php?fa= PAGE.view&pageId=45591.

2. Yaacov Katz, "PA police behind Ido Zoldan's shooting," *Jerusalem Post*, December 2, 2007, http://www.jpost.com/servlet/Satellite?cid= 1195546785899&pagename=JPost%2FJPArticle%2FshowFull.

3. Efrat Weiss, "Suspected killers of Israeli settler indicted," *Ynetnews.com*, January 14, 2008, http://www.ynet.co.il/english/articles/ 0,7340,L-3494137,00.html.

4. Hillel Fendel, "Responses to capture of PA policemen/murderers," *Israel National News*, December 3, 2007, http://www.israelnationalnews.com/ News/News.aspx/124455.

5. Joseph Farah, "Is U.S. hiding Arafat murders?" *WorldNetDaily*, January 17, 2001, http://www.wnd.com/index.php?fa=PAGE.view&pageId=7856.

6. U.S. Department of State, "Foreign Relations, 1969-1976, Volume E-6, Documents on Africa, 1973-1976, http://www.state.gov/r/pa/ho/frus/nixon/ e6/67234.htm.

7. Mijal Grinberg, Yuval Azoulay, et al., "Jihad claims responsibility for Qassam attack on Sderot," *Haaretz*, September 15, 2008, http://www.haaretz.com/ hasen/spages/1020946.html.

8. *Israel Behind the News*, "Israeli Prime Minister Spokeswoman reassures that Abbas has not sanctioned missile attacks," January 4, 2007, http://israelbehindthenews.com/Archives/Jan-04-07.htm.

9. Herb Keinon and AP, "Kuntar claims Abbas asked for Beirut meeting," *Jerusalem Post*, September 2, 2008, http://www.jpost.com/servlet/ Satellite?pagename=JPost%2FJPArticle%2FShowFull&cid=1220349426258.

10. *WorldNetDaily*, "'Peace partner' celebrates heroic terrorist," WorldNetDaily.com, July 16, 2008, http://www.worldnetdaily.com/ index.php?pageId=69767.

11. Cited in Aaron Klein, "'Peace Partner' websites call Jerusalem attack 'heroic,'" *WorldNetDaily*, March 6, 2008, http://www.worldnetdaily.com/index.php?fa=PAGE.view&pageId=58207.

12. Ibid.

13. Ali Waked, "Report: IDF kills mastermind of Jerusalem terror attack," *Ynetnews.com*, March 12, 2008, http://www.ynet.co.il/english/articles/0,7340,L-3518374,00.html.

14. *Haaretz*, "IDF kills five Palestinian militants in the West Bank," March 12, 2008, http://www.haaretz.com/hasen/spages/963694.html.

15. Mohammed Daraghmeh, "Abbas calls for respect at Fatah rally," Associated Press as published on CBS News Web site, January 11, 2007, http://www.cbsnews.com/stories/2007/01/11/ap/world/mainD8MJ6AT80.shtml.

16. Yaacov Katz, "Ramat Gan terror poison plot uncovered," *Jerusalem Post*, April 10, 2008, http://www.jpost.com/servlet/Satellite?pagename=JPost%2FJPArticle%2FShowFull&cid=1207649983255.

CHAPTER TWO: HOW ISRAEL ALREADY DIVIDED JERUSALEM

1. BBC, "Israel hit by new digger attack," *BBC Online*, July 22, 2008, http://news.bbc.co.uk/2/hi/in_depth/7519404.stm.

2. Rory McCarthy, "Three killed in Jerusalem bulldozer attack," *The Guardian*, July 2, 2008, http://www.guardian.co.uk/world/2008/jul/02/israelandthepalestinians2.

3. Rory McCarthy, Allegra Stratton, et al., "Hamas not claiming responsibility 'yet' for Israeli killings," *The Guardian*, March 7, 2008, http://www.guardian.co.uk/world/2008/mar/07/israelandthepalestinians3.

4. Shahar Ilan, Avi Issacharoff, et al., "Olmert: Living with 270,000 Arabs in Jerusalem means more terror," *Haaretz*, July 28, 2008, http://www.haaretz.com/hasen/spages/1005912.html.

5. Ben Sales, "Danger from the east," *Jerusalem Post*, July 24, 2008, http://www.jpost.com/servlet/Satellite?cid=1215331085507&pagename=JPost%2FJPArticle%2FPrinter.

6. Associated Press, "Clinton: U.S. to support Palestinian state," March 3, 2009, http://www.google.com/hostednews/ap/article/ALeqM5jYWGHTcH7n6ITHFwuTfQzyzEy8lgD96MIALG0.

7. Israel Central Bureau of Statistics, http://www.cbs.gov.il/hodaot2006n/11_06_106b.pdf.

8. Atilla Somfalvi, "Ramon hints division of Jerusalem to be discussed at Annapolis," *Ynetnews.com* July 10, 2007, http://www.ynetnews.com/articles/0,7340,L-3457214,00.html.

9. See JNF Web site at www.jnf.org/about-jnf/.

10. *Israel National News*, "Angry MK's confront police over Jerusalem Jewish no-go zone," August 13, 2008, http://www.israelnationalnews.com/

News/News.aspx/127182.

11. Ibid.

12. Ibid.

13. *WorldNetDaily*, "Report: Files on illegal Arab construction deleted," WorldNetDaily.com, March 3, 2006, http://www.worldnetdaily.com/news/ article.asp?ARTICLE_ID=49090.

14. Israel Ministry of Foreign Affairs, "Material seized at Orient House attests to wide-ranging PA activity in eastern Jerusalem," Israel Ministry of Foreign Affairs Web site, February 27, 2002, http://www.mfa.gov.il/MFA/ Government/Communiques/2002/Material+seized+at+Orient+House+ attests+to+wide-ra.htm.

CHAPTER THREE: PLOWSHARES BEATEN INTO SWORDS IN GAZA

1. CNN, "Israeli flag lowered over Gaza," CNN.com, September 12, 2005, http://edition.cnn.com/2005/WORLD/meast/09/11/gaza/index.html.

2. Ryan Jones, "Palestinians burn Gaza synagogues," Jerusalem Newswire, September 12, 2008, http://www.jnewswire.com/article/597.

3. Ibid.

4. Ali Waked, "Hamas leaders pray in Gaza synagogue," *Ynetnews.com*, September 12, 2005, http://www.ynetnews.com/articles/0,7340,L-3141220,00.html.

5. *WorldNetDaily*, "'Terror U' sets up shop in former Jewish city," WorldNetDaily.com, March 1, 2007, http://www.worldnetdaily.com/ index.php?pageId=40424.

6. *WorldNetDaily*, "Hamas prepares rocket war in ex-Jewish city," WorldNetDaily.com, March 26, 2007, http://www.worldnetdaily.com/ index.php?pageId=40787.

7. *Ynetnews*, "Gush Katif evacuees suffering financial, medical problems," July 23, 2008, http://www.ynetnews.com/articles/0,7340,L-3572021,00.html.

8. See Maagar Mahot Institute study published at http://gushkatifbook.com/ 2008/07/23/three-years-after-the-gaza-expulsion/.

9. Gush Katif Committee Special Report, "22 months without a home," May 2007, http://www.katifund.org/upload/mazav%20%20eng2.pdf.

10. *WorldNetDaily*, "Israeli teen refugees attempt suicide, drop out," WorldNetDaily.com, July 6, 2006, http://www.worldnetdaily.com/news/ article.asp?ARTICLE_ID=50930.

11. *WorldNetDaily*, "Israeli soldiers refuse to expel Jews," WorldNetDaily.com, August 6, 2007, http://www.wnd.com/index.php? fa=PAGE.view&pageId=42918.

12. Herb Keinon, "1 in 3 Israelis: Troops mustn't evacuate Golan," *Jerusalem Post*, November 24, 2008, http://www.jpost.com/servlet/Satellite? cid=1226404822719&pagename=JPost%2FJPArticle%2FshowFull.

CHAPTER FOUR: ISRAEL'S WAR AGAINST THE JEWS

1. Caroline Glick, "The two-pronged assault on Religious Zionism," *Jewish Press*, May 29, 2008.

2. Scott Wilson, "Jewish settler kills four Israeli Arabs in attack on bus," *Washington Post*, August 5, 2005, http://www.washingtonpost.com/wp-dyn/content/article/2005/08/04/AR2005080401350.html.

3. *WorldNetDaily*, "Israel orders rabbi out of oldest Jewish city," WorldNetDaily.com, August 9, 2007, http://www.wnd.com/index.php?fa=PAGE.view&pageId=42968.

4. *Shturem Chabad*, "Mobile Chabad ordered out!" August 9, 2007, http://www.shturem.org/index.php?section=news&id=17743.

5. *WorldNetDaily*, "West Bank withdrawal 'within days'", WorldNetDaily.com, February 17, 2006, http://www.worldnetdaily.com/news/article.asp?ARTICLE_ID=48870.

6. Hillel Fendel, "Hundreds Injured in Brutal Demolition of Nine Jewish Homes," *Israel National News*, February 1, 2006, http://www.israelnationalnews.com/News/News.aspx/97735.

7. Nadav Shragai, "Cop convicted for assaulting protestor at 2006 Amona evacuation," *Haaretz*, July 22, 2008, http://www.haaretz.com/hasen/spages/1004152.html.

8. Ibid.

9. BBC News, "Shepherd 'not killed by settler,'" BBC News Online, September 29, 2008, http://news.bbc.co.uk/2/hi/middle_east/7642586.stm.

10. "PM: Evil wind of extremism threatens Israeli democracy," *Jerusalem Post*, September 28, 2008, http://www.jpost.com/servlet/Satellite?pagename=JPost%2FJPArticle%2FShowFull&cid=1222017412369.

11. Yuval Azoulay, "Defense Minister: Violent settlers must be punished," *Haaretz*, September 28, 2008, http://www.haaretz.com/hasen/spages/1025123.html.

12. Ibid.

13. *Haaretz*, "Rightist MK: Attack on leftist prof. being used as excuse to sully settlers," October 10, 2008, http://www.haaretz.com/hasen/pages/ShArt.jhtml?itemNo=1025896.

14. Nadav Shragai, "Settler leader: Shin Bet behind attack on Sternhell," *Haaretz*, October 15, 2008, http://www.haaretz.com/hasen/spages/1026301.html.

15. Isabel Kershner, "Radical settlers take on Israel," September 25, 2008, *New York Times*, http://www.nytimes.com/2008/09/26/world/middleeast/26settlers.html?_r=1&bl&ex=1222574400&en=cd491cbff8aac3b9&ei=5087%0A.

16. *Israel Insider*, "IDF to disband elite religious fighting units, says timing is 'coincidence,'" January 25, 2005, http://web.israelinsider.com/Articles/Politics/4876.htm.

17. Yossi Yehoshua, "Combat service for women," *Ynetnews.com*, September 17, 2007, http://www.ynetnews.com/articles/0,7340,L-3450272,00.html.

18. *Israel National News*, "Hesder Yeshivot, the Disengagement—and the Students," July 7, 2005.

CHAPTER FIVE: ABANDONING THE TEMPLE MOUNT

1. Shmuel Berkovitz, *How Dreadful Is This Place!: Holiness, Politics and Justice in Jerusalem and the Holy Places in Israel* (Jerusalem: Carta Press, 2006).

2. Dore Gold, *The Fight for Jerusalem: Radical Islam, the West and the Future of the Holy City* (Washington, D.C.: Regnery Publishing, Inc, 2007).

3. Berkovitz, *How Dreadful Is This Place!*

4. Benny Morris, "Camp David and After, An Exchange," *NY Review of Books*, 49 no. 10 (June 13, 2002).

5. *WorldNetDaily*, "Jewish Temples never existed, says top Palestinian negotiator," WorldNetDaily.com, November 6, 2008, http://www.worldnetdaily.com/index.php?pageId=80382.

6. Aaron Klein, "Israel 'allowing Muslims to destroy Temple wall'," *WorldNetDaily.com*, August 30, 2007, http://www.wnd.com/index.php?fa=PAGE.view&pageId=43286.

7. Nadav Shragai, "First Temple artifacts found in dirt removed from Temple Mount," *Haaretz*, October 19, 2006, http://www.haaretz.com/hasen/pages/ShArt.jhtml?itemNo=776922.

8. Ezra HaLevi, "Dumped Temple Mount rubble yields Jewish artifacts," *Israel National News*, April 14, 2005.

9. "Artifacts with links to Bible unearthed," *Washington Times*, January 2, 2006, http://www.washingtontimes.com/news/2006/jan/02/20060102-123421-5168r.

10. Roee Nahmias, "Parts of new podium arrive at al-Aqsa Mosque," *Ynetnews.com*, January 24, 2007, http://www.ynetnews.com/articles/0,7340,L-3356436,00.html.

11. *WorldNetDaily*, "Israel allows minaret over Temple Mount," WorldNetDaily.com, February 1, 2007, http://www.worldnetdaily.com/news/article.asp?ARTICLE_ID=54056.

12. Etgar Lefkovitz, "Jordan plans new Temple Mt. minaret," *Jerusalem Post*, October 11, 2006.

13. *WorldNetDaily*, "Hamas broadcasts from Temple Mount on Jewish holiday," WorldNetDaily.com, December 19, 2007, http://www.worldnetdaily.com/news/article.asp?ARTICLE_ID=59276.

CHAPTER SIX: JOSEPH'S TOMB TRAVESTY

1. Genesis Rabbah, 79.7.

2. Hillel Lieberman, "Battle in Shechem—Eyewitness Report," September 26, 1996, available online at http://philologos.org/bpr/files/s020.htm.

3. *WorldNetDaily*, "Palestinians burn Joseph's Tomb," WorldNetDaily.com, February 12, 2008.

4. Ibid.

5. *WorldNetDaily*, "Joseph's Tomb synagogue destroyed by Israeli forces," WorldNetDaily.com, July 31, 2007.

6. Ibid.

7. The only news media outlet I could find that covered the story besides my own reporting was the nationalist *Arutz Sheva* news Web site.

CHAPTER SEVEN: HOW THE U.S. FUNDS PALESTINIAN TERRORISM

1. Isabel Kershner, "Israel aids Palestinians with arms," *New York Times*, September 5, 2008 http://www.nytimes.com/2008/09/06/world/middleeast/06mideast.html?_r=1&ref=middleeast.

2. Richard Boudreaux, "Israel OK's weapons for Abbas' police," *Los Angeles Times*, sec. A-3, November 22, 2007.

3. Paul Morro, "U.S. Foreign Aid to the Palestinians," CRS Report for Congress, October 9, 2007, Order Code RS22370.

4. Associated Press, "U.S. to sharply reduce funds for Palestinians," *International Herald Tribune*, March 21, 2007, http://www.iht.com/articles/2007/03/21/news/mideast.php.

5. Reuters, "U.S. cuts back plan to bolster Abbas' forces, offers $59 million," *Haaretz*, March 27, 2007, http://www.haaretz.com/hasen/spages/842627.html.

6. Ibid.

7. Reuters, "Hamas takes control of Gaza," *USA Today*, June 15, 2007, http://www.usatoday.com/news/world/2007-06-14-gaza_N.htm.

8. *World Tribune*, "Hamas attempts mass casualty attack on Israeli border post," April 21, 2008, http://www.worldtribune.com/worldtribune/WTARC/2008/me_hamas0072_04_21.asp.

CHAPTER EIGHT: THE UN "REFUGEE" CRISIS THAT KEEPS ON GIVING

1. UNRWA, "Total registered refugees per country and area," Work publication, Table 10, June 30, 2008, http://www.un.org/unrwa/publications/pdf/rr_countryandarea.pdf.

2. Eli Hertz, *Myths and Facts*, January 2006.

3. According to the UN Mediator on Palestine, Ralph Bunche, in 1948, the figure was 472,000. In 1949, the United Nations Conciliation Commission put the number at 726,000. UNRWA on its Web site cites 914,000.

4. Mideast Web.

5. The Palestine Remembered Web site, for example, speaks of preserving the memory of the "726,000 Palestinian refugees who were ethnically cleansed from their homes...as a result of the 1948 war."

6. Reported in: Ephraim Karsh, "1948, Israel and the Palestinians—the True Story," commentarymagazine.com, May 2008. Annotated. Karsh is head of Mediterranean Studies at King's College, University of London.

7. Ibid.

8. Ibid.

9. Ibid.

10. This is confirmed by Cunningham's observation in an official *communiqué* to London, cited by palestinefacts.org, that "British authorities in Haifa have formed the impression that total evacuation is being urged on the Haifa Arabs from higher Arab quarters and that the townsfolk themselves are against it."

11. Karsh, "1948, Israel and the Palestinians—the True Story."

12. PalestineFacts.org.

13. Ibid.

14. From the UN General Assembly, Official Record, 5th session, Ad Hoc Political Committee 31st Meeting, November 11, 1950.

15. The Palestinian Refugees FACTFILES, Palestinian Liberation Organization, Department of Refugee Affairs, Ramallah, 2000, 22.

16. Arlene Kushner, "UNRWA Overview and Policy Critique," The Center for Near East Policy Research, October 2008.

17. *Al-Misri*, October 11, 1949.

18. *Al-Ziyyad* April 6, 1950.

19. Kushner, "UNRWA Overview and Policy Critique."

20. The State of the World's Refugees—Chapter 1, "The Early Years."

21. It is pointless to speak of "nationality," as Palestine was not a sovereign state when the Arabs fled.

22. The State of the World's Refugees—Chapter 1, The Early Years.

23. Karsh, "1948, Israel and the Palestinians—the True Story."

24. Joan Peters, *From Time Immemorial* (Chicago: JKAP Publications, 1984).

25. There is yet another reason why the population has increased to this number: While UNRWA originally registered only those within the area they serviced and who were presumably eligible for relief, in 1994 the agency expanded the eligibility for registration to those outside the areas it services. Ingrid Bassner Jaradat, Director of the Palestinian organization BADIL–Resource Center for Palestinian Residency and Refugee Rights, in e-mail communication with researcher Arlene Kushner, has admitted that this had a political dimension.

26. The irony here is that when the resolution was passed, Arab states voted against it because of its implicit recognition of Israel. (Law professor Ruth Lapidoth, cited in *American Thinker*, October 27, 2008.) But then the Arabs returned to it to utilize one phrase as suited their purposes.

27. BADIL Information & Discussion Brief No. 6.

28. Mohammed Daraghmeh, "Teaching the refugee issue at UNRWA," *Jerusalem Times*, June, 22, 2001.

29. The document can be retrieved at: www.un.org/documents/ga/res/40/a40r165.htm.

30. Arlene Kushner, "Why Does UNRWA exist?" *Jerusalem Post*, October 27, 2005.

31. See www.badil.org/Publications/Other/Refugees/Workshop/wkshop2.htm for study.

32. See http://www.impact-se.org/ for the report in its entirety.

33. *Al-Watan* (Kuwait), June, 11, 2003: www.al-watan.com/data/20030611/index.asp?content=outstate2. See also *Filastin Al-Muslima* (Lebanon) July 2003, page five, www.fm-m.com\2003\jul2003\pdf\p5.pdf. Details—vote by area and names of candidates—are available.

34. Jerusalem Media and Communications Center.

35. Palestine Web site: http://www.multaqa.org/access/persons.php?c=a.

36. www.khayma.com/islamicblock/about.htm.

37. Interview with Ahmed Casiso, Islamic Bloc supervisor of twenty summer camps for three thousand junior high school and high school students run in 2004, found on www.alkotla.net/details.asp?id=268.

38. In 2003, this was on the Web site of the prime minister of Israel.

39. Arlene Kushner, "UNRWA. The United Nations Relief and Works Agency for Palestinian Refugees in the Near East. Links to Terrorism," Jersulem Summit, available at http://www.jerusalemsummit.org/eng/refugees_kushner.php.

40. Charles Radin, "UN Role in Palestinian Camps in Dispute," *Boston Globe*, July 8, 2002.

41. Israel Ministry of Foreign Affairs, "Briefing by Deputy Prime Minister Natan Sharansky, Battalion Commander Colonel Hilik Sofer, Lt. Colonel Itai Landsberg, Major Rafi Laderman," April 19, 2002, http://www.mfa.gov.il/MFA/Government/Speeches%20by%20Israeli%20leaders/2002/Briefing%20by%20Deputy%20PM%20Natan%20Sharansky-%20Col%20Hilik%20S.

42. Posted on the IDF Web site, http://dover.idf.il/IDF/.

43. Kushner, "UNRWA Overview and Policy Critique."

44. Reuven Ehrlich, Ph.D., Editor, "Special Information Paper," Intelligence and Terrorism Information Center at the Center for Special Studies, December 2002.

45. Kushner, "UNRWA Overview and Policy Critique," Appendix I, for some instances of camp involvement and involvement of camp residents in terrorism emanating from Gaza.

CHAPTER NINE: HAMAS STATE IN JERUSALEM, WEST BANK?

1. *WorldNetDaily*, "Hamas's West Bank battle plan exposed," WorldNetDaily.com, October 6, 2005, http://www.worldnetdaily.com/index.php?pageId=32690.

2. *WorldNetDaily*, "U.S. backed Fatah admits infiltration by Hamas," WorldNetDaily.com, July 27, 2007.

3. Hanan Greenberg, "Palestinian officers deploy in Jenin," *Ynetnews.com*, May 3, 2008, http://www.ynet.co.il/english/articles/0,7340,L-3538863,00.html.

4. *WorldNetDaily*, "Israeli leader: I speak for my nation," WorldNetDaily.com, November 29, 2007, http://www.wnd.com/index.php?fa=PAGE.view&pageId=44800.

5. "Address to Delegates at the United Jewish Communities (UJC) General Assembly," November 13, 2007, available at the State Department Web site: http://www.state.gov/secretary/rm/2007/11/95103.htm.

6. *WorldNetDaily*, "Israelis: Don't even think about dividing Jerusalem," WorldNetDaily.com, October 18, 2007, http://www.wnd.com/news/article.asp?ARTICLE_ID=58211.

7. Ronny Sofer, "When leftist meets evacuees," *Ynetnews.com*, April 28, 2006, http://www.ynetnews.com/articles/0,7340,L-3245036,00.html.

8. Smadar Peri, "King Abdullah: I oppose unilateral pullout," *Ynetnews.com*, June 7, 2006, http://www.ynetnews.com/articles/0,7340,L-3259866,00.html.

CHAPTER TEN: LOSING LEBANON

1. Conal Urquhart, Chris McGreal, "Israelis invade Lebanon after soldiers are seized," *The Guardian*, July 12, 2006, http://www.guardian.co.uk/world/2006/jul/12/israelandthepalestinians.lebanon.

2. Alon, Gideon; Aluf Benn, Amos Harel, Yoav Stern, "Israel holds Lebanon government responsible for Hezbollah attack". *Haaretz*, July 13, 2006, http://www.haaretz.com/hasen/pages/ShArt.jhtml?itemNo=737687&contrassID=1&subContrassID=0&sbSubContrassID=0.

3. Associated Press, "Israel authorizes 'severe' response to abductions," CNN.com, http://edition.cnn.com/2006/WORLD/meast/07/12/mideast/.

4. Israeli Cabinet Communiqué. Israeli Ministry of Foreign Affairs release of July 16, 2006.

5. Richard A. Oppel, Greg Myre, "Rocket barrage kills 15 Israelis close to border," *New York Times*, August 6, 2006, http://www.nytimes.com/2006/08/07/world/middleeast/07mideast.html?_r=1.

CHAPTER ELEVEN: ROMANCING SYRIA

1. Randall Mikkelsen, "Syrian reactor capacity was 1-2 weapons/year: CIA," Reuters, April 28, 2008, http://www.reuters.com/article/topNews/idUSN2819854620080429.

2. Full text of the statement by White House press secretary Dana Perino on alleged Syrian and North Korean nuclear as published on BBC News Web site: http://news.bbc.co.uk/2/hi/middle_east/7366176.stm.

3. *Jerusalem Post*, "Olmert says he is ready to make peace with Syria," September 17, 2007.

4. Aluf Benn, Barak Ravid, and Shmuel Rosner, "Bush advisor downplays role of joint statement at conference," *Haaretz*, December 26, 2007, http://www.haaretz.com/hasen/spages/928106.html.

5. Barak Ravid, "On eve of Assad visit to Moscow, Israel and Russia discuss security," *Haaretz*, August 21, 2008, http://www.haaretz.com/hasen/spages/1013616.html.

6. The Jewish Virtual Library, a division of the American-Israeli Cooperative Enterprise, has an excellent compilation of Golan history available online at http://www.jewishvirtuallibrary.org/jsource/Peace/golantoc.html.

7. *Jewish News Weekly*, "Shorts: War aftermath," August 18, 2006, http://www.jewishsf.com/content/2-0-/module/displaystory/story_id/30071/edition_id/566/format/html/displaystory.html.

CHAPTER TWELVE: IRAN PURSUES ARMAGEDDON

1. Full PDF of the National Intelligence Estimate available online on the U.S. government's Director of National Intelligence Web site at: http://www.dni.gov/press_releases/20071203_release.pdf.

2. Leonard Doyle, "Bush sends high-level envoy to avoid conflict with Iran," *Independent*, July 17, 2008, http://www.independent.co.uk/news/world/politics/bush-sends-highlevel-envoy-to-avoid-conflict-with-iran-869733.html.

3. Marie Colvin, "Hamas wages Iran's proxy war on Israel," *Sunday Times*, March 9, 2008, http://www.timesonline.co.uk/tol/news/world/middle_east/article3512014.ece.

4. Ibid.

5. *WorldNetDaily*, "Jesus, Mahdi both coming, says Iran's Ahmadinejad," WorldNetDaily.com, December 19, 2006, http://www.wnd.com/news/article.asp?ARTICLE_ID=53430.

6. Intelligence and Terrorism Information Center at the Center for Special Studies, C.S.S. Report, September 11, 2006.

7. *WorldNetDaily*, "'Hezbollah youth scouts' train in terrorism,'" WorldNetDaily.com, September 14, 2006, http://www.worldnetdaily.com/

news/article.asp?ARTICLE_ID=51968.

8. C.S.S., Report of September 11, 2006.

9. Aaron Klein, "War dead flown to Iran," *New York Sun*, July 24, 2006, http://www.nysun.com/foreign/war-dead-flown-to-iran/36557.

10. Mirella Hodeib, "Nasrallah vows 'colossal surprise' if Israel attacks," *Daily Star* (Lebanon), August 15, 2007, http://www.dailystar.com.lb/article.asp?edition_id=1&categ_id=2&article_id=84551.

11. Parisa Hafezi, "Iran's atomic work has 'no reverse gear,'" Reuters, February 25, 2007, http://uk.reuters.com/article/topNews/idUKBLA53622220070225.

12. BBC News, "Iran defiant on nuclear programme," *BBC News Online*, February 25, 2007, http://news.bbc.co.uk/2/hi/middle_east/6395203.stm.

CHAPTER THIRTEEN: HAMAS HANDSHAKE ON WHITE HOUSE LAWN?

1. Associated Press, "Carter embraces Hamas politician," MSNBC.com, April 15, 2008, http://www.msnbc.msn.com/id/24128928.

2. Iramar Marcus, Barbara Crook, "Islam will enter every house…," Palestinian Media Watch Web site, March 28, 2007, http://pmw.org.il/bulletins_mar2007.htm#b260307.

3. Mahmoud al-Zahar, "No peace without Hamas," *Washington Post*, April 17, 2008, http://www.washingtonpost.com/wp-dyn/content/article/2008/04/16/AR2008041602899.html.

4. Haroon Saddique, "Carter: Hamas will accept Israel's right to live in peace," *The Guardian*, April 21, 2008, http://www.guardian.co.uk/world/2008/apr/21/israelandthepalestinians.usa?gusrc=rss&feed=networkfront.

5. Tim Butcher, "Hamas will make deal with Israel, Carter says," *Daily Telegraph*, April 22, 2008, http://www.telegraph.co.uk/news/1896766/Hamas-will-make-deal-with-Israel-says-Jimmy-Carter.html.

6. Associated Press, "Haniyeh: We'll accept a state for a 10-year truce," *Jerusalem Post*, January 20, 2007, http://www.jpost.com/servlet/Satellite?pagename=JPost%2FJPArticle%2FShowFull&cid=1167467776076.

7. Steven Erlanger, "France admits contacts with Hamas," *New York Times*, May 20, 2008, http://www.nytimes.com/2008/05/20/world/europe/20france.html?_r=1.

8. Aaron Klein, "Hamas seeks Israel's destruction despite French talks, Denies Paris diplomat's claim terrorist group will recognize Jewish state, *WorldNetDaily*, May 19, 2008, http://www.worldnetdaily.com/index.php?fa=PAGE.view&pageId=64782.

9. Ibid.

10. Khaled Abu Toameh, "Hamas pleased with European 'U-turn,'" *Jerusalem Post*, August 15, 2007, http://www.jpost.com/servlet/Satellite?pagename=JPost%2FJPArticle%2FShowFull&cid=1186557450129.

11. BBC News, "Norway-Hamas links anger Israel," BBC News Online, March 20, 2007, http://news.bbc.co.uk/2/hi/middle_east/6470669.stm.

12. U.S. State Department, "Text of November 9, 2007 interview with the *Dallas Morning News*," U.S. State Department Web site, http://www.state.gov/secretary/rm/2007/11/94868.htm.

13. U.S. State Department, "Text of June 8, 2007 interview with the *NY Daily News* editorial board," State Department Web site, http://www.state.gov/secretary/rm/2007/06/86255.htm.

14. David Brooks, "Obama admires Bush," *New York Times*, May 16, 2008, http://www.nytimes.com/2008/05/16/opinion/16brooks.html?_r=3&partner=rssnyt&emc=rss&oref=slogin&oref=slogin.

15. *Jerusalem Post*, "Al-Hayat: 'Obama's advisors met with Hamas prior to US elections," November 11, 2008, http://www.jpost.com/servlet/Satellite?cid=1225910089559&pagename=JPost/JPArticle/ShowFull.

16. Ibid.

17. *USA Today*, "Sen. Kerry visits Gaza, avoids Hamas," Associated Press reprint, February 19, 2009, http://www.usatoday.com/news/world/2009-02-19-kerry-gaza_N.htm.

18. Fox News, "Kerry turns over Hamas letter to U.S. consulate," FoxNews.com, February 20, 2009, http://www.foxnews.com/politics/2009/02/20/kerry-acting-mailman-hamas.

19. Sue Pleming, "Clinton says no U.S. funds will go to Hamas," Reuters UK, March 2, 2009, http://uk.reuters.com/article/homepageCrisis/idUKN02355696._CH_.2420

20. Adam Entous, "Exclusive: Money trail to Hamas begins with Israeli banks," Reuters, September 27, 2007, http://www.reuters.com/article/latestCrisis/idUSL03139119.

CHAPTER FOURTEEN: THE GAZA WAR: AGAIN ISRAEL FAILS TO WIN

1. Fox News, "Olmert delivers 'Last Minute' warning to Gaza," FoxNews.com, December 25, 2008, http://www.foxnews.com/story/0,2933,472856,00.html.

2. Roni Sofer with Reuters, "Hamas' Meshaal says group will not renew truce with Israel," Ynetnews.com, December 14, 2008, http://www.ynet.co.il/english/articles/0,7340,L-3638320,00.html.

3. CNN, "Carter meets with political leader of Hamas in Syria," CNN.com, December 14, 2008, http://edition.cnn.com/2008/WORLD/meast/12/14/carter.hamas/index.html.

4. Yaacov Katz, "A year's intel gathering yields 'alpha hits'," *Jerusalem Post*, December 26, 2008, http://www.jpost.com/servlet/Satellite?cid=1230111714969&pagename=JPost%2FJPArticle%2FshowFull.

5. Associated Press as reprinted on FoxNews.com, "Israel 'at war to the bitter end,' strikes key Hamas sites," FoxNews.com, December 29, 2008, http://www.foxnews.com/story/0,2933,473448,00.html.

6. Herb Keinon, "Olmert calls a halt to assault in Gaza," *Jerusalem Post*, January 18, 2009, http://www.jpost.com/servlet/Satellite?cid= 1232100163477&pagename=JPost%2FJPArticle%2FShowFull.

7. Aluf Benn, "Israel declares victory in Gaza, but at what cost?" *Haaretz*, January 18, 2009, http://www.haaretz.com/hasen/spages/1056248.html.

8. Philip Webster, "Hamas must be brought into peace process, says Tony Blair," *Times Online*, January 31, 2009, http://www.timesonline.co.uk/ tol/news/politics/article5621184.ece.